W9-AUV-356

CALIFIA WOMEN

CALIFIA WOMEN

*Feminist Education against
Sexism, Classism, and Racism*

CLARK A. POMERLEAU

UNIVERSITY OF TEXAS PRESS *Austin*

Requests for permission to reproduce material from this work should be sent to:
    Permissions
    University of Texas Press
    P.O. Box 7819
    Austin, TX 78713-7819
    http://utpress.utexas.edu/index.php/rp-form

♾ The paper used in this book meets the minimum requirements of ANSI/NISO
Z39.48-1992 (R1997) (Permanence of Paper).

LIBRARY OF CONGRESS CATALOGING-IN-PUBLICATION DATA

Pomerleau, Clark A.
    Califia women : feminist education against sexism, classism, and racism / Clark A.
Pomerleau. — First edition.
        p.   cm
    Includes bibliographical references and index.
    ISBN 978-0-292-75294-8 (cl. : alk. paper)
    1. Feminism and education—California—History—20th century.   2. Women's
studies—California—History—20th century.   3. Community education—
California—History—20th century.   I. Title.
    LC197.P66 2013
    370.82—dc23   2013021090

doi:10.7560/752948

MY GRATITUDE GOES TO MY FAMILY FOR TEACHING ME COMPASSIONATE LOVE, FAIRNESS, AND THE PURSUIT OF LEARNING. THAT FOUNDATION PREPARED ME TO APPRECIATE THE DIVERSITY CHAMPIONS AND CHOSEN FAMILY WHO HAVE WALKED THIS PATH WITH ME.

CONTENTS

"WELL, WHAT ARE YOU LOOKING FOR?" That abrupt question from archivist and Latina lesbian feminist activist Yolanda Retter Vargas, along with my answer, initiated this book. As someone interested in U.S. social movements for civil rights and liberation, I wanted to research in Los Angeles's two most promising archives for late-twentieth-century multi-issue feminist or queer groups. Retter Vargas immediately shot back, "That's Califia Community. Do you want me to set up interviews?"

In 2000, the ONE National Gay and Lesbian Archive at the University of Southern California (USC) and the independently run June L. Mazer Lesbian Collection provided initial grounding for this study of a feminist community education experiment and its times. Only three published essays existed on Califia.[1] Retter Vargas introduced me to former collective members and steady participants, who led me to others, including one-time attendees.

Archives dedicated to social movements counter forces that downplay such movements as sources of new ideas and societal change. Heated debate erupted in the early 1980s when Congress formally honored the significance of the African American civil rights movement by setting aside a national holiday named for Dr. Martin Luther King Jr. It took until the twenty-first century for all states to recognize the holiday. United States history courses I took in the 1970s through the mid-1990s rarely acknowledged the impact of social movements and often relegated women's historical roles to sewing a flag, guiding explorers, and being the wives or mothers of prominent men. During graduate study in women's studies and in women, gender, and sexuality history, I found it impressive to see committed volunteers like Jo Duffy running the June L. Mazer Lesbian Collection or USC staff archivists maintaining the ONE National Gay and Lesbian Archive.

Early in my research, I took to heart Nancy Whittier's argument that "any study of radical feminism is . . . by necessity, a local case study."[2] The case study of Califia Community tests generalizations in national overviews about expressions of feminism in the 1970s and 1980s. This assessment of Califia Community's development in the context of feminism at that time intervenes against dismissive stereotypes by those who came of age after the 1970s by showing that there is much to learn from 1970s–1980s community activism, dynamics of feminism and antiracism within social movements, and national politics. This book details how feminists educated themselves outside of university courses.

Participants in Califia Community's education experiment (1975–1987) organized more than a dozen week-long summer conference camps and over a dozen long-weekend sessions during summers and Thanksgivings, with about 100–250 women and their children at each camp. They tried to strengthen interpersonal relations and leadership skills to promote organizing for change. Attendance varied from year to year, so the total number of "Califia women," as they called themselves, is difficult to determine exactly; I estimate well over 2,000 but under 5,000. Sampling through referrals worked well to find women who were part of sometimes hidden populations based on their political and social views. Relationships that had lasted fifteen to thirty years revealed part of the social networking among women that was crucial to the growth of feminism and typical of many social justice movements. Referrals and overlap in what women remembered as important helped me to identify which collective members and long-term teachers had made the greatest impacts. I have used interviews to show the development of the group in its times rather than to represent every woman's important contribution.

Feminist oral history methods gave my research agenda the flexibility to incorporate topics that narrators considered important. Sherna Berger Gluck and Daphne Patai collected formative advice in *Women's Words*[3] to look for subjective meaning and emotion. My first question was, "What do you think are the most important things to focus on if someone is going to assess Califia Community?" Narrators used the open-ended questions to raise issues that moved beyond my initial inquiries and exposed unexpected connections. For example, the context of feminists' first speakouts about rape and domestic violence influenced the perceived need for safe space. Prioritizing a safe temporary separate space influenced debates over whom to include, together with an age cutoff for boys that still allowed mothers to be involved, as well as disagreements over how to convey anger, under what circumstances to engage in sexuality, and what role spiritual rituals should play in a feminist community space. *Women's Words* directs interviewers to check their own perceptions of the stories narrators tell against the narrators' expression of their feelings, attitudes, or values and the meanings narrators attach to events. Some Califia women thoughtfully clarified how their views changed over time. I tried to balance explaining their points of view with historical analysis regarding how representative of the times their ideas or activities were and the consequences of such mindsets and actions. Areas where emotions ran high after twenty years merited special analysis, and ways women understood the end of the educational project in 1987 show the intractability of racism and issues of race and socioeconomic insecurity in the context of conservative political gains.

This project depended on Califia narrators' feminist passion, memories, and interest in preserving struggles that women waged to better society. They gave their time and support generously. Five graciously opened their homes to me when I made interview trips, and others made similar offers of a place to stay. Some have chosen to remain in contact. They have changed me by exposing me to feminist wisdom about interpersonal dynamics that they developed through their experiential learning and prompted me to consider the need for solidarity over sameness.

In addition to the Califia Community participants, ONE archivist Retter Vargas, and Mazer volunteer Duffy, my family, colleagues, and friends improved each stage of this work. I am indebted to Martha Parrent Pomerleau, my mother, for transcribing most of the interviews. She and I were then able to converse about feminism along with my father, Wayne Paul Pomerleau. Professors Karen S. Anderson, Elizabeth Lapovsky Kennedy, Sarah (Sally) Deutsch, and J. Reeve Huston provided invaluable assistance in the early stages of the project. Members of the Gender in U.S. History writers' group at the University of Arizona gave wonderful feedback, especially Anderson, Deutsch, Katherine Morrissey, Lydia Otero, Michelle Berry, Meghan Winchel, Mike Rembis, and Adam Geary. Merryl Sloane generously copyedited an early version. Friends gave feedback after I overhauled the chapters for the manuscript, especially Elizabeth Turner, Diane Wiener, Morgan O'Donnell, Donna Drucker, and Tomi Fatunde. Courtney E. Jacobs helped me enhance photographs for the book. I greatly appreciate the support of Theresa May and the staff at the University of Texas Press.

The University of Arizona gave me my first funding with travel stipends through the Women's Studies Advisory Council and the Graduate and Professional Student Travel Grant Fund. The Western History Association's Coalition for Western Women's History awarded me the Irene Ledesma Prize in 2002 to cover equipment, an interview trip, and interview tape shipping. The University of Arizona's Department of History gave me a Research Travel Grant for the summer of 2002 and the Elizabeth Lantin Ramenofsky Grant for a final research trip in the summer of 2003. The University of North Texas awarded me a Junior Faculty Summer Research Fellowship for the summer of 2008.

CALIFIA WOMEN

CALIFIA COMMUNITY IN
SOCIAL MOVEMENT HISTORY

THIS STUDY REVEALS HOW COMMUNITY EDUCATION fit into feminist institution building. In response to entrenched inequalities in the post–World War II United States, Americans who supported gender equality built on political opportunities to find each other and create the country's largest social movement.[1] By the 1970s, the proliferation of feminist organizations in Los Angeles was representative of the nation's largest cities. Southern California feminists built on previous leftist education experiments to plan Califia Community in 1975. They drew on their social networks to bring women (and their children) together for a week or long weekend to learn from each other's experiences, imagine and live an alternative to mainstream society, frame issues, and organize to change the social order. For a decade of summers, Califia Community collective members facilitated conferences at campsites that alleviated mainstream pressures. The experience strengthened many women's sense of shared culture and collective identity as "Califia women."

Califia Community is significant both in its own right and as a lens on its times. There has been little study of sustained grassroots feminist educational activism outside of the formation of college courses, even though the feminists who considered themselves "second wave" were dedicated to community-based consciousness raising, leadership training, organizing, and revision of knowledge about women and gender.[2] Grassroots groups that did community education tended to be significantly smaller than Califia Community and usually lasted fewer than five years, while women-only trade programs outside established vocational training venues have received scant scholarly attention.

This study extends beyond most previous scholarship's focus on the late 1960s and early 1970s, widely acknowledged leaders, and the East Coast or Midwest. Scholarship on feminism of the 1960s–1980s continues to need case studies that correct generalizations based on national overviews.

Local-level dynamics confirm the multiplicity of competing views that feminists generated. Analyzing Califia Community helps to explain how New Left political and countercultural concerns influenced multi-issue feminists to blend tactics and goals in practices that they and later scholars have classified separately as "radical feminism," "cultural feminism," and "separatism." Early participants at Califia had a range of gender expressions, sexual orientations, class backgrounds, and races/ethnicities. Leaders built on that diversity and were especially concerned to advance antiracism and coalition work among races and ethnicities. Over their decade of conferences, Califia women developed their training on identity variation in ways that help clarify issues of feminists' differing sexual orientations, classes, and races.

The Califia experiment illustrates that 1970s feminists often mobilized women from overlapping social networks, built institutions with volunteer-based resources, and sustained interest through strong social relationships, a shared sense of culture, and the powerful emotions feminists felt when working together against injustices. Califia women adapted their priorities over time in response to their participation in feminist debates and to external pressures from right-wing organizing. Looking at Califia in relation to nationwide developments reveals how feminists expanded their content and tactics, the strengths and weaknesses of lenses like identity politics and methods like consciousness-raising and consensus, and ways in which members of the Right repeatedly attacked feminism. Many of these issues remain salient.

Across the United States, the number of participants in feminist groups and the movement's visibility to mainstream Americans expanded enormously over the 1960s, 1970s, and 1980s. Betty Brooks, who helped establish and run Califia Community, spoke to the ways in which many women felt swept up in a collective movement that altered the course of their lives.

> There was a *giant wave* that was happening. And I guess I could *say* that that *wave* picked *me* up, although I was already *in* the ocean of women's liberation. You know there's two aspects of all this—women's *rights* work and women's *liberation*. And so *I* would say . . . that the most *important* thing that Califia did was *really* to raise women's consciousness about their own individual liberation *and* the connection to the big "isms," . . . which *surround* us like *smog*, which are sexism, racism, and class. And it was that *younger* generation of women, the second wave of feminists, the people who had been in the political liberation movements of the '60s, that focused in. . . . They walked out of *mainstream* politics and said that the "personal is political." So that Califia was picking that up. We were really the only

radical group of people [in southern California] trying to do that kind of work—to try to *raise* people's *consciousness* in a *different* way than just keeping it in a small group. I mean, we really want to pick up the big stuff.
BETTY BROOKS (CALIFIA COMMUNITY FOUNDER AND COLLECTIVE MEMBER, 1975–1983)[3]

Brooks's use of a wave metaphor encapsulates some complexities of participants' thinking. She distinguished between a great wave that picked her up and being "already *in* the ocean of women's liberation." Differentiating work to gain rights from liberation, Brooks honed in on the radical aspect of movement struggle that did not pursue goals by reforming law and engaging in mainstream politics. She characterized Califia's work as continuing to politicize what had been ignored as personal, a concept widely attributed to "the second wave of feminists." Brooks identified second wave feminists as "that *younger* generation of women . . . who had been in the political liberation movements of the '60s," in contrast to the work of women who came of age after the suffrage movement and preceded 1960s movement work.

Recent scholarly trends that reject the 1968 term "the second feminist wave" raise legitimate concerns that grouping feminist activism into a first and second wave focuses on the same women to the exclusion of others and fails to recognize connections to activism outside the periods 1848–1920 and 1960–1980s. Historically, people have attempted to advance gender equality at other times, have formed multi-issue groups with tactics that subsequent activists claimed to have invented, and/or have done so without self-identifying as feminist.[4]

Brooks's usage pushes us to consider multiple ways of using "wave" as an analogy. Periods with large numbers of participants have not precluded work outside those times. Like the Chicago Women's Liberation Union graphic, "Many Waves, One Ocean,"[5] Brooks described the activism of different groups of women as the waves within one ocean of women's liberation. This metaphor fits with social movement scholars who take an inclusive view of strands of progressive activism. Van Gosse's definition of "New Left" includes many aspects of progressive organizing with roots in 1940s dissent. Likewise, scholars such as A. Finn Enke show that one can simultaneously recognize that a period had a massive outpouring of feminist activity and include a variety of participants who contributed to expanding opportunities for women.[6] The oceanic waters of activist interest in gender equality remain whether in a shoal created by backlash, cresting, or falling back into that water.

Brooks was part of a "political generation" that developed a collective activist identity in relation to societal conditions. Califia Community helped bring women into that political generation regardless of whether they were in their late teens, thirties, or sixties at the time. Jo Reger refers to the women who joined feminist activism in the late 1960s through 1980s as the "second wave generation."[7] This work will refer to the decades in which Califia's activity took place because the wave metaphor can intensify a sense of generational division. Feminist activists since 2000 have continued to face dilemmas that activists confronted over a generation ago, and while disidentification with an older political generation is typical, actually addressing continuing problems requires learning from past tactics and goals.

Most explanations of the origins of initial feminist activists consider the argument famously put forward in Sara Evans's *Personal Politics*.[8] Women's participation in the civil rights movement and New Left student organizing to expand democratic participation and end war in Vietnam gave women activists organizing skills, a language to analyze oppression, and experience with gender discrimination that led some to form separate groups dedicated to challenging gender inequality. These women were a large part of early organizing.

Government-sponsored work was another initial place where like-minded women and men met, and their frustration led them to form non-government organizations. Pressure on President John F. Kennedy in 1961 led him to agree to form the President's Commission on the Status of Women, and state commissions formed where women and men shared an interest in equalizing conditions for women. The passage of the Civil Rights Act of 1964 with the addition of "sex" as a protected category made the consequential formation of the Equal Employment Opportunity Commission (EEOC) look like a place to address discrimination against women. EEOC members' early reluctance to investigate sex discrimination complaints, however, resulted in the formation—by women and men—of the National Organization for Women (NOW) in 1966 so there would be a national group devoted to women's rights.[9]

By the mid-1970s, feminists found each other through national and state initiatives for legal changes and through small groups that flourished in larger cities. In California, the state's President's Commission on the Status of Women and NOW chapters were the earliest visible spaces where work for women's equality occurred. Los Angeles, for example, had one of the most radical chapters of NOW in the country.[10] L.A. also developed a dense network of smaller organizations with overlapping membership for political change and social networking.

Women often had previous New Left experience when they joined feminist groups in the 1960s. In contrast, feminism was the first organizing experience for many female participants who joined groups in the 1970s and 1980s. As the movement gained momentum, it drew in women of various ages. Individual feminists often worked for reform and revolution simultaneously, joining groups like NOW as well as women-only consciousness-raising groups and transferring tactics from one struggle to the other.[11] Califia Community was one of many spaces girls and grandmothers went who wanted to have fun, revolutionize people's self-perception, and fundamentally alter how people interacted with each other in society rather than working through established parliamentary procedure, lobbying, and other democratic processes.

Scholars like Benita Roth, Kimberly Springer, Winifred Breines, Anne Valk, and Maylei Blackwell have explored alternative routes by laying out how racial division among the New Left, the civil rights movement, Black Power, and Chicanismo led American women to move from cogendered activism to develop forms of feminism partly divided by race or ethnicity.[12] Breines takes seriously the role of socialist feminists while, too often, scholars of feminisms diminish their impact or leave them out altogether. She also extends the scope of time to include the early 1980s and ties multicultural feminism to third wave feminists. Valk shows for black and white feminists in Washington, DC, that "these divergent streams of activism merged" and that "these branches of feminism provided a foundation for further women's movements that extended into the 1980s and beyond."[13] Using Califia Community as indicative of the way feminism developed in its second decade addresses increasing coalition work among feminists of color and continued attempts of white feminists to grapple with racism and work together with women of color.[14]

The white women who founded Califia Community considered gender and sexual orientation primary oppressions while they also addressed class, race, and, ultimately, other identities. Those women of color who crossed L.A.'s racial divide to participate tended to view the camps as more intensively radical spaces than was generally available. They attended, in part, to further their feminist education, develop leadership, network with like-minded feminists and lesbians of color, and get allies for coalition work.[15] Califia women of color often valued both coalitions across race and multi-issue feminism.

Consciousness-raising (CR) was foundational to feminist education. Women across the country recognized similarities in their experiences and analyzed the systemic nature of sexism as a basis for strategizing ways to address individual and institutional bias. New York Radical Women popularized CR in 1968 after members withdrew from male activists' sexist attitudes. They drew on a Maoist Chinese Revolution concept of "speaking bitterness" to share thoughts, experiences, and views about male oppression in order to develop individual confidence and group bonding as a precursor for deciding what action to take. The method spread quickly, and within two years women across the continent met in small CR discussion sessions within larger organizations like NOW or in autonomous grassroots groups.[16] Women found that authoritative research and policy overlooked sexism, whereas CR validated arguing based on women's lived experience with misogyny. Early CR members criticized their CR groups for failing to discuss the experience of minority women. Such criticism exposed the importance of diverse experience for CR to produce inclusive analysis.[17] This was a lesson feminist groups nationwide struggled with repeatedly because the comfort of organizing by commonalities in identity as well as the ways women generalized from similarities in experience made it challenging to integrate differing experiences. Califia Community and its offshoot, White Women Against Racism (WWAR, founded between 1981 and 1982), benefitted from CR as they took the lead locally in addressing multiple oppressions, but Califia and WWAR are also typical of how CR left its assessments unfinished.

The ways feminists chose to intervene to change society led to their dividing feminists into different types. Initially using the term "women's liberation movement," women and some men became more comfortable calling themselves feminist or pro-feminist by the early 1970s. The ways in which people adopted mindsets and tactics were often more fluid than separate categories like socialist, Third World, or multicultural, liberal, radical, cultural, separatist, or lesbian feminist admit. Despite fluidities, the distinctions among these categories are important to understand how feminists did and did not work together.

Socialist feminists argued that "there is no way to understand sexism as it acts on our lives without putting it in the historical context of capitalism."[18] Americans who adopted socialist views as part of the New Left learned Marxist theories about how violent, forcible exploitation and hegemony furthered economic and cultural oppression. Those who then became feminist applied those theories to gender while refusing to compartmentalize or postpone addressing sexism. Socialist feminists tended to see the struggle against public and private inequalities as needing simultaneously to address class inequalities, racism, colonial-imperialism, and sexism and used both reform and revolutionary methods. Socialist feminism attracted mostly—but not solely—white Americans.

Feminists of color drew from their own experience to focus on simultaneous oppressions by gender, race, class, and transnational colonial experience. They formed groups as African, Latina, indigenous, or Asian American feminists, sometimes using the umbrella term Third World feminists to show that their solidarity and ethnic origins lay with formerly colonized developing areas. In the 1980s, multicultural feminism became a more common term. Black and Chicana feminists developed their ideas and actions separately from white-dominated feminisms in the same period rather than being derivative of white-dominated feminisms.[19] Feminists of color often worked within their own race or ethnicity and in solidarity with men of their race or ethnicity, which meant they were less likely to advocate all organizing be separate from men.[20] Black, Chicana, Native American, and Asian American feminists experienced ethnically specific pressures for racial solidarity and demands not to express feminism within gender-inclusive movements because their racial power groups considered feminism a "white thing." The most famous black women's groups formed on the East coast in the late 1960s. Nonetheless, looking at the Western United States, as Ellen DuBois and Vicki Ruiz suggested, "provides an important corrective" for diversifying history. Sources for southern California substantiate that Chicana groups, such as the first-generation college students of Hijas de Cuauhtemoc (1968), formed in the late 1960s, while Asian American and American Indian feminist groups seem to have proliferated later than black and Chicana ones did. First-generation college students initiated an L.A. Asian American women's movement through their cogender work in the Asian American Political Alliance (AAPA). In 1971 and 1972, L.A. Asian American feminists who "wrote regularly for the Asian activist newspaper *Guidra*" produced two special women's issues.[21] American Indian women were among delegates to the 1977 National Women's Conference in Houston, issued a manifesto, and tentatively began establishing women's groups. Women of All Red Nations (WARN) started in 1978 as an extension of the American Indian Movement, and Ohoyo (Choctaw for "woman") formed in Tehlequah, Oklahoma, through a Women's Education Equity Act grant in 1979.[22]

In contrast to socialist and Third World/multicultural feminisms, liberal feminists generally tried to reform the existing social structure through political and legal means that would not displace capitalism. They hoped that expanding representative democracy would address inequalities due to racism, class hierarchy, and imperialism. The largest and longest-lived liberal feminist group is NOW. Feminists who were not in groups like NOW often used "liberal" or "reformist" as an insult to indicate that NOW members' tactics were not geared to producing sufficient change. This generalization is problematic, though, because NOW members helped to achieve changes that fundamentally altered opportunities for women and ideas about appropriate gender behavior, and because some NOW members advocated tactics like "guerrilla, street, and mass actions" more often associated with radical feminism.[23]

Self-described radical feminism and its offshoots considered patriarchy the linchpin holding together all axes of oppression and focused on attacking male-based authority and power to overhaul society completely. The methods radical feminists employed created overlapping forms of feminism—cultural, separatist, and lesbian. Cultural feminism shared a focus on male power and interpreted women and men as having essential differences, whether biological or developed through socialization. A proposed solution to supposed irreconcilable differences was for women to create their own independent institutions (not unlike proposals from Marcus Garvey through the Black Panther Party). Women might enjoy women-only spaces temporarily and remain connected with male loved ones most of the time, but separatist feminism specifically did not support heterosexual relationships. Separatist feminist theory extrapolated on essentialism to posit that even well-intentioned pro-feminist men engaged in sexism and sought to maintain male privilege because men were dependent on women. Marilyn Frye famously reflected that people separate to achieve "independence, liberty, growth, invention, sisterhood, safety, health, or the practice of novel or heretical customs." In advocating that women separate themselves "from men and from institutions, relationships, roles, and activities that are male-defined, male-dominated, and operating for the benefit of males and the maintenance of male privilege," separatist feminists raised and debated the issue of at what age male children would be barred from women-only spaces.[24] Califia, for example, included children ages three through eleven and made twelve the cut-off for male participation, while twelve-year-old girls could choose to attend the adult women's presentations and workshops.

Lesbian feminism overlapped greatly with radical, cultural, and separatist feminisms and began as a critique of the homophobia they said heterosexual feminists in NOW displayed. After NOW officials purged some leaders on charges of lesbianism, former NOW members and gay liberationist women took over the stage at NOW's 1970 New York Congress to read a position paper that characterized women in heterosexual couples as engaging in false consciousness by identifying with male power, ego, status, protection, and acceptance that alienated women from themselves and other women. "The Woman-Identified Woman" position paper argued that lesbian relationships made women's commitment to women for liberation and authenticity primary and so made lesbians vanguard feminists. This argument implied that any woman who was woman-identified could achieve autonomy, but subsequent lesbian feminist theory often considered lesbian relationships a paramount component.[25]

Widespread criticism of cultural feminism continues to deserve reevaluation. In 1975, Brooke Williams of Redstockings coined the term "cultural feminism" to disparage women's formation of women-only spaces as depoliticizing radical feminism. Historian Alice Echols formatively set the decline of radical feminism at 1975.[26] Verta Taylor and Leila Rupp, in contrast, compellingly argue that cultural feminism, especially as lesbians embraced it, helped the women's movement survive amidst conservative gains. The overlapping ideologies of cultural, separatist, and lesbian feminism formed a resistance culture of values, relationships, and institution building that preserved one core of the movement, successfully recruited and raised feminist consciousness, and developed strategies feminists and other movement activists have embraced for political action.[27]

The history of Califia Community as part of feminist movements that were components of New Left organizing helps to rectify gaps in understanding of American history. Mainstream education and the historical record marginalize social movements' influences on societal change although the sources exist. For over one hundred years, Americans who advanced equitable gender, economic, and racial relationships have energetically documented evidence of their struggle. Suffragists Elizabeth Stanton, Susan B. Anthony, and Matilda Gage knew that nineteenth-century journalists and historians neglected to cover women's activities, including details of the important work to gain the vote for women. They published the six-volume *History of Woman Suffrage* as "an arsenal of facts" for the next generation. Most historians ignored the tomes and erased the efforts of Black suffragists like Mary Church Terrell until after the 1970s.[28] Analogously, labor activists published their analyses, circulated songs, and taught their members and members' children, but mainstream histories often failed to give the labor movement its due for gains in American quality of life. Likewise, institutionalizing remembrance of the civil rights movement through the Martin Luther King Jr. holiday tends to reduce the movement to one great man and simultaneously to ignore the complexities King championed that fit desegregation and voting rights into a larger picture of economic equality and opposition to the Vietnam War.

Chapter 1 shows the dire need for avowedly feminist radical education by placing the development of feminism and Califia Community in the context of post–World War II inequalities, radical community education, and the explosion of feminist institutions before Califia. Alternative institution building in L.A. reflected how and why feminist work varied nationwide as feminists borrowed and refined each other's ideas to support services for women's safety and health, to determine boundaries of membership in groups, and to try to unite women through shared culture.

Chapter 2 explains the initial significance of creating an educational collective designed to teach women how to work together for grassroots change. Califia founders' motives and their experiences with what they called "the mother of Califia" informed their endeavor to improve feminism by redressing power differentials among women and creating alternative education on a small budget that was compatible with activists' finances. Califia exemplified how feminist groups struggled to accommodate various goals.

The material in Chapters 3 through 5 is organized according to the three main Califia presentation topics about patriarchy, classism, and antiracism because these were major focuses for activism education within feminism. Developments on each topic affected other aspects of feminist thought and practice..

Chapter 3 reveals that attempts to unify women by gender trained participants to defend themselves and rallied women to oppose violence against women and children. Califia's education reproduced tensions among feminists based on sexual and gender expressions and foreclosed most cross-gender work. Advocacy of lesbian feminist separatist ideology deserves attention because it produced energetic institution-building and spurred reevaluation of who threatened whom and who needed protection in society. Theorizing gender and sexuality as most important also produced grave limitations when other women felt that their socioeconomic class and/or race were major factors in their lives.

Chapter 4 argues that Califia Community's experientially based analysis of class fostered interpersonal relations by teaching adults to reassess how applicable the classed values they learned as children remained in their current lives. The focus on the interpersonal, however, left participants unconnected to labor or welfare rights organizing to reform class inequalities. This was typical of most feminist activists of the time and reflected the difficulties of dealing with neoliberal policies, individuals' economic insecurity as the social welfare net unraveled, and the tenuousness of actual work among feminist, labor, and welfare groups.

Chapter 5 demonstrates that the development of Califia's antiracism presentation and multiracial participation exemplified increases in feminist antiracist work while mainstream America deemphasized how intractable racism has been. Califia started with white founders, and racial homogeneity was common to groups in southern California and nationwide. This chapter explains the gains for women of color who attended Califia, the challenges for feminists of color who chose to lead the antiracism presentations, and the tensions over white participants' unexamined views about race and to whom the group "belonged."

Chapter 6 concludes that the decline of Califia mirrored the demise of many feminist groups by the mid-1980s due to the hostile political-economic climate and internal pressures. New Right attacks on public education disrupted feminist education inside and outside universities by purging female professors with grassroots connections. Middle-aged white activists burnt out while younger feminists of color struggled to balance their own economic needs with the demands of adapting Califia to women of color audiences. Feminists split over identity and developments in sexual politics, including the place for lesbians in gay organizations in the midst of antigay campaigns and government neglect of the AIDS epidemic.

CHAPTER I

THE NEED FOR COMMUNITY
EDUCATION PROJECTS

HISTORICAL ASPECTS OF AMERICAN SOCIETAL INEQUALITIES and radical educators' interventions help to contextualize feminist institution building. Post–World War II discrimination provided the milieu for New Left agitation, but longer-term frustrations about mainstream education created lines of radical pedagogy that stretched from the nineteenth century to 1960s movements. In response, women raised their awareness of inequalities, equipped themselves with practical skills, and formed women-run institutions that could sustain a sense of community and provide a base from which to address societal disparities. Thus, this chapter combines temporal, thematic, and spatial contexts to set up the relationships among postwar conditions, sexism specific to traditional education, radical community education antecedents, and foundational organizing in Los Angeles.

POSTWAR INEQUALITIES

After World War II, Americans faced many forms of discrimination, and campaigns for equality that led to legislative and cultural change are widely documented. Popular culture myths about women persist, however, despite the best efforts of scholars like Joanne Meyerowitz, Alice Kessler-Harris, and Stephanie Cootz to debunk them.[1] It is crucial to know the conditions against which feminists fought in order to understand the impact of organizing.

Personnel from the federal government, defense-related industries, and mainstream media created a propaganda campaign in 1945 as powerful as the "Rosie the Riveter" wartime campaign to recruit women into jobs and auxiliary military units. The campaign to return women to the home and economic and legal dependence on husbands proclaimed the necessity that women exclusively be homemaker wives and mothers. Although the percentage of wives in the workforce doubled between 1940 and 1960 from 15 percent to 30 percent,[2] the ideal that women be like the June Cleaver character on *Leave It to Beaver* foreclosed the possibility of well-paying, high-status jobs for most women. Messages to marry early and be consumers for their families laid a foundation for discontent both among the women who had succeeded in jobs previously defined as "male" and among their daughters.[3] The image of the happy homemaker perpetuated a false assumption men had touted since the late nineteenth century: that husbands needed careers to support their family, while if women got job training, they worked temporarily until marriage or childbirth.[4] In fact, millions of women filled jobs created by postwar business expansion. Aggressive marketing and extension of credit heightened demand for consumer goods, which increased the need for women's income. With close to one quarter of Americans in substandard housing with inadequate food and clothing, wages and credit were crucial to the support of many married and single women.[5]

Legal and business practices contributed to disparities in rights. Until 1963, it was legal to pay women less than men for the same work. Companies ran newspaper job advertisements on pages that were segregated by sex and usually relegated women to lower-paying, lower-status jobs than men had. No laws prevented gender discrimination in employment. Companies routinely fired pregnant women on the assumption that they would and should forsake wage and salaried work for full-time child rearing. Legally women could not hold head of household status, could be denied credit or loans in their own name after marriage, and were expected to take their husband's last name. The efforts to shield women from life outside the home extended to barring them from serving on juries in some states. Women were largely excluded from positions of power. They hardly ever ran big corporations or universities, rarely served in Congress, were not ordained as ministers, did not anchor newscasts, and seldom held other leadership roles. Government and media leaders largely disregarded that the home was not always a haven. Before the late 1970s, police and neighbors usually considered "wife beating" an unfortunate private concern and did not intervene. Until feminists applied the criminal legal term "battery," created the concepts of "marital rape" and "sexual harassment," and started to establish battered women's shelters in 1973, there was little recourse in the judicial system. Americans often thought victims of rape and harassment somehow "asked for it." Paradoxically for a society that touted male breadwinning heads for nuclear families, judges usually did not enforce rulings that men pay child support and alimony if couples divorced.[6]

Today Americans have a right to basic feminist legal gains such as non-discriminatory hiring practices, equal pay, maternity leave, and access to birth control, laws against preventing women from serving on juries or refusing married women loans, and judicial processes to redress sexual harassment, sexual assault, and nonpayment of child support. Universities were important sites of inequality because postwar society increasingly touted college degrees as a prerequisite for success.

EDUCATIONAL SEXISM

While laws and mores have shifted in the years since the 1960s–1970s, explicitly feminist community organizations are less prolific now than they were during that time. In the twenty-first century, students of all genders across the United States can learn together in feminist-inspired university courses. Some feminists, especially those within academia, believed that a way to preserve feminism was to infuse it into the university system. That strategic choice was not a foregone conclusion. In the late 1960s and 1970s, feminists organized in differing but complementary ways based on their recognition that university culture acted on mainstream sexist biases.

> "*History* was terribly devoid of what *women* were doing while all these *wars* were happening and all these *male heroes* were doing all their actions and everything. . . . And we didn't *do* anything. But it's because men *looked* at what we've been doing and didn't think it was *important*. . . . So we needed to *talk* about that. History was *empty* for us."
> DIANE F. GERMAIN (CALIFIA COMMUNITY COLLECTIVE MEMBER 1981–1983).[7]

For Diane Germain, Califia Community represented a way to validate her and other women's historical agency after an education from the mid-1940s through the mid-1960s that failed to mention women. Women and male supporters developed educational programs inside and outside the university system in order to establish a place in history and to preserve gains against opposition. Califia Community's decade-long volunteer-run education stood in contrast to the careers of feminist professors and the institutionalization of Women's Studies programs that have been documented as well as the generation of books and articles that have now gained inclusion in many surveys of U.S. society.[8]

Founders held Califia Community's weeklong or long-weekend summer conferences in temporary spaces that were only for women and children. They raised women's consciousness about various forms of inequality and strategized how to improve conditions for women. The decision not to link the "Amazon training camps" to already-established universities and newly developing Women's Studies programs made sense in light of its founders' experiences with university systems. Where to locate feminism fit into a broad debate over whether to work within or outside the systems that needed reform.

Universities exemplified male-dominated space that taught and enforced an ideal that primarily defined women as "housewives" and mothers, an ideology Betty Friedan called "the feminine mystique." During the late 1800s and early 1900s, women became a minority of undergraduates, graduate students and university professors, but Depression-era gender assumptions exacerbated the prioritization of educating and hiring men over women. After World War II, 2,232,000 male veterans and 64,728 female veterans gained college experience through the G.I. Bill, including white and ethnic minority Americans from working-class backgrounds who could not otherwise have afforded higher education. The influx of male veterans led to overcrowding in universities, and colleges solved this problem by favoring the guaranteed tuition of G.I. Bill students over nonveterans, especially rejecting women's applications.[9] This unintended consequence of the G.I. Bill, combined with successful efforts to push women out of careers in favor of domestic duties and secondary jobs, further diminished educational gains for women. The percentage of college students who were women declined from 47 percent in 1920 to 34.2 percent in 1958.[10] While women of the 1920s earned half the bachelor degrees conferred, females earned only 24 percent in the 1950s. By the 1970s, two generations of women like Diane Germain had experienced the marginalizing effects of this system.

Educational reform to include a wider array of students and curriculum change became a big part of the buzz for post-1945 societal change. By 1970, G.I. Bill students from three wars included veterans from socio-economically disadvantaged backgrounds. These first generation working-class students' experiences did not necessarily mesh with institutionalized middle-class biases. During the Vietnam era, increasing numbers of students wanted to change what university courses taught as they took to heart American ideals of representative democracy. Civil Rights activists recognized that addressing education inequalities was crucial to career advancement and voting rights that were restricted to separate and unequal literacy tests.

After activism and implementation of the 1965 Voting Rights Act guaranteed access to polling places, Americans continued to struggle to integrate K–12 education. Black Power and Chicanismo adherents included educational reform in their mission. They argued that a Eurocentric curriculum prevented Americans from learning racial and ethnic minorities' contributions to civilization. Radicalized minority students read up on their own history and literature and began to create alternative schools so as not to rely on a racist system. Their extracurricular learning included non-Western influences such as Chinese Chairman Mao's *Little Red Book*, domestic manifestos that promoted ethnic unity and self-determination (e.g., black nationalism, Chicanismo, Red Power), and creating their own alternative political journals as vehicles for their message. At Oakland's founding chapter of the Black Panther Party, for example, older youths led other children in revolutionary songs. A Harlem Panther woman told reporters they were educating community members about the inherent inequalities capitalism hid behind American racism.[11]

Feminist education was the latest in a series of monumental examples of people addressing glaring gaps in traditional education, challenging quotas and discrimination in higher education, and the dearth of information on women's contributions to western culture. They wanted education to be more relevant to their lives and to lead to successful careers. Women were able to resist being funneled into nursing, home economics, or secretarial work by building on the 1957 call to educate men and women in math and science to prepare the United States for its space-race competition with the USSR.[12]

Expanding 1960s universities granted unequal access to graduate training and hiring, which created a scarcity of women faculty. Universities grew due to four main factors: baby boomers started to reach college age, the federal government increased educational funding in response to population and the space race against the Soviet Union, the economy boomed, and a draft during the Vietnam conflict encouraged some young men to enroll to gain deferments. Women slowly benefited as students and finally reached 45 percent of the undergraduate population in 1976. These students, however, had a lower percentage of female professors to mentor them than their grandmothers' generation had. Colleges typically had a higher percentage of female faculty members in the 1920s than in the late 1960s and early 1970s and often had no female full professors.[13]

Hiring practices did not initially reflect transformations in the student body. University personnel nationwide employed legal and conventional tactics to minimize admitting women and ethnic minorities to graduate schools and hiring them as professors. In interviews of academic women, they describe gender-based obstacles they faced even when that is not the focus of their stories. They remember programs rejected them to avoid the funding dilemma of giving women fellowships instead of men, having women teach male undergraduates or the possibility that female students would become pregnant.[14] When admitted, some were the only women in courses where their peers were "extraordinarily hostile to women being in their environment" or were one of a small handful of female graduate students.[15] They earned coveted fellowships despite quotas to restrict women from applying. In the 1950s and early 1960s, before mandated national searches or affirmative action, chairmen could simply ask colleagues at other schools to send one of their graduate students—the epitome of an old-boys network. Departments openly rejected female applicants because the department had a policy against hiring women, they did not hire "housewives," or some male faculty did not want to work with a woman. Women who became professors sometimes spoke positively about their male advisors. They complained in hindsight that otherwise supportive mentors did not put much effort into their female students' job searches because mentors generally assumed that colleges would not hire women or would hire them at a lower level than they deserved.[16] Female professors who looked back critically considered it commonplace for male professors' letters of recommendation to focus on women's appearance and behavior in ways that could undermine their candidacy. One male advisor claimed in the mid-1960s that his advisee "seems really quite normal, and I think would fit in easily." Another praised his student as "pretty, some might say beautiful" while a negative recommendation disparaged the candidate as "the wheel horse of any committee she serves on."[17] Academic husbands and wives faced gender bias when departments or schools consistently instituted nepotism rules against the female professor to retain her husband. On rare occasions, the husband resigned in protest. One husband suggested his wife call Betty Friedan because the National Organization for Women (NOW) wanted the executive order against employment sex discrimination to extend to universities. The origin of NOW merits further attention later as a source of feminist organizing.[18]

Departments routinely hired women for lower salaries. This remained permissible after 1969 because the Equal Pay Act did not include professionals. Sometimes departments' standards for advancement included gender bias such as not recognizing women's suffrage as a viable area for historical research.[19] A woman in one particularly hostile department had senior colleagues who pretended she was invisible and a chairman who denied her tenure after he chose three of his close friends to review her and neglected to mention any of her publications. In other cases, the fact that professional conferences rarely accepted panels with women presenters and that professional journals were far less likely to publish articles written by women worked together with claims that accepting women professors meant "lowering standards."[20] Many state schools only hired women part-time to minimize salaries and benefits, and some blacklisted women who protested that policy. By the late 1970s and 1980s, female faculty members worked together to gain space in professional conferences, replace the old boys' network with national searches and more transparent hiring practices, chart noncompliance with affirmative action and bring successful class-action lawsuits to force equal salaries.

In retrospect, the 1970s wrought significant positive changes for women in academia. Women academics, allied university men, feminist organizations like NOW, and sympathetic politicians created a climate that fostered Women's Studies programs, courses with more balanced gender content, and the status of women in academic and professional fields. Over the 1970s, the proportion of female students rose from nine to 25 percent in medical school and from 10 to 36 percent in law school.[21] Often those who fought to bring feminism into academia were already professors. Elizabeth Lapovsky Kennedy, for example, said that in contrast to fears that universities would never support women's education and would co-opt feminists' work to compromise their goals: "I was too much of a pragmatist to be attracted to this way of thinking. Where would the funds come from for an alternative institution?" A taxpayer and professor at a public university, she wanted her tax dollars to support better education for all women by infusing feminism into the curriculum.[22]

RADICAL COMMUNITY EDUCATION ANTECEDENTS

Before the massive expansion of New Left social movements that changed college enrollment, curriculum, and hiring, at least three types of Americans created leftist community education that overlapped. In the face of strong opposition from dominant society some immigrant Americans, American Communists and Socialists, and radical American Christians employed community education projects to try to put into practice their political, economic, and cultural analyses. Radical educators have shared the view that traditional education preserves the status quo by fitting students into the economic and social system of their nation. Americans reinvented a concept for adult community education outside an academic system of grades and degrees that originated with a nineteenth-century radical Christian in Denmark. Immigrants to America revised the Danish folk schools.

Both the Communist and Socialist Parties benefitted from immigrant Americans' educational spaces. In 1931–1932, Myles Horton researched the Danish model to create a school that intersected with other radical leftist endeavors and helped to shape the civil rights movement. Leftists' work then influenced feminist education.

Nikolaj Frederik Severin Grundtvig created the idea for a Danish folk school system. He developed radical Christian educational and political views from prioritizing the Bible and democratic discussion over authoritative pronouncements. Grundtvig completed Lutheran seminary and worked in Denmark as a tutor and historian until he was old enough to be ordained. His award-winning sermon at his father's church gained him ordination in 1811, but the published sermon rankled his bishop. Grundtvig argued that rationalist pride corrupted ecclesiastical authorities, which led them to stray from Biblical meaning. He resigned four years into his first church appointment in 1826 when a professor of theology successfully sued him for libel after Grundtvig published a similar attack on theologians. Nonetheless, Denmark's absolute monarch funded Grundtvig's varied research. Seeing the open-ended conversational style at Trinity College in Cambridge, England in 1831 helped Grundtvig develop ideas for adult education.[23] He valued its free inquiry and relatively equal teacher-student exchange.[24] Grundtvig promoted the idea that ordinary people held valuable wisdom, so adults should continue learning primarily through discussions drawn from life where each person taught and learned. Followers initiated Denmark's first folk school with farmers in mind in 1844. After the Danish king's death, Grundtvig gained election to Parliament and helped to promote increased representative democracy. He was the only man to write a favorable review of the first Danish published call for women's equal rights. His folk school idea blossomed in the 1860s[25] and preserved Danish language and culture, including music, while "advancing the economic and political interests of their students." By the 1900s, the folk school concept had spread to Germany, Norway, Sweden, Finland, and England.[26]

For twenty years on either side of 1900, the United States experienced massive immigration. New Americans who wanted to preserve their language, culture, and religious traditions sometimes settled together and formed mutual aid societies for the adults and programs for their children. Finnish Community Halls and Jewish Hebrew Schools, for example, worked against the erasure of ethnic distinctions. Folk school pedagogy for adult learning influenced educational practices devoted to imparting cultural knowledge and strengthening ethnic ties for children. Anti-assimilationist education overlapped with socialist or communist ideologies among community members who learned those political ideas in Europe or embraced them in the United States in response to American class hierarchy and anti-immigrant sentiment. New York City, for example, had over 4,000 students just in the Communist-supporting Yiddish language schools. The New York area also had many Jewish camps by the 1920s where children escaped anti-Semitism and enjoyed summer recreation along with religious, Zionist, and/or Socialist instruction.[27]

From the early 1900s to the 1940s, Socialist and Communist Americans organized the largest left wing of the United States. Adult members borrowed mainstream models to create youth programs that sought to help their children become revolutionary Americans who could turn "political and economic analysis into a way of life."[28] Socialist Sunday schools before World War I appropriated hymn and catechism formats to teach youth. The Communist Party U.S.A. developed the Young Pioneers of America in 1926 as an alternative to the Boy Scouts of America, and its leaders encouraged members to observe urban poverty, unionize child workers while demanding playgrounds, free school lunches, and the abolition of child labor, and become autonomous from their schools' and even parents' teachings. The 1930s Red Falcons provided a Socialist alternative to the Young Pioneers. Youth magazines, books, and summer camps that were kids-only or family resorts provided further venues for inculcating children with their Communist or Socialist parents' values.

Curricula harkened to immigrant pasts and thoroughly American presents while leading the way for pluralism. Leftist Americans' programs and leadership development echoed adult folk schools by encouraging children to initiate activities and become officers or organizers and by including projects on the history and culture of sponsoring ethnic groups. Simultaneously, they mirrored fraternal lodge practices in the children's groups and borrowed hiking and camping information from the YMCA and Boy Scouts. At least one camp introduced Woody Guthrie's folk music as a basis for radical political culture. The camps taught girls to be as involved as boys. Programming for youths and adults sometimes promoted multiculturalism by teaching about different white ethnicities and creating rare interracial spaces for black-white solidarity that taught about the contributions African Americans have made to U.S. society. This provided space for black Americans to meet respectful whites for the first time, and Communist-sponsored children's books were among the only ones with minority characters before the 1960s. By 1940, close to 20,000 youth were in the Communist Children's Movement from coast to coast.[29] Scholars have traced the influence of "Red-diaper babies" on the movements to extend participatory democracy in the 1960s. Respect and inclusion were also part of the labor and civil rights work of the Highlander Folk School and the publishing of founding feminist historian Gerda Lerner before spreading through 1970s feminist education via scholarship by Lerner and other feminists who had Communist ties or through the transfer of experience from civil rights and other New Left work.

Highlander Folk School (HFS) combined radical Christianity with goals of participatory democracy and economic justice. Generations of labor and civil rights proponents developed their strategies at HFS, making the school's influences, pedagogy, and results crucial context for community education and social movement work.

Founder Myles Horton grew up in Appalachian Tennessee with Presbyterian schoolteacher parents who fed and clothed white and black poor people in the area.[30] He involved himself in Christian endeavors like Vacation Bible School and the YMCA while he attended the Presbyterian-founded Cumberland College and then worked with theology professor Reinhold Niebuhr during graduate school. Horton saw a need for adult education unbounded from university constraints to help Appalachian people value their culture, think through how to deal collectively with economic and political problems, and organize for change.[31] After countless discussions eventually led him to observe Danish folk schools, Horton cofounded HFS in 1932 and devoted his life to this "rural settlement house."[32] Like the Danish system, HFS included music and drama from the beginning to "cultivate the spirit and soul" and to put people's experiences into kinesthetic performances that engaged people to understand emotional interests.[33] When Zilphia Johnson attended in 1935, her music and drama training and radical Presbyterian perspective infused HFS. Horton and Johnson married, and she worked at HFS for the rest of her life, teaching drama, collecting folk songs, and contributing to the process of converting hymns, ballads, and popular music into protest songs such as "We Shall Not Be Moved." Zilphia Horton learned the black hymn "We Shall Overcome" when white tobacco worker strikers taught it to Highlander participants. She simplified the melody and added verses. The labor movement used the song, and then members of the Student Nonviolent Coordinating Committee and the Southern Christian Leadership Conference picked it up from HFS. Along the way, different song leaders added verses, and it became the most widely used civil rights song in history.[34]

Because HFS's mission was "to assist in the defense and expansion of political and economic democracy," and the teachers supported local strikes, conservative politicians, segregationists, and employers tarred HFS as a "Communist Training School."[35] In 1981, Bill Moyers asked Horton what principles had influenced him and whether he had ever been Communist. Horton traced his impetus to his characterization of the New Testament as about love and the Hebrew Scriptures as about creation. He said, "You can't be a revolutionary, you can't want to change society if you don't love people. . . . love people, that's right out of the Bible. . . . God was a creator. If you're going to be with people, born in God's image, then you've got to be creators, you can't be followers, you know or puppets. . . ." Horton avowed he was never Communist. The Communist Party head had retracted an invitation to join, saying that with all of Horton's ideas, they could not trust him to toe the party line.[36]

He and other teaching staff developed one- or two-week programs based on needs that community members expressed. Adult students lived and learned together quickly, analyzing their own lived experiences that were meaningful to them. They talked about what they were doing in their community and problems they hoped to solve.[37] Rather than impart knowledge in regimented schools to train people into managerial and employee positions within a system Horton found exploitative, HFS teachers facilitated people's creative thinking, pluralistic ideas, and power to make decisions. Teachers summarized discussion to keep the analysis moving and sometimes contributed their own experience to the mix. This ensured that the teaching was not doctrinaire. Horton also distinguished radical education from organizing, saying that organizers could achieve a specific, limited goal efficiently and justify not involving people in a process based on how the end result would benefit them. In contrast, in radical education it was essential that everyone participate, lead, and learn problem-solving skills.[38]

Highlander yielded results; they gave people a place to develop their projects, supported local initiatives, and created space for interracial respect. After violating Tennessee's law against integrated schools for nine years, HFS started laying the groundwork in 1953 to end segregation. *Brown v. Board of Education* was under Supreme Court review. Rosa Parks supplemented her NAACP training by attending HFS in 1955 and said, "That was the first time in my life I had lived in an atmosphere of complete equality with the members of the other race." The school hired her as a speaker-recruiter after her Montgomery, Alabama, employer fired her in retaliation for her refusal to move from her bus seat. Other black leaders echoed Parks's sentiment. Septima Clark and Essau Jenkins attended a workshop and then encouraged Clark's cousin, Bernice Robinson, to go. All were impressed to find white Southerners who could live with black Southerners as equals. In 1956, HFS loaned Jenkins money to buy a schoolhouse, where

Robinson taught night classes for other black residents near Charleston, South Carolina, so they could fulfill the literacy test requirement for voting. The "Citizenship Schools" asked students what they wanted to learn, carrying on HFS's pedagogy, and Clark convinced Martin Luther King to adopt and spread citizenship schools through the Southern Christian Leadership Conference in 1961. Horton pushed sit-in students to defend their concepts of nonviolence and civil disobedience, and students at HFS produced guidelines for future protests. The HFS workshops also spoke to the place of whites in the civil rights movement and coordinated six-week sessions of interracial living for black, white, Native American, and Mexican American high school students in 1960.[39] Although racial nationalism withdrew from the interracial "beloved community" concept, feminists struggled to recreate it.

Education was a key part of activist reform. Locating feminist education at the community level outside of campuses drew on radical education principles as a strategic response to imposing campuses and the prevalence of hostility feminist women received from men and women who resisted change.

REPRESENTATIVE FEMINIST INSTITUTION BUILDING

Activists challenged society when they promoted alternatives to traditional ways of thinking. A dense variety of feminist institutions formed in major cities across the United States through the 1970s and 1980s. The range of institutions, organizations, and events that L.A. feminists created were typical of those that raised awareness, framed issues, and shored up a sense of community in major cities.

A series of community centers overlapped in different areas of L.A., which became spaces to advertise other feminist endeavors like Califia Community. Lesbian feminists distinguished themselves from the gay liberation movement by leaving the Gay Liberation Front–inspired Gay Services Center on Westlake.[40] The Los Angeles Women's Center was considered radical and welcomed lesbians in 1970; one member remembered women there being "very Maoist."[41] Del Whan, who had been in the Peace Corps, civil rights, and antiwar movements, founded the Gay Women's Service Center in 1971 on Glendale Boulevard in Echo Park. An early leader there, Sharon Raphael, recorded that the Gay Women's Service Center was the first lesbian-only social service agency, and that it provided bail, release from mental institutions, and transitional housing as well as social events.[42] Sisters Liberation House on South Oxford Street by downtown followed

the next year. The Westside Women's Center at Second and Hill Streets in Santa Monica[43] (1972) housed two programs that merit attention—the Radical Feminist Therapy Collective (1972) and Fat Underground (1972). In the 1980s more community centers arose that deliberately tried to include women of color from the start: Commonground (1983), Connexxus (opened January 1985), and Connexxus East (1987).[44]

Concerns about mental health care at the Gay Women's Service Center and the Westside Women's Center reflected how criticism of sexism within the mental and physical health industries had reached a national audience. Boston women's frustration with condescending doctors led them to publish the famous and still printed *Our Bodies, Ourselves* in 1969 to inform women about how to control their health care. By 1973, 1,200 women's health groups in the United States provided services and education.[45] Critiques such as Kay Weiss's "What Medical Students Learn" (1975) followed objections to sexist Freudian stereotypes that feminists had made in the United States since Betty Friedan's *The Feminine Mystique*. Weiss revealed demeaning misogyny in a widely used obstetrics and gynecological textbook. The authors of *Obstetrics and Gynecology* claimed women were childlike, wanted "a masochistic surrender to the man," and "an element of rape," and needed psychiatric care if they did not always attain orgasm through vaginal stimulation. A survey of twenty-seven other gynecological texts by Diana Scully and Pauline Bart in 1973 corroborated that not one

[i]ncorporated Kinsey's 1953 findings that orgasm without stimulation [of the clitoris] "is a physical and physiological impossibility for nearly all females" or Masters and Johnson's 1966 findings . . . that although orgasm is felt in the vagina, the feeling derives from stimulation of clitoral nerves.

Men had taken over women's health by the late nineteenth century, and their successors continued turn-of-the-century misinformation that supported men's pleasure while pathologizing women. More broadly, physicians, 90 percent of whom were male, dangerously dismissed women's physical complaints as psychosomatic and withheld information, preventing women from making informed decisions about their treatment.[46]

In the context of women's health work, two politicized health groups were highly influential in southern California. The Radical Feminist Therapy Collective (RFTC) and Fat Underground (FU) both initiated radical education that permeated other feminist spaces, including Califia.

The RFTC originated in 1972 as a way to "teach radical therapy tools, problem solving skills, and do political consciousness raising and community organizing in the context of lesbian feminist politics."[47] A group of L.A. women traveled to Claude Steiner's Berkeley-based Radical Psychiatry Center for training. Returning to form RFTC, they extended radical psychiatry's rejection of trends in therapy that pathologized people to pressure them into conforming to society. Members taught women to define themselves and to oppose the persecution of a society that had labeled them "sick" based on being frustrated, uppity, lesbian, or fat. The collective valued woman-identification regardless of women's sexual orientation. Unlike traditional therapy, RFTC defended its rejection of impartiality. Members argued that raising consciousness and advocating for women's interests required taking stands. Over the years, RFTC mediated L.A. feminists' conflicts and raised consciousnesses, especially about body image. Simultaneously, though, some L.A.-area feminists were wary of the RFTC members' rejection of impartiality. Women experienced pressure to conform to feminist ideals in the 1970s. RFTC members, like other feminists, assumed that once women's eyes were opened to the oppressive origins of practices, nobody would in good conscience choose to continue practices like shaving their legs. The difference between RFTC women and other feminists was that the peer counselors "knew everyone's secrets."[48]

Fat Underground (FU) developed from RFTC in its first year to demystify oppression against fat people. It was the first fat liberation group in the country. Reclaiming the term "fat" and opposing euphemisms like "overweight" as negative, FU became the most significant force against bigotry based on people's looks in a city known for celebrity beauty. Radical therapy asserted that oppressors portrayed their control as benefiting the oppressed, thus mystifying oppression. Judy Freespirit and Aldebaran ran into the limits of that model when other collective founders balked at them speaking as a team at a local college. Collective members feared that having two fat representatives could discredit the group. In search of a successful diet, Aldebaran ran across Llewellyn Louderback's 1970 *Fat Power*. Louderback blamed the diet industry for fat discrimination. He found evidence in public health documents that fat was due to biology rather than overeating and that almost all doctor-supervised diets failed over the long term. Medical studies before the proliferation of high-fructose corn syrup and other massive changes to the American diet correlated health problems like heart attacks with fat people in judgmental societies that advocated dieting rather than fat people whose societies did not consider weight negative. Contrasting biological and environmental factors, he concluded that prejudice against fat people was one more example of a societal problem rather than a personal failing.

Like Louderback, Freespirit and Aldebaran accepted some premises of medical science in order to politicize fat oppression, criticize powerful institutions, and gain supporters. They first joined the National Association to Aid Fat Americans (NAAFA) and created an L.A. chapter. Their group charged "doctors, psychologists, and public health officials . . . [with] concealing and distorting the facts about fat that were contained in their own professional research journals. In doing so, they betrayed [fat people] and played into the hands of the multibillion dollar weight-loss industry." By 1973, Lynn Mabel-Lois (aka Lynn McAffee) taught members to research medical journals. Like gay men and lesbians who successfully challenged the American Psychiatric Association's designation of homosexuality as a mental illness that year, NAAFA-LA combated the conflation of scientific and moralizing discourses, which asserted that fat people were gluttons who created their health problems, so people should control their weight through dieting. Fat liberation arrived at a wholly positive position like gay liberation's "gay is good" and discounted all potential health problems associated with being fat. Probably to avoid the retort that Americans' unhealthy lifestyle made them fat, the group did not weigh in on the rising availability of high-calorie, low-nutrition foods.

The beginning of their slew of position papers and appearances on talk shows prompted the main NAAFA office to order them to quiet down and disguise their feminism.[49] Instead, the group quit NAAFA. Four of the women and one man whose membership was brief took the name Fat Underground (FU), with initials that expressed their attitude.[50] FU reclaimed the word "fat," while "Underground" conjured images of the underground railroad with their CR rescuing others from enslavement to the diet industry but also sounded like the violent Weather Underground. Its nonviolent members attacked a multibillion-dollar dieting industry in an anticapitalist "communiqué" (published article) with lines such as the following:

Most of the popular knowledge about fatness is mystification. This mystification is backed up by the medical profession and capitalist interests. The anti-fat stance of capitalism—the interests of the fashion and diet-food industries, for example—would be easy for most radicals to accept as oppressive.[51]

FU broadened from CR to approaching others in southern California. Freespirit and Aldebaran guided RFTC to start a Fat Women's Problem-Solving Group. Fat-positive CR discouraged dieting as ineffective and taught women to speak up for their right to health care without pressure from doctors to diet.[52] Ariana Manov prompted discussion of why they did not talk about sex or relate to others or each other sexually. Why did they fulfill the "sexless fat girl" stereotype in the midst of "the sex-drenched environment of the 1970s"? Over the course of 1974, the group took secluded retreats and worked to love their bodies by recuperating an aesthetic based on ancient earth mother goddess images like the Venus of Willendorf. This imagery supplemented the Amazon warrior motif within the feminist community.[53]

FU supported healthy lives with good relationships to food regardless of weight gain or loss and appeared at a Women's Equality Day and in the pages of *Sister* by the autumn of 1974.[54] FU members harassed local weight-loss clinics by attending introductory lectures and using the question-and-answer portion to attack the programs' medical theories and success rates. They denounced weight-loss surgeries like intestinal bypass and jaw wiring as barbaric, dangerous mutilations.[55] By 1976, FU members spoke regularly at California State University at Long Beach (CSULB) Women's Studies classes. At the first Califia Community camp Freespirit saw women supporting the diet industry by buying diet soda pop and encouraging each other in weight loss. According to Ariana Manov, "[S]he got so pissed off that she drove off the mountain and came *back* to L.A. and got the Fat Underground . . . videotape that was made, and took it back up to Califia Community."[56] It would have taken about two hours to drive the sixty-plus miles round-trip. The video proclaimed the fat liberation manifesto: fatphobic ridicule supports false claims of the diet industry in the face of evidence "*that over 95% of all weight-loss programs, when evaluated over a five-year period, fail utterly* [italics in original]," "fat people are entitled to human respect and recognition," and discrimination must end.[57] After a visual presentation, FU members led discussions during the first three to four years of Califia. Other women began noticing fat liberation and writing articles to *The Lesbian Tide*.[58] FU members connected "fatness" to disability and theorized that disability was a social construction that created oppressed minorities out of those who did not fall within the norms society created. Their views on disability mirrored broader demands for disability access at a time when women-only spaces like Califia and women's music festivals were leading the way in laying down wheelchair accessibility routes, incorporating American Sign Language interpreters, and considering whether spaces were safe and pedagogically inclusive for blind women. Former FU members directly influenced Califia camps and continued to write and speak out for fat liberation into the early 1980s from both coasts, serving as models for continued fat liberation work.[59]

Educating women to control their medical and mental health and reject size constraints expressed the growing perception that women must organize against harmful, misogynous mainstream norms. Women's safety was paramount for feminists of the 1960s through 1980s, and they pro-actively supported and strengthened women to combat male violence. Feminists started antirape speak-outs in 1971 and battered women's shelters in 1973. They initiated a twenty-year campaign to get state-by-state legislation criminalizing rape within marriage and worked with police officers, hospital staff, and judges to change the ways they treated women who were raped or experienced domestic violence. Examples of such work in Los Angeles were the L.A. Coalition Against Assaults Against Women (1973), Women Against Violence Against Women (1976), the San Fernando Valley Rape Crisis Center (1981), and the development of Take Back the Night Marches from 1980 on.

Lesbian feminists did a lot of the organizing in L.A., including conferences that drew women together across state and national lines and across ideological divides. The Gay Women's West Coast Conference of 1971 attracted homophile women from Daughters of Bilitis accustomed to middle-class civil rights organizing and lesbian feminists who danced shirtless.[60] The West Coast Lesbian Conference (1973) boasted almost 2,000 attendees from several countries and twenty-six states, which was awe-inspiring for women who had never seen more than a few lesbians together at one time. Lesbians also enjoyed the NOW Sexuality and Lesbianism Task Force Conference in 1974. In subsequent years, L.A. hosted the National Lesbian Feminist Organization founding conference (1978), Gay and Lesbian Life-styles Conference (1980), National Lesbians of Color Conference (1983), International Lesbian and Gay People of Color Conference (1986), and the West Coast Conference and Celebration By and For Old Lesbians (1987). Many of these conferences met in different large cities different years.

At the West Coast Lesbian Conference, a dispute over what makes some-one a woman split participants in a way that portended continued debate. Robin Morgan used her keynote address at the West Coast Lesbian Conference to stir hostility against conference organizer, Beth Elliot, because Elliot had been labeled male at birth. Elliot was an active feminist and a Daughters of Bilitis member working for lesbian rights before she helped create the conference. Referring to Elliot, Morgan charged,

> Where the Man is concerned, we must not be separate fingers but one fist.
> . . . I charge him as an opportunist, an infiltrator, and a destroyer—with the mentality of a rapist.
> And you know who he is. Now. You can let him into your workshops—or you can deal with him.[61]

Given her record of feminist work, if Elliot was "an infiltrator, and a destroyer," she certainly was delaying her calculated blow. Morgan's insistence on denying Elliot's self-identification as a woman by referring to her with male pronouns and the label "the Man" indicated a belief that the male sex label that male doctors imposed at birth was an indelible mark of enemy status. The majority of the feminists present supported Elliot's participation in her own conference in two votes "overwhelmingly" and "3 to 1 in favor of Beth performing," but "the San Francisco Gutter Dykes" continued to agitate against her. Another conference organizer, Barbara McLean, reviewed the conference and responded to biologizing arguments like, "He has a *prick*! That makes him a man" with "That's bullshit! Anatomy is NOT destiny."[62] Both Morgan and McLean participated in separatism, but McLean demonstrated a social constructionist understanding of Elliot transition from male to female (MTF) opposed to Morgan's essentialist position. Before the pressure to expel Elliot, the conference-planning women worked congenially and clearly considered Elliot a woman rather than doomed by biology to live as a misogynous man.

Morgan and other attendees' hostility to MTF trans women is significant not only for its essentialism but because early anti-trans incidents involved outsiders stirring up conflict and being unwilling to listen to people's experience. Five years after the Morgan incident, Janice Raymond sent the women's music collective, Olivia Records, a draft of her dissertation chapter in which she attacked their music engineer, Sandy Stone, as a threat to womanhood. Stone was labeled male at birth and raised a boy but identified as a lesbian feminist woman. Olivia Records employees, like the West Coast Lesbian Conference organizers, supported Stone as a woman and argued that she trained other women after getting experience the music industry usually denied to women. Raymond's publication of *The Transsexual Empire* led lesbian consumers to threaten a boycott, and Stone left her collective.[63]

Raymond became famous by gathering the conversations that percolated since 1971 and advocating trans-exclusion from feminism. A feminist press reissued *The Transsexual Empire* in 1994, but the fifteenth anniversary edition added nothing to the debate and simply perpetuated misinformation, including the continued assertion that female-to-male (FTM) trans men were not a significant phenomenon. Raymond claimed that there were scant female-to-male (FTM) transsexuals compared to male-to-female transsexuals because FTMs were "the *token* that saves the face for the male 'transsexual empire.'"[64]

Listening to trans experience was crucial to understanding gender variation and the limits of one's own experiential knowledge. After Califia collective member, Betty Jetter, trained to be a counselor at the Gay Community Service Center (GCSC) in the late 1970s, a person labeled female at birth came to Jetter wanting to be recognized as a man. Jetter realized, "Of course, I was nowhere near *fit* to counsel *her* [*sic*]. So I *did* give her [*sic*] to a woman who had done a lot of that kind of counseling." Another collective member, Josy Catoggio, noted that she

> didn't really *get* it until I met transgendered people and *talked* with them. [laugh] *Again*, like every other *issue*, if it wasn't part of my experience, I was *ignorant* and *loud* about it like I am about everything. [laugh] And people would tell me, "You're *wrong*, girl! You don't know what you're talking about. Listen to *my* experience and *then* you decide."[65]

There is humility in Jetter and Catoggio recognizing the limits of their experience based on their expertise in a form of feminism founded on a gender binary.

By the mid-1970s, avowedly political groups like NOW coexisted with community centers, conferences, and increasingly identity- or interest-specific small groups, sharing overlapping attendance and agendas. For example, lesbian women formed Southern California Women for Understanding (SCWU) in 1976 because gay men with whom they had worked in the Whitman-Radclyffe Foundation since the early 1970s refused to recognize a women's caucus. SCWU was an example of a group that, using a relatively generic name, primarily catered to white, middle-class, lesbian professionals for socializing and networking parties but could mobilize politically. SCWU became important as a fund-raising group for a coalition in 1977 that organized to oppose an initiative that would have fired teachers who showed any support for gay and lesbian Americans.[66]

A good example of feminists uniting in a shared interest is women's music. As in other big cities, women's music flourished in Los Angeles. Music festivals produced culture that resonated with women's, and especially lesbian feminists', lives. Singers also saw themselves as spreading feminist messages in a way compatible with CR.[67] A collective started the Los Angeles Women's Community Chorus (LAWCC) between 1976 and 1977, and popular annual concerts added to a growing women's music scene that aroused women's indignation and bound them together with a sense of purpose. LAWCC performed a combination of new standards by Margie Adams, Meg Christian, Cris Williamson, and Bernice Johnson Reagon of Sweet Honey in the Rock,[68] traditional tunes from various cultures,[69] and other songs tailored to feminist concerns. LAWCC women composed Spanish-language songs for the chorus to appeal to and include the large Spanish-speaking minority within the women's movement.[70] In what must have been a charged atmosphere, the chorus sang of women's fury over rape,[71] economic misogyny and sexist gender norms,[72] the outrage of psychiatric violence against women,[73] and inadequate gains toward women's liberation.[74] Rousing, inspirational pieces heralded women's rising expectations and camaraderie through the feminist movement.[75] They educated the audience with songs that glorified women's history, promoted feminist health consciousness, and described the work of Women Against Violence Against Women (WAVAW).[76] Programs included sing-alongs to draw the audience into one unified voice.[77] LAWCC provided women with a shared project, time, space, and identity. Elsa Sue Fisher reveled in LAWCC as a collective member and in Califia as a yearly participant. She remembered applying some of the Califia workshop issues at LAWCC retreats: "Gazillions of women were in LAWCC and Califia."[78] The desire for the shared dynamic between LAWCC and Califia may have influenced women to try out and remain involved in both as sustained or recurring women's spaces.[79]

With the increase in CR, networking, and feminist forums, Los Angeles became a vibrant center for feminist businesses. Bars like Seventh Circle, Bacchanal, Joanie Presents, Cork Room (1971), and The Woman's Saloon (1975) connected lesbian feminists to a previous tradition of locating gay and lesbian socializing in taverns. Women's garage shops and other businesses marketed services to feminist women.

Feminist spirituality provided a safe space for women to revive their faith if it had been damaged by misogynistic organized religion. The growth of women's spirituality in the L.A. area rejected patriarchal religious structures in favor of feminist spiritual lives that connected with other feminist politics. Zsuzsanna "Z" Budapest encouraged women to link spiritual growth with feminist principles and politics. She left a depressing marriage for lesbianism in 1970, came out as a witch in 1971, and started holding sabbats that saw exponential growth. She founded the Susan B. Anthony Coven number 1 as high priestess. By 1974, Budapest opened the Feminist Wicca store where she sold supplies and read tarot cards. Many in the feminist community rallied to her support in April 1975 when an undercover policewoman arrested Budapest for fortune telling based on a seldom-invoked old municipal ordinance. Some feminists felt the ordinance conflicted with a state law that only banned fortune telling with intent to defraud. The ensuing case raised the issue of the First Amendment right to religious practice and the role of payment for religious services. The judge argued that divining for profit did not fall under First Amendment protection. An exposé in *The Lesbian Tide* claimed the prosecutor was consistently sarcastic, derisive, and bent on discrediting Dianic witchcraft as a religion. Since "Wicca is an organized religion and has been recognized as such by the State of California" and tarot reading "plays an important part in the work and rituals of the Wiccan religion," *The Lesbian Tide* concluded, "Z's story is another incident illustrating increasing political harassment of feminist activists."[80] Found guilty, she appealed without success three years later after realizing that Los Angeles sold licenses for fortune telling in addition to upholding a law against it.[81]

Feminist Wicca under Budapest's leadership captured tensions between culture and politics. A Wiccan supporter argued that the Dianic tradition was "the ideal religion for feminist women actively seeking change" because it validated women's power, intuition, self-confidence, and responsibility while promoting sisterhood through rituals. Such spirituality could be "a great sustainer" and increase women's power by supporting women against patriarchal norms.[82] A woman who had felt ashamed of having facial hair found Budapest's "matriarchal herstory . . . of ancient wise wimmin who sported their beards proudly as symbols of their wisdom and veneration" to be an overwhelmingly validating introduction to understanding oppression based on looks. Like fat liberationists, this woman started raising people's consciousness on the streets in the feminist publication called *The Lesbian Tide*.[83] Proponents of feminist spirituality posed their beliefs as a necessary support to and integral part of political work.

Wicca also became a livelihood for Budapest and reflected tensions between spreading information to support revolution and gaining profits from one's work.[84] Budapest complained bitterly in an article that the southern California movement should support her "Magical Goddess Slide Show" presentation with speaking fees comparable to the $750 she said she got in Michigan. That would allow her "a reasonable living in exchange for [her] work" of reenergizing audiences and stimulating new thoughts. In an accompanying rebuttal, the *Tide* Collective vehemently disagreed with Budapest's focus on certain women as stars rather than on organizers.[85] The newspaper's collective was reiterating a distinction that nationally known feminist Rita Mae Brown had made between leaders who rose from the ranks and media-appointed stars. The feminist movement had lasted more than a decade by 1977 with little in the way of big-money contributions because of the dedication of thousands of volunteer organizers and workers. Likewise, Califia would side with volunteerism.

By the mid-1970s women in large cities and some college towns could structure their lives around women. Los Angeles women could bank at the Feminist Credit Union, learn carpentry and other home-building skills from Building Women, hire feminist service providers like Dianic Mechanics through the L.A. Women's Yellow Pages, practice woman-centered spirituality at the Feminist Wicca, support feminist bookstores like Sisterhood Bookstore (1972) and music through Olivia Records, and take women-only vacations on Womantours.

Lesbian feminists and straight feminist allies celebrated the thrill of a sense of women's community even as they grappled with internal and external contradictions that produced divisions. All-women spaces generated supportive, engaging discussions that touched women's lives and yielded new analyses of the world in order to challenge patriarchy. Feminists trained women to fight for themselves physically and intellectually. Women's culture had its own lesbian feminist language, music, and events. There were avenues for political activism from legal reform to guerrilla speak-outs. The women who participated, however, brought differences in their backgrounds and lifestyles, which became sources of division as women politicized their lives. How could a theory of oppression that took sexism as paramount adequately cover diverse issues without becoming too diffuse to address everything? Feminists struggled to define the boundaries of their army to include as many potential fighters as possible without introducing diversions from living in an unequal society or provocateurs. How could they survive in an unreformed world and simultaneously disassociate themselves from the forces they felt shackled them—badly behaving men and heteropatriarchal institutions, including class structure and racial hierarchy?

CHAPTER 2

FOUNDING, FUN, AND FRICTION

I think [Califia] was a great pioneering *experiment and* brought women together *in dealing in holistic ways with our minds, bodies, and spirits and did a lot of* innovative, creative, exciting, imaginative *stuff about bringing women together. It was Amazon* summer *camp. It was* great! *I mean it was a* fabulous *time to both do serious political work and have discussions and also to* celebrate *and* dance *and enjoy each other's company and* enjoy *each other's mind* and *bodies. So I think Califia was a noble experiment in that regard.*

ARIANA MANOV (CALIFIA PARTICIPANT 1976–1978/1979)

WOMAN-IDENTIFICATION AND ALTERNATIVE EDUCATION

The ability to find woman-focused separate spaces appealed to some who dealt with negative male behavior in their workplaces or family lives. This chapter makes five major arguments. The backgrounds and goals of Califia Community's first two founders, Betty Willis Brooks and Marilyn Murphy, make their desire to reach beyond their campuses understandable. Founders distinguished their endeavor from a previous feminist educational experiment's conflicts and advertised in L.A.'s extensive feminist networks. The initial sense of excitement, wonder, and anxiety women felt at finding like-minded women with new ideas for living during Califia's first three years of conferences (1976–1978) illustrate American feminists' search for community and counter-cultural attempts to reassess conventional wisdom and provide alternative solutions. Because participants' feminist ideologies overlapped but contrasted with each other, they struggled to accommodate various goals. Their emotional highs and lows reflected the "personal politics" and "sisterhood" assumptions behind feminist organizing.

Betty Brooks traced her starting point to the emancipatory possibility of religion, so her initial activism was within her church. She grew up in a white middle-class family that emphasized the importance of Protestant church life in segregated Louisiana. Brooks recalled that when she was a new mother in California, "I was trying to figure out what I *believed*, what I was going to *do* with the rest of my *life*." She and acquaintances attended the Ecumenical Institute in Chicago in the late 1960s. Like the HFS, The Ecumenical Institute provided residential learning that included seeing gender and racial parity in action. Brooks returned to California and worked for two years introducing inclusive language into her church but concluded that liberal Protestants "were still terribly male dominated, and I was moving in a very different direction." She put feminist ideas into practice as an assistant professor of physical education at California State University in Long Beach (CSULB) and thought about ways to expand feminist education beyond the academy.[1]

From the institute Brooks developed a mission to combat rape. Although Brooks was not L.A.'s first self-defense teacher, she became "a one-woman self-defense, consciousness-raising and training system, teaching hundreds of women how to protect themselves."[2] As early as 1973, she taught her "dirty street fighting" at the Westside Women's Center and elsewhere. Women's spaces like the Center could help put women at ease while they learned to protect themselves from male violence. Brooks combined standard information with pedagogy specific to women. In addition to advising surprise attacks against the vulnerable points along an assailant's vertical centerline (eyes, nose, windpipe, groin, knees, shins, insteps), Brooks showed women how to turn men's strength and balance against them, instructed them to tap into an attacker's guilt, and called a deep scream to draw help and give an assailant pause "the ovarian yell." Brooks challenged women to "turn fear into anger into action." Faced with the widespread phenomenon that women were reluctant to act, Brooks asked women to examine why they would defend their children and not themselves.[3]

Brooks's self-defense training was part of citywide and national goals for ensuring women's safety. In 1973, the Los Angeles Women's Union and the Westside Women's Center included antirape programs that coordinated rape-crisis counseling services and tried to strengthen rape laws against the popular view that rape victims somehow asked for abuse.[4] That year a citywide conference established the Los Angeles Coalition on Assaults Against Women (LACAAW). Betty had all two hundred conference participants practice "dirty street fighting." She organized the Downey-Whittier hotline for rape victims.[5] By 1976, LACAAW had state funding for the Los

Angeles Rape Crisis Center's twenty-four-hour hotline, counseling, and community education.[6] LACAAW continues to operate.

Brooks modeled her feminist mission of preparing women physically and mentally through her outspoken personality and high energy. As such, she seemed a beacon to some and a glaring problem to others. She started the first feminist bookstore in conservative Orange County in 1974. Brooks named Persephone's Place after the Greco-Roman myth, in which Hades kidnapped and raped earth mother Demeter's daughter. Brooks wanted to educate women, "so no woman would be pulled into Hades." The bookstore doubled as a women's center with lectures but folded after a year.[7] Six months into its existence, CSULB's Physical Education Department denied her a permanent teaching position. The L.A. feminist newspaper, *Sister*, reported this as a purge of feminists and detailed Brooks's university accomplishments. She had developed courses, and a large majority of colleagues had elected her to the Women's Studies Steering Committee to agitate for parity in budgets for men and women's athletics. Brooks's committee fact-finding revealed that men's athletics got ten times the funding women's did although only the women's teams won championships. The Committee Against Sexism in Employment backed Brooks, and her case revealed inconsistencies in assessing qualifications for teaching and tenure.[8] Brooks retained her job after a fight. She continued to teach self-defense, developing an Association of Self-Defense Instructors and helping to form a growing antirape network in the wider Los Angeles area. She also initiated courses on women's sexuality. In addition to weekend extension classes, Brooks and sociology professor Linda Shaw developed a course called "Women and Their Bodies" in 1975. The course dealt with bodily oppression through the commercialization of women and emphasis on their appearance as well as tackling women's health, sexual lifestyles, and sexuality for pleasure. FU presented there. By 1976 Brooks was an assistant professor in Women's Studies and continued her community education by helping to found Califia Community.[9]

It was at Persephone's Place that Brooks and Marilyn Murphy met. Murphy was also active inside and outside the university and a charismatic leader. A "recovering Catholic" from New York City, Murphy grew up before Vatican II changes in a state where the Catholic Church had a long history of vigorously opposing women's reproductive rights. Her memories of her working-class Irish- and Italian-American upbringing in Catholic elementary school included interpreting the roles for priests and nuns, boys and girls as unfair. She had felt isolated as a wife and mother in Oklahoma but enjoyed a circle of women friends for a time until, one by one, they turned to psychoanalysis to address their dissatisfaction and fell away. Murphy put her faith in feminism and rejected religion or counseling as paths to social justice. A move to California gave Murphy the chance to attend college, and by 1969 she threw herself into writing, community teaching, and organizing. She was part of the Orange County Women's Liberation Center, Orange County/Laguna Beach NOW, and California Women in Higher Education. As one of the first publicly feminist Ph.D. candidates in southern California, she participated in speakers' bureaus, giving talks at least twice a week. Resistance to her feminist dissertation ultimately ended her doctoral study and left her with a fiery interest in preserving feminism outside of university constraints.[10]

They, like other feminists who created feminist educational space separate from colleges, cited not only fears of co-optation but also the desire to reach the diversity of women beyond university spaces. College campuses, as emblems of privilege, could be daunting places to enter for women from working-class backgrounds without higher education, so barriers to access ran counter to goals of class and racial inclusion. By the early 1970s, affirmative action programs in California actively recruited women of color. Those students remembered finding themselves awash amidst a sea of white faces and struggling to find people of their own race and ethnicity. A few African American women in the Sunbelt Southeast could tap into the long history of black colleges, but blacks and Chicanas remained vastly underrepresented at the university level in the 1960s and 1970s. Los Angeles–area artist Judy Baca "would never see a Mexican or a black person or anybody of color" on her public college campus in the 1960s. Chicana leaders whom Benita Roth interviewed reported that California colleges' Educational Opportunity Programs recruited them, but they joined Chicanismo and created campus organizations in response to isolation and first experiences with racism.[11] In the collective consciousness, college campuses in the 1960s, especially state schools in California, were bastions of radical change. Less remembered are the ways they remained foreign, hostile territory for minorities.

LEARNING FROM SAGARIS

Brooks and Murphy had talked about starting some kind of feminist education program on the West Coast since they became friends in 1974 at Persephone's, and their early planning sought to address minority-status divisions.[12] When L.A.'s lesbian feminist monthly, *The Lesbian Tide*, announced in January 1975 that a Vermont-based, collective-run feminist institution called Sagaris would open that summer "to bring together the foremost feminist thinkers so that they can communicate with and teach other women," Brooks and Murphy decided to go.[13] The provisional Califia collective (before their first public meeting) grew from southern California women's attendance at this event, which used a college setting for extracurricular feminism.

Sagaris planners expressed the tensions Brooks and Murphy felt between the academy and community. They created an extracurricular space to give participants intensive study with leading feminists. Dissatisfied with feminist studies at Goddard College in Lyndonville, Vermont, local women started planning Sagaris in 1973 as a model of feminist education without institutional constraints. They solicited funding from individuals. When that left them short, after much debate, the Sagaris collective also asked foundations for funding.[14] Brooks and Murphy attended the first session together, along with Marilyn Pearsol from Los Angeles and Jodie Timms of San Diego. Sagaris held two five-week sessions on the college campus, which were open to 120 participants each.[15] The collective charged a sliding-scale tuition fee that topped off at $700 per session and gave scholarships and child care duty work exchanges to recruit minority and working-class women. They offered living space in the dorms, child care, and classes taught by such luminaries as Rita Mae Brown on leadership, Charlotte Bunch on organizing, Mary Daly on knowledge, Emily Medvec on economics, Candace Falk on socialist feminism, Ti-Grace Atkinson on theoretical thinking, and Alix Kates Shulman on anarchist feminism. During the first session, collective members and participants raised concerns that went unresolved: that the collective did not sufficiently support lesbians, that working-class and middle-class participants were divided, that rifts over child care pitted mothers against those who resented added child care duties, and that individuals' disruptions drained energy from the group.[16]

The women who formed the first Califia collective took care to learn from these divisions by explicitly addressing class and keeping costs down, so that women could attend without work exchange. Califia Community founders continued Sagaris's recognition that it was important to organize feminist education that went beyond local consciousness-raising and remained outside of male-dominated spaces to prevent co-optation. Califia, however, would side with radical peer education pedagogy against imitating university power differentials created by the teacher/student dynamic. This is an example of how feminists exchanged ideas from coast to coast to learn from each other's experiences.

The second session, which Sagaris planner, fundraiser, and future Cali-

fia collective member Josy Catoggio attended,[17] degenerated into paranoia
and opposing factions who debated whether Sagaris collective members
should have solicited and taken a $5,000 grant from the *Ms.* Foundation
for the first session and another $10,000 for the second. The radical fem-
inist group Redstockings issued a press release on May 9, 1975 "accusing
Ms. Magazine editor Gloria Steinem of having once been involved with a
CIA front," which "insinuated that *Ms. Magazine* was part of a CIA strategy to replace radical feminism with liberal feminism." Steinem had not
dignified the false charge with a denial, so some Sagaris presenters objected
to *Ms.* funding.[18] During a six-hour debate between Ti-Grace Atkinson and
Joan Peters, Atkinson argued, "You can't take that money. The Redstockings have just accused Gloria Steinem of being a CIA agent. The money
is tainted, that money is suspect, and you're going to pollute Sagaris with
it."[19] Catoggio explained why the majority of the Sagaris participants voted
to retain financial support:

> And, of course, we couldn't have *survived* without that money. We'd al-
> ready *spent* it. So it was *never* even an *issue.* And they ultimately decided
> that they shouldn't even have opened that issue to debate because it wasn't
> our decision to make as a community. . . . And *working-class* women who
> were there, like *Dorothy Allison* . . . would say, "Look! It's a question of
> *survival,* you know. If you want this to happen, the money has to come
> from *somewhere.*" Some feminist groups were taking money from the *Play-*
> *boy* Foundation. Now *I* thought that was *much* more outrageous than the
> *Ms.* Foundation.[20]

Catoggio's memory highlighted elements of authority and the classed nature of the debate over principles, as published assessments of Sagaris have
not. Although some women at the first session found the Sagaris collective
too controlling, the collective felt a burden of responsibility. Members repeatedly begged feminists in cities nationwide to donate funds for an educational experience they hoped would link theorists with grassroots activists to shape the course of feminism.[21] With the second session upon
them, there was no time for fundraising. Working-class feminists experienced with how distressing budget constraints could be may have been
more pragmatic about making up for insufficient contributions by solicit-
ing the funds from what was widely considered the "liberal" feminist *Ms.*
Magazine.

Pragmatism did not reassure those whose principles were offended by
rumored connections to the CIA. "Ti-Grace Atkinson, Alix Kates Shul-

man, Susan Sherman, and Marilyn Webb—and about twenty students seceded from the school to form the August 7th Survival Community."[22] They held classes at a place they rented in town. Peters described complete polarization, hero worship by students, fistfights, and a sense that Sagaris had become "the establishment" to be fought.[23] Catoggio, Peters, Falk, Webb, and many others at Sagaris came to believe that FBI infiltrators furthered the conflicts as they did in many movement groups.[24] Catoggio explained how infiltration worked:

> [T]hey support the person who has the most extreme point of view and encourage them to not work with the others because they won't come around completely. . . . It literally divided into the Ti-Grace Atkinson followers, who named themselves the August 7th something 'cause that was the date that they actually walked out on the rest of us. . . . There were two women that nobody knew. And they were from California, interestingly enough, but nobody from California knew them either. And they were pretty quiet except that they would really sort of encourage Ti-Grace to stick to her guns and don't work with those other people, so that—the point of which—you couldn't go to her classes unless you signed this sort of little loyalty oath.[25]

Although it remains unclear whether government agents targeted Sagaris, Catoggio's assessment of how infiltration worked explains the apparent irrationality and destructive consequences of secession. Senate hearings in 1976 exposed what movement people had suspected for over a decade. The FBI had engaged in covert operations since 1963 against the civil rights movement, student movements, and feminist organizations. Using techniques developed from wartime counter-intelligence, the FBI violated First Amendment rights of speech and association. Among the methods the FBI used were "instigating 'personal conflicts or animosities'" and "creating the impression that leaders are 'informants for the Bureau or other law enforcement agencies.'"[26] As part of a decade-long trend of bureaucratizing surveillance, the FBI wasted thousands of dollars of taxpayer money and agents' time compiling useless data to argue that Americans who dissented from mainstream politics were a danger to national security.[27] As it did with civil rights and leftist groups, the FBI did try to monitor women's liberation groups and disrupt actions that could threaten the status quo.[28] In a vicious cycle, societal oppression bred feminist distrust while goals of recruitment and radical democracy left feminist groups exposed to government counterintelligence programs, which further encouraged distrust.

Given the mores of the 1960s and 1970s, it is easy to understand why American women and pro-feminist men saw the need to intervene against sexism. In addition to laudable work feminists accomplished in legal and institutional reform, women created temporary separate space where they raised each other's consciousness and organized with limited harassment from antifeminists. They could retire to there when misogynistic daily interactions drained them and could use the places as bases for recruiting others to their cause. That said, identity and power differences among women were consistent problems because feminists had grown up learning larger society's oppressive attitudes. Feminists frequently organized not only by gender but also by other identity factors or ideological perspectives. Sagaris, and Brooks, Murphy, and other Califia founders' interest in attending it as a model to develop in California, show that feminists recognized the importance of education within a temporary separate space to avoid cooptation and encourage CR, leadership training, and action planning. Sagaris is an example of how power differentials by teacher/student, financially independent/"work-study," and oppressor/oppressed identities were critiqued but were instrumental in unraveling the educational project. The speculation of government provocateurs resonated because feminists already had experience with FBI surveillance and had good reason to suspect federal agents would wield power against them.

"CALIFIA COMMUNITY IS THE DAUGHTER OF SAGARIS"

There were numerous attempts to form community education experiments for societal transformation. Charlotte Perkins Gilman's *Women and Economics* proposed in 1898 that families live communally, so women and men could divide household duties and collectively raise and educate children without sexist socialization. Although Califia founders mainly drew from the Ecumenical Institute, Sagaris and other feminist groups to create Califia Community, the civil rights movement had produced early examples. Laurel Falls Camp started in 1920. Later, under Lillian Smith's guidance, the camp used play to raise white girls' consciousness about the indignities of segregation. The Highlander Folk School's adult pedagogy was critical to union activism in the 1930s and 1940s, civil rights in the 1950s and 1960s, and environmentalism in the 1970s and 1980s.[29]

Brooks, true to her expansive vision, returned from Sagaris ready to pioneer a better educational model by drawing on her background with the Ecumenical Institute.[30] The perspectives of those who made up the original collective determined Califia's direction. Brooks got Murphy, Marilyn

Pearsol, and Jodie Timms to attend planning meetings with other feminists across California. The initial meeting places they chose were neither feminist strongholds nor areas known for diversity. Instead, La Jolla (between Los Angeles and San Diego) and Morro Bay (between Los Angeles and San Francisco) were geographically convenient to those who expressed interest and were pleasant beachfront locations.[31] Soon they recognized that, unlike Vermont's Sagaris collective, California was too large to combine its southern and northern feminists.[32] Instead, these four solicited every feminist group they could think of in the Los Angeles to San Diego area and put a notice in *Sister*, which led to a forty-four-woman meeting at the Women's Building in L.A. Six joined as collective members.[33] Murphy retrospectively described their project thus: "Califia Community is the daughter of Sagaris and, like most daughters, is very like and very unlike her mother."[34] The southern California context inevitably affected the course of Califia's education.

Like Sagaris and other 1970s feminist groups, the collective agreed on a name linked to Greco-Roman myths of warrior goddesses, but, unlike their East Coast progenitor, the California experiment projected western inclusiveness. Pearsol thought up the name. Murphy explained in 1983:

> We call ourselves *Califia* because she is the legendary Black Amazon/Goddess for whom California was originally named. We call our organization *Community* to express our commitment to the development of an *informed* community spirit among Califia women which recognizes and affirms our differences as we celebrate our sisterhood. Califia Community is committed to the development of a multicultural community of the spirit of women through feminist education.[35]

This white-founded, radical feminist group's name emphasized cultural contact with Spanish conquest in that Hernán Cortés is reported to have named the area California in 1519 after a place in a popular Spanish romance novel.[36] The mythical Califia Amazons, who lived without men, mirrored a separatist aspect. Murphy's statement theoretically honored women of color (mythically black or geographically American Indian) and lesbians (through the lesbian associations with "Amazon") as foundational contributors to society while recognizing that differences prevented women from uniting for positive change. The term "multicultural" is more reflective of the 1980s, but the commitment to lesbians was foundational, and Brooks credited Murphy with injecting early interest in class and race.[37]

To form an informed community, collective members fashioned feminist pedagogy that circumscribed their degree of control and promoted shared responsibility. Unlike Sagaris, the Califia collective's temporary community avoided a firm division between authoritative teachers and dependent students; their goal was that "all the teachers are the taught and all the taught are the teachers."[38] This motto expressed feminist CR-based education that valued every woman's personal experience and collectively analyzed that experience to reveal the bases of oppression, so that women could devise actions to oppose oppression.[39] Califia teachers sought interactive forms of presentation that allowed free exchange and "co-investigation" of ideas and problems rather than a strict teacher-student hierarchy in which teachers authoritatively determined all curricula and bestowed the information that ignorant, passive students meekly memorized and repeated.[40]

To this end, collective members provided structure and left opportunities for others to contribute. The collective organized year-round, allotted the time available during the sessions, and taught major presentations. Timms promoted wider participation with small-group activities instead of lecture format. Mary Glavin integrated charts, drama, and language, including diagnostic tools by which women determined their class backgrounds as a precursor to speaking from their own experiences. Brochures and camp announcements encouraged women to sign up to teach their own workshops and bring whatever expertise and skills they had to share. Califia also held a nightly community meeting where women could put anything on the agenda for discussion. Janet Stambolian coordinated a talent show and banquet to add participatory fun.[41] Through these activities, the collective created what schools of education later called "learner-centered education" by gearing information and critical thinking to visual, kinesthetic, and auditory learners with a high level of involvement.

Striving to include as many participants as possible, the collective focused on how to reduce costs and open attendance to less-privileged feminists. Califia founders rejected the Sagaris model of two five-week sessions. Josy Catoggio labeled such long sessions "elitist" because working-class women would lose pay or be fired if absent from jobs for so long. She had only been able to attend because she was temporarily unemployed. After Sagaris, Catoggio rode across the United States with a woman and gave her gas money to see how well Califia's proposal for a "leaderless," cheaper, and more accessible educational experience would go.[42] The Califia collective members scheduled two to four conferences per summer. Some were weeklong while others were over a weekend. This provided an intensive environment where women could learn to live together and work out ways to fight societal pressures from family, work, and contact with men, all of

which they escaped temporarily.[43] By locating weeklong educational sessions at area campsites instead of college campuses or hotels and weekend
conferences at camps or women's centers, early Califia camps could isolate up to 250 women and children from dominant society on the cheap.[44]
For the first three years, collective members rented de Benneville Pines
camp in Angelus Oaks, California from the Unitarian-Universalist Church,
and Califia women drove ninety miles east of L.A. to the secluded forested
mountains.[45]

The reduced time and camp setting drastically cut the Sagaris fee (up to
$700) and gave Califia founders flexibility to recruit lower-income women.
Their choices made Califia available to more women and sparked early conversations about how class background affected women's ability to access
what they want. For the first camp in 1976, Califia charged $75 as a reg-
ular price, a $50 low-income fee, and $25 for accompanying children plus
a $10 deposit that defrayed initial costs. Middle-class collective members
such as Betty Brooks considered the sliding scale very successful. Alice Myers found costs too inexpensive to pass up. Participant Jane Bernstein attended Califia from 1977 to 1982 although she was a new nurse and found
it difficult to find the time and money.[46] In contrast to the perspectives of
those raised middle-class, classism presenters Ahshe Green and Josy Catoggio believed

> [s]liding scale privileged downwardly mobile middle-class women—
> 'cause they're the people that feel comfortable asking for it. Working-class
> women—our reality is, "If I can't afford it, I don't get to have it." . . . But
> with sliding scales, what it would do is it would privilege the women who
> felt comfortable enough and entitled enough, who were downwardly mo-
> bile, to ask for the low end of the sliding scale, even though they could
> choose to make more money if they worked more hours or worked in a
> job they didn't necessarily love as opposed to being voluntarily under-
> employed—which a lot of women were in those days.[47]

One of the missions of feminist work over the 1970s and 1980s was to encourage women to access their sense of entitlement to equal treatment, so
that was a conversational process over Califia's decade of existence. Women
who could not afford the low-income fee, whom Brooks calculated were at
least a quarter of attendees, paid only room and board and could work out
a payment schedule. There were no scholarships because collective members felt that they implied that some women were more deserving than others, a process of discernment tainted by dominant-culture norms. Instead,

brochures starting in 1978 urged women who could to donate more to cover others' attendance costs.[48] Rejecting Sagaris's work-exchange system, Califia required that all participants sign up for shifts that covered the physical and emotional maintenance work of cooking, cleanup, child care, and peer counseling. The only paid staff consisted of a head cook, child-care coordinator and assistants, a female lifeguard to replace the male lifeguard that campsites provided, and later an American Sign Language (ASL) interpreter.[49] Sue Dunne and Shirley Virgil insisted on vegetarian menus that reflected healthy eating and a "commitment to the preservation of life," which combined radical ecological feminist principles with another cost-cutting practicality.[50] The collective's decisions combined feminist ideology, volunteerism, and financial accessibility to open Califia to as many women as possible.

Getting the word out to the feminist and lesbian communities was the next step for inclusion. In addition to advertising in *The Lesbian News*, collective members assembled mailing lists they got from other groups, and individuals told everyone they knew to come.[51] Murphy told other NOW members like Betty Jetter, other women at a lesbian rap group she and Jane Bernstein attended in 1977 at the L.A. Gay Community Services Center, and all the women who went to CR sessions she held at her home.[52] Elsa Fisher called a contact number and talked directly to Murphy, which led her to attend the first camp in July 1976, room with Catoggio, and begin a close friendship. She told Muriel Fisher, "Mother this is something you have to do," and her lesbian mother loved it.[53] Lois Bencangey remembered someone storming through a Southern California Women for Understanding (SCWU) meeting with flyers and deciding on the spot with her companion at the time, María Dolores Díaz, to go to a Califia camp in 1978.[54] Many others learned about Califia from the rave reviews of women who attended the year before.[55] Like so many grassroots feminist organizations, Califia operated extensively through personal contacts, interaction with other feminist spaces, and the advertising opportunities that lesbian publications provided.

Planners anticipated uniting attendees through feminist education on the differences and privileges that divided women and prevented them from working together for social change. The specific educational content coalesced over time. Initially the collective billed itself as giving daily presentations on "history, sexuality, spirituality, class, ethics, race, political and economic systems, organizing skill[s] and strategies—specifically as they relate to the social and political struggles throughout the world."[56] Both Brooks and Murphy wrote around 1982 that the original collective finally decided to focus on sexism, racism, and classism, with the term "sexism" representing interrelated points of sexual orientation, homophobia, hetero-sexism, and misogynist appropriation of women's bodies.[57] Almost all nar-rators independently volunteered this triad. Brooks credited Murphy for helping the original collective "understand that we must always deal with race and class as central issues that divide women as we look at sexism."[58] The 1979 brochure corroborates their memories: "sessions will be orga-nized to provide time for in depth discussions of essential feminist issues: sexism, racism, class, sexual preference, colonization of our bodies."[59] Cali-fia reflected feminist attempts to understand identities and sites of oppres-sion as interrelated. Understandably, the group picked fault lines that were divisive throughout U.S. society and thus, not surprisingly, within social movements. Like other feminists of the time, they grappled with how static or malleable identities were and how experience related to expertise.

Califia's initial collective had impressive ambitions that resonated with feminist goals nationwide. Like other organizers, Califia collective mem-bers sought to build a sense of community where women could count on each other personally and politically. Califia was typical of blending radi-cal, cultural, separatist, and lesbian feminisms by emphasizing what women shared in order to encourage them to unite for change. Califia differed from some groups, though, in that participants simultaneously addressed head-on societal rifts among people by sexual orientation, race, class, age, and marital/parental status. Presenters analyzed power relations that Ameri-cans often ignored. As an alternative educational space, Califia drew on the broader movements' uses of CR, participatory and experiential learn-ing, a radically egalitarian collective structure without officers, and consen-sus decision-making to promote valuing women's experiences and abilities. Califia presenters sought to create a climate where women could unlearn biases and support those whose backgrounds dominant society disparaged.

THE DRAWS FOR CALIFIA WOMEN

Califia camps blended serious consciousness-raising with vacation time that included plenty of entertainment and inspiration. Narrators lightheart-edly described Califia as an "Amazon summer camp" or "a week in the woods with 150 women" where "playfulness of people could come out."[60] Of nineteen women who attended camps between 1976 and 1978, thirteen (68 percent) remarked on the importance of having an all-women's space where they built safety, trust, and freedom outside confining mainstream norms.[61] Ten attendees (53 percent) reflected that Califia produced some of their most important and lasting relationships.[62] Marilyn Murphy's partner, Irene Weiss, and sister Jeanne Murphy said women developed group identification as "Califia women," a community affiliation that transcended the specific conferences they attended to bond them with others who went across the years.[63]

What made Califia so special to its participants? Women were most struck by the emotional boost of a week or long weekend working and living with other women away from men out in nature without societal restrictions. Elsa Fisher was thrilled from the first day of the first camp in 1976. She reflected back,

> Oh there was *nothing* that could compare with what Califia provided. . . . *living* together, *eating* together, *working* together, doing *really emotional work* together. When you work *emotionally with* other people, the *bond* is so *intense*. And there are *friends* that I made at Califia that are still the *dearest* friends in my *life*.[64]

The importance of a live-in learning environment for Fisher was amplified by her dyslexia. Teachers who were unequipped to address learning disabilities had dismissed her as "stupid."[65] She said, "I'm a non-reader, non-writer, and everything I do—*all* my learning—comes from people. . . . this is my bliss—community and groups."[66] Califia was also transformational for women who were more used to learning in isolation and organizational meetings. Betty Jetter read feminist books and worked in NOW for years before Murphy invited her to attend the first Califia conference of July 1976. A key importance of the camps for Jetter was "finding *other feminist women* to be with. It *felt* like coming *home*. This is where I *belonged*. And I felt like, especially the *radical* feminist women. I became *radicalized* very quickly. . . . I made *lots* of *good friends* that are *very* important to me because they *think* like *I* do."[67] Jane Bernstein, likewise, remembered an after-party for Califia in 1977 where she thought, "my God, these are my *people*."[68]

Strong affinity led women to return to Califia summer after summer. Diane F. Germain attended the third year of Califia in 1978 and was so excited that she continued until the end of the original Califia in November 1985 and joined the collective in 1981. She explained her desire to return year after year:

> it was *so wonderful* to go to *camp*. It was *so exciting*. It was *so neat*. It was every kind of thing *I like*—you know, being out in the *woods* and having a big *swimming pool* and everybody was *naked* and it was just *women* and we didn't have people *telling* us what to *do*. . . . *bonfires* and *marshmallows* at

night and *singing* and making *art* and just *talking* from morning 'til night. It's *eating* in this big gigantic *room* where everybody's *talking* and *eating*, and you have all these women to choose from. Did you want to sit with the *political* group or the women of *color* or did you want to sit at the table with the *kids* and. . . . It was really, really *exciting* and *wonderful* and *fun*. . . . I just couldn't *wait* to go again.[69]

Germain summed up points many narrators remembered: camp activities, women-only space, freedom to go naked, the exciting range of women and children with whom one could associate.

The camps fostered an array of women's relationships from activist colleagues to friends to romantic partners and supported sexual exploration by shutting out mainstream discrimination and separating the children from the adults. The collective tried to balance freedom and privacy for women with respect for the children by grouping the kids together in their own camp at the edge and specifying times when the children swam separately or joined the adults for evening entertainment. Lois Bencangey stressed,

it could be a very proper place, and the children were very respected, but if you wanted to explore your lesbian sexuality or your sexuality as a woman, this was a place where you could do it. Such a free atmosphere and this was the seventies, so my ideas about monogamy and relationships to women changed a lot there. Almost nothing, to talk about anyway, was taboo. So it was a place to bring your questions and bounce your ideas about, and to have fun in a safe environment.[70]

The sexual revolution, the development of a feminist health movement, and gay and lesbian liberation supported teaching about women's and lesbian sexuality. Brooks's crusade for women's defense and sexual autonomy led her to put together a slide show to illustrate how varied women's genitalia were.[71] Germain deemed the closely cropped "cunt slides" a tool against internalized repression. Their very name reclaimed a derogatory word hurled at women. Assembling slides of vulva variation countered the homogeneity of mainstream pornographic images and addressed the dearth of accessible educational material depicting women's bodies. The first viewing at Califia elicited initial titters and then suffocating silence and tension. So on the fourth slide, French-Canadian Germain called out, "Oh my God! My French teacher!" Everyone burst into laughter, breaking the tension and promoting discussion about women's bodily variety.[72] Narrators remembered the cunt slides fondly. A spontaneous guessing game became a raucous part of the viewing at the Women's Building, better known for exhibits of Judy Chicago's art. Women asserted to whom vulvas belonged based on the presence of fingers with nail polish, Band-Aids, or dirty nails.[73] Women's laughter, assertions of intimate knowledge, and joy at release from hushed privacy made the cunt slides comparable to speculum demonstrations performed throughout the women's movement. Both broke through imposed ignorance and shame about women's sexualized bodies.

Other sexuality workshops also celebrated a combination of diversity and empowerment. In one, women brainstormed a list of pressures that "all women" felt about their sexuality compared to pressures that lesbians and straight women felt in the movement because of their sexuality. They then contemplated revolutionary changes that could be made in sexuality, current tools for realizing them, and possible future control of technology and their bodies.[74] A questionnaire elicited discussion on a variety of sexual attitudes and practices.[75] Other workshops featured the G-spot, female ejaculation, masturbation techniques, and ben wah balls.[76] Jane Bernstein laughed at her ignorance about the vagina as she learned about the G-spot and female ejaculation at Califia instead of nursing school.[77] These workshops produced sexual knowledge for and by women to overturn reticence society mandated.

Educational programming encouraged women to explore desire and sexual techniques. Lesbian feminists have been stereotyped as sex-negative, prioritizing ideology over sexual expression. In the 1970s, however, lesbian feminist-identified women like Brooks positively sought to develop women's sexuality and advocated that women learn their bodies and experiment with other women. Brooks asserted, "Everybody was *screwing* their heads off. Everybody was *sleeping* with whomever they could *sleep* with. . . . Remember *this* was the time when there was a *lot* of non-monogamy. No AIDS."[78] Karen Merry agreed that many women heeded the call to experiment. She recounted a tale of meeting a sex teacher the first year Merry went to camp. After a wonderful workshop, Merry "ended up speaking/ sleeping with her that night. That was a *very fun night*."[79]

Numerous women enjoyed exploring lesbian sexuality at Califia.[80] In fact, a number of narrators were in the process of coming out when they first attended Califia.[81] "Brought out" was the term used when an established lesbian had sex with a woman who had never been with another woman but recognized herself as lesbian. Jetter described how unstable this sexual labeling was:

> [T]his woman from *England* came over here. I brought her out. But *she* went to [the West Coast Women's Music and Comedy Festival beforehand in 1980], and she joined the lesbian group. And they didn't want her to *be*

in that lesbian group because she was heterosexual. She says, "Now *wait* a second!" She said, "*I* plan on *never* having sex with a man again in my *life*. Just 'cause I haven't had sex with a *woman* doesn't mean I don't *belong* here." And she says, "How come you lesbians here, who call yourselves lesbians, say 'Oh, yes, and I had sex with men too?'"

Jetter concluded that sexuality is not "cut and dried."[82] Brooks corroborated, placing Califia within the broader culture and her views on sexual liberation:

> I mean if you get *liberated* with your *sexuality*, then *you* might . . . be sleeping with *men*; you might be sleeping with *women*; you might be doing all *kinds* of things. It was *not* a *rigidity*. It was a much more fluid *nature* of it. Now many women who were there [at Califia]—that was not *true* [pause] because *suddenly* they said, "Oh, my goodness. Maybe I'm a *lesbian*." I mean *that* was a *big* deal.[83]

Califia was an unofficial lesbian space open to straight and questioning women. Califia could serve as a place to experiment with lesbian feminist ideology and sexuality. The running joke was that "when the campouts began, eighty percent of the women were lesbians, and when they ended, ninety-five percent were."[84] Women who professed long-term lesbian identities told this joke, which speaks to their belief that one could adopt lesbianism as a better political-sexual choice.

Califia was also one of many spaces women experimented with relationship styles in the 1970s and 1980s. Monogamous women who attended were sometimes puzzled by nonmonogamy and worried women might disregard the fact that others were committed to one woman. Germain remembered a lot of discussion about nonmonogamy. She did not feel safe seeing women hit on another woman's girlfriend.[85] Between these poles of behavior were women who started long-term relationships at Califia conferences. Bonnie Kaufmann (pseudonym), for example, had attended one of Murphy's feminist consciousness soirées and befriended Kathy Sabry (pseudonym) there. Kaufmann stressed that Califia changed her life because the camp was the place she and Sabry started dating. They had been together for over twenty-five years when interviewed for this book.[86] As is the case with most Americans' early dating experience, many more narrators who started or further developed relationships at Califia sustained extended but not life-long partnerships.

Isolation from city life for a week at a woodsy campsite freed women

to connect with nature, their bodies, and each other. Bencangey specifically linked the campsites to feminist spirituality: "And you had nature all
around you. And you had to connect with it. . . . Plus it makes you remember that we're human animals, and that we're really part of nature, which
goes right along with a lot of feminist thinking about religion and spirituality, that we all come from the goddess, like a drop of water flowing to
the ocean."[87] Wanda Jewell, who also appreciated Wiccan ideas, remembered the de Benneville forestland camps made it "much easier to take in
new ideas" because women were together in a beautiful place with clean air.

Manov summed up the connections women made among rural air quality, women's energy, and bodily freedom when she considered effects of the
camp setting:

> Well, I *loved* being in the *woods* and with the cold, crisp, clean air and the
> *good* smells and the *getting* up; and just the *woman* energy at Califia was al-
> ways a real *high* for me. . . . I mean, just being with all those women walk-
> ing around topless if they chose to, and being able to sleep together and
> stay up all night, and I don't mean sleep together in a sex way, although
> that happened at Califia a lot. There were real erotic, pulsing undercurrents
> around a *lot* of Califia Community experiences for a *lot* of women. But *that*
> notwithstanding, I'm talking about just the *sharing*, getting up and *fixing*
> breakfast together and *brushing* your teeth side by side and *hanging* out late
> at night around the camp fire and *taking* long walks and so on. The fact
> that we were in a setting where we had *some* privacy, not entirely but *some*
> privacy, and could really be fully *ourselves* and where your body type was
> OK and where people weren't dressing up. I mean, some of the lipstick les-
> bians were still wearing lipstick and . . . getting up in the morning and put-
> ting on their make-up before they came to workshops. But for the large
> part we were all being pretty much who we *were* and not being judgmen-
> tal of each other and wearing *comfortable* clothes. There's a *casualness* and
> a *grace* about women's *bodies* when we're not under scrutiny by *men* and
> we're not expected to perform according to certain roles and *wear* certain
> clothes. . . .[88]

Associations among nature, women's energy, and bodily freedom were
memorable draws for many women throughout the decade of Califia
camps. Narrators found a completely new sense of freedom in being able
to go without clothing away from men's sexualizing gaze. For many, their
own comfort increased and they saw women of different ages and sizes in
an atmosphere where participants were vocally supportive of body varia-

tions.[89] The continual presence of an older woman who cooked topless, for example, gave Germain hope that she could age well.[90]

Nudity in feminist spaces extended beyond isolated, (temporary) women's land to urban cultural events like the West Coast Women's Music Festival, one of many expressions of women's music festivals across the country.[91] In the early years of Califia, it was not yet clear that comfort with nudity was marked by other identity factors, but later attendees indicated that de facto racial segregation in Los Angeles, like that in many major U.S. cities, affected experiences with feminism and lesbian feminism. Lydia Otero remembered at Califia in 1980 or 1981:

> [T]here were women walking around with their tops off, which I'd never seen before. At that time, I remember feeling uncomfortable. . . . I guess a lot of people had gone to those women's music things and they were used to seeing women topless and stuff like that. I sure wasn't going to go topless, and nobody that I went with ever took off their clothes. We were all actually saying, "These white women are crazy!" . . . So it might be a cultural thing in terms [of] having that freedom to take off your top, and . . . it's certainly more prevalent amongst *white* women, I think.[92]

Weiss agreed that white participants embraced nudity more warmly than did women of color because "that was too intimate for some of [the women of color], too close to the non–women of color."[93] California culture was revealing, not only with a warm climate and beaches but also with nude beaches and nudist camps that led the way for expressions of nudity at concerts and on campuses. Nudity, however, represented sexuality in popular culture, and women of color burdened by sexualizing stereotypes and unseen power dynamics resisted exposing themselves to white women's gazes. Despite the presence of toplessness in various spaces, those women of color narrators who attended Califia after 1978 continued to be bemused in their interviews at the interest white women showed in going topless or naked. For the women of color, lack of interest in disrobing seemed to connect to their negative assessment that white women sexualized them, whereas white women expressed no unease about nudity amid "real erotic, pulsing undercurrents."[94]

TRANSFORMATIVE FUN

The ways that Califia combined cultural and activist objectives make it ideal for understanding debates over what weight feminists gave to forming separatist culture and/or political action after 1975.[95] Early collective members adopted a trend of seeking a separate space for women and their children. Away from men and male children twelve years old and older, women could feel safe to explore, strengthen themselves, and form women's culture while gaining the tools they needed to unite for social change. Irene Weiss remembered, "Women made *big* changes in their lives after Califia. A *lot* of them moved across the *country*, gave up *partners*, got *new* partners, changed their *jobs*, dropped out, dropped in." Weiss said most of the women who came to Califia identifying as heterosexual became lesbian, and some expressed that they had longed for the support and close ties between women that they had never had before but saw at Califia.[96] Up-ending one's own life was momentous, but Brooks called stopping at becoming lesbian and exploring sexuality "*lifestyle* lesbianism." She wanted to know "what *other* stuff are you *doing*? Are you fighting any of the other *real* heavy-duty *oppressive parts* of a society that's holding *everybody* down?"

Fun community-forming aspects of Califia were important for the ways participants sought out like-minded women, found a reinvigorating retreat from mainstream hostility, hoped for an environment that would accept and support them for who they were, and gained space to reinforce their identities as feminists and sometimes as lesbians. Relief and tensions over identity and group formation can be seen among other beleaguered populations that organized based on a minority identity. The fun encouraged imaginative thinking and continued ideas for change. Disagreement over how to behave within feminist circles and how to intervene in society, however, could devastate those who needed a sense of solidarity and affirmation.[97]

Women found relief from the hard emotional work concerning sexism, classism, and racism through recreation and bonded while doing chores. They enjoyed the outdoors, hiking, swimming, and sitting around a campfire singing songs to guitar accompaniment and dancing.[98] Joy Fisher reviewed the second conference experience of 1976 in *The Lesbian Tide*. She described "the revolution" as consisting of attendees listening to Alix Dobkin's *Lavender Jane Loves Women* while working together in the kitchen because that united women.[99] Weiss, who joined the collective in 1978, also joyfully recalled the radio or tape cassettes playing during kitchen duty: "we were all *dancing* in the *kitchen*, while we were cooking and cleaning up."[100] Murphy recognized that even the four to six hours of kitchen duty fostered "camaraderie" and became a get-away for women who were overwhelmed by the intensity of Califia.[101]

Inspired by the first camp and wanting to commemorate Califia's goals,

Jetter created a melody to which others wrote lyrics. "The Song of Unity (A Woman's Anthem)" recalled the turmoil, joy, sisterhood, pride, and hope for changing the world that Califia contained:

Woman loving tough and caring, sister pain and triumph sharing
Proud our woman's bodies bearing, sisters dream and do and dare
We will grow and we will build tomorrow, People whole and space that's free
And together raise our separate voices, in a Song of Unity

When the darkness seems to fill the hour
Woman Power will prevail
Neither class nor age shall make a difference
Sisterhood will never fail

Like the mission of Califia, "The Song of Unity" displayed the struggle to overcome mainstream derogation of women by taking pride in their bodies and supporting each other through their pain. The authors of the song listed class and age as salient identity factors that divided women and concluded, "Sisterhood will never fail." The juxtaposition of sexism unifying women while class and age divided them only partially covered what would crystallize into the three major presentations. The focus on age reflected the reality that Califia presentations were open to females twelve years old and up, with middle-aged mothers like Brooks, Murphy, and Jetter employing their years of feminist experience to teach neophytes:

All our children will embrace the truth
And their paths will be revealed
And the visions that we've all been seeing
Will become alive and real

We will take our power and we'll live it
Find our strength and freely give
To the sisters yet to be awakened
To the dream they might all live[102]

The lyrics reflect Califia collective members' interest in accommodating mothers with three- through eleven-year-old children by sharing childcare duties. Not only were the camp's informative CR sessions supposed to generate a shared vision from personal experience, but the physical presence and participation of children and their interaction with feminists besides their mothers held out the possibility of creating an intergenerational community of shared responsibility and mission. Narrators recalled that their kids would go home and play "feminist bookstore" and "Califia Community" or would enjoin their mothers to listen nondefensively to resolve disagreements, asking mothers to "listen like at Califia." In a period before much discussion of different types of families, children got to be with other kids who had lesbian mothers and/or blended families.[103]

This focus on group assistance appeared in the final verse, as the authors promised to share their message with women who had not yet had exposure to feminism. Women's music commonly had a theme of breaking out of individualizing models of personal pain to participate in collective work for change. This was central to Califia's mission.

In addition to spontaneous composition, retrospectives on workshops illustrated the topics that participants considered fun and important. Joy Fisher's review characterized the camp as perhaps "typical of the West Coast" in its "proliferation of workshops on relationships—how to have them, how to avoid them, how to mediate them, how to recover from them. (As the week wore on, women began to leave the cabins, two-by-two, bedrools [sic] under their arms, undoubtedly for a little field study.)."[104] Jewell remembered many workshops on self-care such as massage, women's health, and spirituality. Themes of relationship, self-care, and spirituality fit squarely into cultural feminist goals of nurturing women and personal transformation.[105]

During a camp session in 1977, Z Budapest gave a packed workshop on women's spirituality, which exposed tensions over the proper expression of feminism. For Jewell, a feminist perspective on spirituality constituted "very exciting times because instead of having a patriarchal structure of men's religions and politics, we could go to a place that was completely about women. So it was incredibly refreshing and life-changing."[106] Jewell and other women integrated aspects of feminist Wiccan paganism, astrology, goddess worship, and Native American spirituality into their lives and, so, joined a vibrant spiritual community. Budapest, an engaging speaker, encouraged women to link spiritual growth with feminist principles and politics.

Budapest's Wiccan organized religion brought about controversy. Not all welcomed the presence of witches or any religion at Califia. Joy Fisher described a banquet that women organized midweek, "complete with a receiving line of witches. . . . By the end of the week, I was weary of witchcraft—not one more witches' circle would I snail in."[107] Jetter, an avowed atheist who prided herself on rational thought, had never known witches really existed. More than twenty-five years later, she wanted to go on record about Wiccans:

> And *every* time *all* the community was there at the same time, *somehow* I found myself in a *ritual* I didn't know I was going to *be* in. *Form* a circle. *Hold hands. Do* this, that, and the other thing. You know, five or ten minutes all of a sudden you're *doing* something you don't know what you're *doing* it for. And about the *third* time I was *starting* to get the idea that *I* didn't really want to be *doing* this, that they were *doing* this to me without my *permission*. I saw a woman standing on the sidelines for the *third* time with this. And finally after that third time I went over to her, and I said, "*How come* you never *participate* in that?" And she said, "I'm not going to be involved in anything as stupid as *that*." But the *fourth* time was really what *blew me away*. There was a woman there who was a *tiny* woman, maybe ninety pounds dripping *wet*, and all of a sudden there were *two* rows of women *serpentining* around the room, and they *lifted* this woman over [their] head[s] and everybody was *passing* her down this serpentine line. And at the end she comes off the line. And *this* ritual was a *woman* giving birth to herself.

Jetter canvassed and found others were also confused and irked. Jetter then complained publicly at a nightly community meeting that these ceremonies were unjustified and done without the participants' permission. She stressed that witches should "at least *say* you're going to do these rituals and do you *want* to participate." Eventually, over the years, she found that the presence of witches subsided. Jetter speculated that they might not have found Califia welcoming until its very last years.[108] It is not surprising that lesbian feminist Wiccan practitioners "came out of the woodwork" to attend Califia camps.[109] The second-year brochure claimed that spirituality would be part of Califia, and its natural setting was conducive to nature-based religions.

Contrary to Jewell's enthusiasm and Jetter's disgust, Weiss and Brooks acknowledged but played down the presence of witches at Califia as part of the larger feminist debate over what counted as political and what place cultural feminists had in a movement for social justice. Weiss remembered that some women loved the rituals Budapest did in the couple of years she attended Califia and that on evaluation forms some wanted more spirituality presentations.[110] Interviewing Brooks with her partner, Silvia Russell, Russell's interest in spirituality prodded Brooks to discuss Wicca. After initially saying there was no spirituality, Brooks suggested that some people did things in the woods but avowed that Califia was "*very* very secular." Russell prodded, "Any *witches* at that time?" and Brooks recalled that many women were witches doing rituals. Although Brooks initially forgot and then de-emphasized witchcraft, she argued cultural feminism in general contributed to movement work:

> And they need to have a place where they're *nurtured*, and then they need to be given the *tools* to then move out and do other things. So *often*, groups just become *nurturing* places and nothing is really ever *demanded* or nothing ever *comes* of it. And *that* may be good in its own *self*. Psychologists say that's good *in and of* its own self, but I've always wanted to make something *happen*.[111]

The trajectory that Brooks plotted with personal well-being as a stage before action indicated her prioritization of action. Josy Catoggio and Ariana Manov eventually came to view emotional support, well-rounded lives, and activism as mutually necessary:

> You had no right to more than the *bare minimum* as long as there were people who didn't have the *bare* minimum. And so a *lot* of us were living in this *intense, passionate, political space* where we didn't take the *time* to *rest* or to *have relationships* or to *feed* or *nurture* ourselves. And a lot of us were acting in ways that Ariana *now* describes as an *awful* lot like using activism as your sort of drug of *choice* to avoid dealing with whatever in your life you don't want to *deal* with.[112]

These avowed activists supported cultural feminism. They saw it had positive effects and assessed that a single-minded focus on political or social causes was detrimental to women.

When individuals burned out, their withdrawal could destroy the group effort. How much energy to spend on oneself and on the betterment of one's world was impossible to resolve, but it related to the place of spirituality in cultural and/or political feminism. The public avowal of matriarchal religions and nondominant spiritual practices promoted the formation of collective identity and pitted spiritualists against their opponents in a political contestation of dominant categories. Despite the apparent decline in witches attending Califia conferences, the debate over whether spirituality was a distraction or made a significant contribution to women's well-being and political activism would continue.

FALSE STARTS AND FRICTION

Spirituality hardly represented the only bone of contention in Califia or feminism nationwide. Although Califia tried to operate through consensus, conflicts erupted in the first three years over how decisions were made and over unexamined power dynamics. A lofty plan for sustained community demonstrated some of the practical limits of cultural feminism. Turmoil followed discussions about the role of the community in caring for itself and for individuals as well as the authority of the collective vis-à-vis participants. These areas of friction underscore the idealism and diversity of programs American feminists undertook.

A group of women at Califia's first conference at de Benneville Pines camp in Angelus Oaks, California spearheaded a project for permanent women's land. They took the Califia experience and pledged to prevent class problems and to incorporate environmentalism. Their plan advanced the possibilities of withdrawing support from the dominant society or regenerating women's feminist energies and equipping them to continue the struggle. Over the next months, *The Lesbian Tide* reported on the development of the Califia land project, which was slated to buy eighteen acres in Sonoma County.[113] A group of women who called themselves the Malibu/Califia Land Management collective purchased land in Malibu for "an educational conference and healing center for women."[114] Within a month, several of these Califia women closed on twelve-and-a-half acres and planned to use it "for only one retreat for Califia members before [reselling it] to purchase a communal living area here in Los Angeles for the larger membership of Califia Community" because the land they had gotten had insufficient buildings. One of the investors related that they had developed a model of collective living that would eliminate tenant/owner situations. Some women's lands formed land trusts or nonprofit organizations for collective control, but the article left the Malibu/Califia plan unclear, and only explained that $3,000 to $5,000 partial interests in the proposed land would be sold to women in the larger community.[115] The Malibu/Califia Land collective appeared to have shifted from acreage modeled on 1960s back to the land rural countercultural communes to trying to reproduce urban feminist communal living on a grander scale than the Furies collective in Washington, D.C. had. Soon afterward, the plans for permanent communal living dissipated. Brooks believed that they could not keep up with the payments. After weathering being fired and the closure of her bookstore, she "wasn't going to touch it."[116] Although Califia participants did not create urban or rural collective living, groups of women

across the country turned their attention toward other women and away
from mainstream society by forming women's lands that have been well
documented.[117]

Califia participants were divided, anyway, over the value in withdrawing from society instead of continuing to engage for change.[118] Catoggio
continued to feel some guilt that experiencing Califia's temporary reprieve
from patriarchy raised expectations too high:

> A *lot* of women would come [to a Califia conference] and would *radically*
> change their lives because of *that* experience. They would *go* home and
> *leave* their husbands and come *out* of the closet and *work* in a factory be-
> cause . . . we *created* the illusion . . . that there was this women's commu-
> nity to come out *into* because Califia was *it*. But Califia was *temporary*. . . .
> it was *so traumatic* for people to come *out* of that and *back* into their *lives*,
> which now looked like *shit* to them 'cause they could see *all* the ways in
> which they were oppressed and had made compromises. And, you know,
> they'd been to *utopia* and they thought utopia still *existed* somewhere here
> in Los *Angeles*, and if they left their husbands and kids and whatever, that
> there would be this women's community to *join*. . . . And women would
> sort of *dismantle* their middle-class *lives*, even if they'd worked for years to
> *achieve* that, 'cause they suddenly couldn't stand being with their husbands,
> and they wanted to come out as a *lesbian*, and they thought there was this
> mythical feminist lesbian community that would embrace them with open
> *arms* and help them find a *job* and get *settled* and *live* in their house.[119]

There was no formal "community" of women who guaranteed to support newcomers with temporary housing, career training, and job placement. Women who did completely upend their lives, however, reported that
emotional support sustained them, and they attained more fulfilling lives.
Sometimes women who embraced lesbian identities and divorced their husbands wanted permanent women's land. In the long-term, though, they
got credentials for jobs, often in human services fields like counseling or
teaching, where they applied social justice principles about radical therapy,
sexism, classism, and racism they learned at Califia.

At the second de Benneville Pines camp session of 1977, tensions
erupted over how to balance the needs of an attendee remembered as "Sappha" with the requirements of the other hundred or so participants. Disagreement epitomized debates about disability issues, allegiance to western
medicine or alternative medicine, group responsibility, and the authority
of the collective. Jane Bernstein and Betty Jetter labeled Sappha "schizo-

phrenic" and blamed herbalists for convincing her to stop her medication cold turkey and switch to herbs during the June session.[120] The implication was that green tea could cure schizophrenia.[121] Sappha went off her drugs, went home, and came back two weeks later for the July Califia, which Jetter attended.[122] Narrators described Sappha as roaming, babbling, screaming all night, and exhibiting lowered inhibitions.[123] Jetter remembered that the green tea proponents tried to care for her but were asking for volunteers by the third night. At every night's community meeting, participants spent hours debating what to do about Sappha.

At stake was fear of complicity with a mental health profession that popular culture increasingly problematized and that leading feminists condemned. Jack Nicholson's recent performance in *One Flew over the Cuckoo's Nest* (1975) plumbed the depths of unchecked repression in mental institutions. Participants had just heard Ahshe Green's convincing class analysis of mental illness, in which she stressed that the middle class defined appropriate behavior and health, leaving all working-class people susceptible to the charge that they were crazy and the fear of being "locked up [to] just die rotting in a mental institution."[124] Green's examples of violent outbursts born of frustration about experiencing inequality and her continuous return to the theme of power differentials must have resonated with some who continually felt out of place. Women invoked personal experience and, as Manov remembered, "there were women who had been screwed over by the patriarchy and been locked up in *mental* wards who were *bound* and *determined* to keep this woman from having that *happen* at *Califia* of all places."[125] They found authoritative support in *Women and Madness* (1972) where feminist Phyllis Chesler indicted psychiatric theory and practice as brutally sexist.[126]

When middle-class men defined norms of appropriate behavior, did their mental illness labels even correspond to real phenomena or did they simply constrain women and other men whose unruliness otherwise threatened to upset polite society? What were the implications for everyone when people learned about comfort and dis-ease within a hierarchical societal construction? At the time, Manov was in good company in asserting that mental illness did not exist.[127] Others, like Bernstein and Elsa Fisher, wanted to get Sappha hospitalized and back on her medication because they felt ill-equipped to help her and recognized that she was in distress.[128] Both they and Sappha seemed ill at ease with the situation. Karen Merry had the unique perspective that women at Califia also feared involving authorities because it could have imperiled the camp and jeopardized the safety of the other women there. As a social worker, she advised people on their options for getting Sappha help.[129] For about four days the debate and care shifts continued as Sappha's behavior disrupted this temporary community.[130]

The collective members finally asked Sappha to leave because they could not do any of the planned educational work, and a couple of women drove her down the mountain.[131] Manov believed that those women continued to nurse Sappha rather than risk care from the dominant society. Later Manov reassessed the episode, believing that mental illness was a biochemical reality. She worried that ultimately area feminists may have blamed the victim for not improving. She recalled rumors that Sappha floated around without the intervention she needed and "wreaked *havoc* on a lot of women" who did not know how to care for her.[132] The tragic story of Sappha is one example of the unintended effects of throwing everything into question and trying to reform the world while living in an unreformed society. As progressives reassessed norms and created new standards of behavior, they rightly questioned mental illness standards. The mental health industry had a long history of harming women, and social conservatives tended to call into question the sanity of people who behaved unusually and wanted change. Feminists did not want to perpetuate harm and delegitimization. In the long run, compassionate views toward those who most visibly could not fit in society fed a whole field of feminist social work and therapy. In the short run, it was impossible to accommodate the needs of women like Sappha with others' learned discomfort and lack of experience with mentally ill people.

In the wake of the exhausting second session with Sappha, some leaders proposed that the collective divest itself of power over what programs to organize or present so as not to be "elitist." The collective was still firmly divided after ten hours of argument and, resorting to a vote, the no-structure side won. Making a clear argument for structure, Murphy recounted, "The following morning, two hundred women, new to Califia, were met by exhausted collective members and a schedule consisting only of meals for the week. From the chaos of the next few days, after which the original schedule was followed, several Califia policies were determined." Not only did structure during the first two days allow participants to become acclimated and to start thinking about how they wanted Califia to develop, structure met the collective members' political needs. The inauspicious night-before vote reaffirmed collective members' insistence on reaching all decisions by consensus and began a commitment to finishing structure and content changes before the last meeting.[133] Consensus was a time-consuming alternative to representative democracy used by some feminist and New Left groups. Everyone on the nine- to eighteen-member collective gave input until they shaped a proposal to meet everybody's concerns. Ultimately, everyone agreed to each decision or at least did not block it. Consensus allowed full participation, respectful inclusion for all involved, and much more group cohesion than democratic groups that split into factions and allowed 51 percent of a group to tyrannize the minority. Despite calls to end meetings on time, later collective members joked that meetings continued to privilege those with the most stamina.[134]

Califia's aborted attempt to operate without structure reflected and refined Jo Freeman's evaluation of small groups in "The Tyranny of Structurelessness." Freeman found CR groups' time-intensive participatory process incompatible with organizing concrete projects that required specific tasks. In addition, some feminists' resistance to choosing representatives or leaders led reporters to choose "stars," whom some feminists then condemned as "elitists." Freeman argued that feminist groups structured themselves according to friendship networks with exclusive informal communication networks. Such a structure required a narrow function, a small and homogeneous group, high communication, and low skill specialization.[135] Although the Califia collective reproduced concerns about taking too much power, its system challenged many of Freeman's conclusions. Members tried to ensure inclusion in decision-making by using consensus and setting up various sites for discussion about policy at the camps and between camps. In ensuing years, they expanded diversity in the collective and started projects that addressed men's violence and whites' racism.

Collective meetings and camp community meetings were the primary sites for decision-making. Numerous narrators saw the community meetings as exciting examples of taking one's power. Looking back, most narrators saw consensus as a humane and community-building alternative to oppressive hierarchy, a tool that was applicable some of the time but that needed to be used in conjunction with making power and responsibility commensurate.[136] For Jewell and Carla Seco (pseudonym), process and consensus were the most important things to consider in assessing Califia. Community meetings were one of Jewell's "favorite things because anybody could put up an agenda item." A pad of butcher paper, a facilitator, and a process person guided the discussions after women wrote down the topics and the number of minutes they wanted for each discussion. Community meetings galvanized women, and Jewell saw the meetings shift from passive to passionate discussions over the course of the week.[137] The importance of consensus to Seco lay in the development of trust and communication that it necessitated. Rather than strategizing and lobbying for votes, even the potentially negative consensus aspect of talking each other to death shared more of people's underlying rationales.[138]

Consensus required that women exhibit convincing articulation, and in an unequal society, there were limits to its democratizing effects although it exceeded current political norms. Catoggio defended consensus against executive decisions and voting, which leave the many losers subject to dictates of the appointed or the majority. In the long run "you end up with a lot of people feeling oppressed and sort of doing various kinds of sabotage—whether consciously or unconsciously." From discussion with Manov, Catoggio concluded that the major drawback to consensus was that it privileged persuasive speakers, so that people would still feel "run over." If they cannot articulate their positions, "then eventually they turn on you and say that *you're* oppressing *them* because you're articulate and strong and sway people to your *side*." Weiss agreed that, in practice, "there are always some people who carry more weight and whose word carried more weight. And sometimes that was Marilyn. Sometimes it was Betty Brooks, who were the two founding members . . . and who had *big* voices [chuckle]." Unlike majority-rule models, feminists hoped to train women to "take their power" by practicing the skills they needed.[139] Later, a younger collective member, Anna María Soto, reminisced that she never felt so sharp and bright and articulate as when she was on the collective.[140] Betty Jetter recognized that women really needed to discuss the issues they felt were pressing. She did not look forward to the tedium and, with years of experience, "always felt like, 'Well, *here* we go again.' And yet I knew [laugh] we *had* to do it." Majority rule would have been "bullying."[141]

Work on the collective trained women to stand up to people, and Weiss noted that there were always "nay-sayers, obstacle-growers." Asked, "So how would that work in the long run with a consensus model?" she quipped, "That's what it did—a *long* run."[142] Collective meetings simply ran on and on because achieving consensus to empower women rather than outvoting them took time. Scoffing at the idea that they ended meetings "on time," she recalled long discussions until the opposition was worn down. Seco qualified such complaints, saying that everyone knew before they joined the collective that they were committing to all-day meetings.[143]

Rather than time constraints causing problems, conflicts repeatedly erupted from unexamined power dynamics and from failures to convince participants to make changes that supported political ideals. Occasionally consensus completely broke down, most dramatically over vegetarian food. Sue Dunne and Shirley Virgil had convinced the initial collective to provide vegetarian meals. They were part of a broader political movement that opposed the postwar meat industry as cruel to animals and ecologically unsound. Their reasoning, however, failed to coincide with the priorities of Brooks and Murphy.

Significantly, no narrators could recap with any conviction the details of the rationales for vegetarianism. The Califia collective mailed a vegetarian announcement to attendees in the packets containing directions to the camp and an overview of events:

> In keeping with the presentation of alternatives to present systems, Califia offers a primarily vegetarian menu for the week. Delicious, balanced seasonal and varied meals will be served, so that you will likely discover that vegetarianism is not only a viable but also a palatable choice of eating habits. There will be a presentation explaining in more detail the various rationales for vegetarianism.[144]

Bernstein, who attended for six years, could reiterate that the camps were vegetarian because it was cheaper and healthier, but she thought it was "funny" and "really insane" that women believed that eating meat contributed to patriarchy.[145] Jetter sequentially linked strict vegetarian ideology with witchcraft as novel views: they "would complain that everybody's *behavior* changed the minute they had their once-a-week meat meal and that they had gotten *crazy*, and see what meat *does* to you and that kind of thing."[146] Clearly, the spiel advocating vegetarianism did not sway the majority of narrators or, probably, participants in general.

Given the times, Frances Moore Lappé's *Diet for a Small Planet* (1971) provided the most widely-read argument for changing eating habits. Lappé condemned inefficient protein production. In the late 1960s, livestock ate more than three-quarters of the grain produced in the United States in a process by which twenty-one pounds of protein fed to cattle became one pound of meat. Both in the United States and in Central American markets bound to U.S. consumption demands, massive land and water resources that could have grown cereals, legumes, and leafy vegetables were diverted to meat and cash crops while millions starved. Lappé estimated:

> [T]he average ratio for protein conversion by livestock in North America is 10 to 1. Applying this ratio to the 20 million tons of protein fed to livestock in 1968 in the U.S., we realize that only 10 percent (or 2 million tons) was retrieved as protein for human consumption [as meat]. Thus, in a single year through this consumption pattern, 18 million tons of protein

becomes inaccessible to man. This amount is equivalent to *90 percent of the yearly world protein* deficit.

In addition to exacerbating world hunger, factory farming hurt the earth through topsoil erosion from overgrazing or excessive plowing and threatened the health of people and other life forms through the concentration of chlorinated pesticides, antibiotics, growth hormones, and mercury up the food chain.[147] Alongside factory farming grew an organic health food movement and a surge in vegetarianism that blended with progressive politics to encourage people to link ecological, political, and humanitarian issues.[148]

Ecologically motivated practices like vegetarianism could seem to be more immediate forms of political action than voting or planning a Marxist revolution and more connected with non-Western, non-Anglo, nonurban models of voluntary simplicity and scaled-back technology.[149] French radical feminist lesbian Françoise d'Eaubonne coined the term ecological feminism in 1974 to draw parallels between male oppression of women and landowners' exploitation of the earth and laborers.[150] Ecofeminism often fit well with Wicca by positing a mystical connection between women and nature.

Such simplicity, however, ran counter to southern California life. Los Angeles in the 1940s and 1950s had spawned fast food restaurants such as McDonald's, the predecessors of Carl's Jr. and Taco Bell, and then Jack in the Box. In 1975, farm activist Jim Hightower had warned about giant corporate homogenization, terming it the "McDonaldization of America."[151] Mirroring Hollywood and all it represented, McDonald's symbolized unhealthy, plastic, homogenized, speeded-up culture to many vegetarians and cultural dissidents.

Feminist Carol Adams drew parallels between meat production and sexism, encapsulating arguments Bernstein and Jetter remembered. Like ecologists and goddess worshippers who saw the earth as a mother, Adams claimed that the "rape of the land by meat-eaters (it requires 6 to 10 times as much land to feed meat-eaters) is taken for granted just as the rape of women is condoned." She compared the colonization of Central and South American countries for meat production to "the colonization of women's energies by American men: neither are allowed self-determination, for that would be injurious to the oppressor's interests." Likewise, Adams connected historically gender-divided hunting and gathering and the western phenomenon of men eating more meat than women to explain male aggression and women's affinity to animals. She posited that rather than a desire to hunt and kill being innate, perhaps "it is meat-eating that causes the violence and aggression exhibited in hunting, sports and wars characteristic of patriarchal society."[152] At Califia, the imposition of vegetarian meals seemed like a needless attack on women's comfort during otherwise stressful weeks because planners did not successfully articulate arguments against the products of factory farming or convince other women that meat-eating furthered male supremacy and nutritional deficits for women.

Unaccustomed cuisine pushed some participants too far outside their comfort range when they were already struggling with the emotional intensity of camp life. Meat had been the center of American meals since colonial times and linked to status; beef industry advertising since the turn of the century had claimed that meat was the key to good health. By 1970, the average American ate 160 pounds of red meat per year; 7 percent of the global population consumed 30 percent of the world's animal food, eating 10 to 12 percent more protein than necessary even by conservative USDA estimates.[153] When vegetarianism first became a feminist issue, Murphy derided it as another "middle-class affectation." By considering downward mobility chic, middle-class feminists rejected norms that working-class families struggled to attain. Food and the equation of meat on the table with middle-class norms in the minds of working-class women were recurring themes in the class background discussion and in interviews. Over the years, collective members from working-class backgrounds like Murphy, Weiss, and Jetter came to see some virtue in vegetarianism, but they personally, along with most middle-class narrators, continued to eat meat. Alice Myers, by contrast, became vegetarian as a direct result of serving as Califia's cook and as one of the presenters on why vegetarianism was *the* feminist food choice.[154]

Califia strayed from vegetarian-only meals by allowing women to bring in food. Dunne and Virgil were only on the collective in 1976 and 1977, and, after they left, Califia conferences incorporated one chicken meal midweek. The presence of meat at meals was as much an affront to vegetarian feminists as diet sodas were to fat liberationists. In 1978, when Murphy was hosting a collective meeting, "vegefems" came to protest the food. Collective meetings were always open to all participants. Jewell remembered that there was no accommodation, and those vegefems never returned to Califia. She felt that when something did not suit Murphy and Brooks's vision, "they were the ones who held the power really in the collective." As a new collective member, Jewell wanted to continue striving for middle ground, but the vegefems were walking out, and "Marilyn's attitude was, 'Well, we're done.'" Jewell was horribly disappointed at the discrepancy between consensus talk and practice.

The four collective members from the founding year (Brooks, Murphy, Perna, and Stambolian) had power not only as founders but because they had experience with feminism, were older than some newer members, and were articulate and self-assured. Brooks and Murphy had achieved enough material success to own homes in which they could host planning meetings. During Jewell's year on the collective in 1978, she experienced such personal conflicts that she left. Twenty-five years later, the events were so painful to two collective members who felt pushed out that they could not give full accounts, but others supported their interpretations. For Jewell, the vegefem incident was one of the last straws that influenced her to quit. Throughout her interview, amid the life-changing joy she received from Califia, Jewell referred to her disappointment with other collective members and the fact that she was not alone.[155]

(UTOPIAN?) SEARCH FOR FEMINIST COMMUNITY

Realities falling short of professed ideals hit new feminists hard. Jewell came out of a marriage into lesbianism, attained a new world view, and anticipated having found a nurturing feminist community after feeling lost. When she encountered trashing and put-downs, the rosy glow dissipated. For her there seemed to be little substance.[156] When Catoggio regretted that Califia might have created an illusion of feminist utopia, she contrasted Jewell's experience with her own. Catoggio was able to move to Los Angeles because she had a friend who could house her in exchange for help with childcare. She felt that middle-class women were not used to taking in women until they could get on their feet. Betty Friedan had described the individualized suburban nuclear family structures that had isolated and infantilized white middle-class wives in *The Feminine Mystique*, but despite the rise of a women's movement that included cultural spaces and social groups, individualism in America was still the norm.

Califia Community's educational plan pointed to new forms of self-conception and interaction to overhaul society both individually and collectively. Feminists reassessed almost everything to live deliberately. In doing so, Califia women created new norms of behavior founded on their personal experiential knowledge and identity formation. Their countercultural values provided safety, freedom, and empowerment for lesbian, fat, poor, and racialized women whom society disparaged. Califia was frequently life-changing and affirming. The collectively examined life also subjected attendees to feminist judgments. Califia women were still working out their analyses and choosing which countercultural theories to utilize. They would especially join work against sexism, campaign against homophobia, and become the leading area speakers against racism. A cultural focus on relationships and self-care provided group support, which sustained energy for political activism. Taking opposition to heteropatriarchy as their starting point had positive implications for connecting sexism to body politics, including disability. The lesbian feminist lens was less useful for articulating other connections convincingly, which weakened their initial perspectives on vegetarianism, class, and race because their theories did not hook well into collective work.

Women came to the conferences and were challenged by all the innovative ideas. Within one week, women were bombarded with all sorts of programs for personal liberation, including lesbianism, fat pride, sexual education and exploration, nudity, understanding and support for working-class women, alternative views on mental illness, Wicca, and consensus alternatives to representative democracy. There seemed to be a plethora of options for participation. They could work on their bodies and spirits through morning yoga, meditation, and self-defense, get schooled in feminist basics, dedicate themselves to stopping violence against women, join FU, enjoy a newfound love, commit themselves to unlearning their racism, become a witch, or at least roll up their sleeves and work together to keep the camp running. Califia, like feminist spaces across the nation, forged a new vocabulary and alternative ways of conceiving the world. Such spaces could be completely alienating or devastating when they could not live up to expectations. Califia could be such a high that women came back session after session to get away from a world that paled by comparison. After its initial years of exploring a multiplicity of new cultural concepts, such returnees began to focus on incorporating more diversity and taking local action.

CHAPTER 3

INTEREST IN WOMEN

FROM ITS INCEPTION TO ITS CONCLUSION, Califia collective members' presentations about sexism sought to unite women based on shared oppression by men and to call Califia women to action. Califia founders and their contemporaries built on earlier feminist critiques to teach women to prioritize women.[1] They addressed patriarchal male domination and heterosexual privilege and debated what constituted aspects of sexism. Feminists in the 1970s–1980s disagreed about the amount of privilege women enjoyed, oppression they faced, and degree they could be good feminists in relation to their gender identity, the gendered behavior they exhibited, sexual attraction, and sexual practices.

This chapter explains Califia's teachings about patriarchy and its connections to feminist trends because Califia was most indicative of its times in debates about sexism, lesbianism, and how to mobilize against misogyny. Founder Marilyn Murphy drew on six years of movement literature that touted lesbianism as a superior emotional and sexual choice for women. By linking lesbianism and homophobia to sexism, Califia women participated in the process of unpacking "sexism" as about more than men oppressing women. Putting lesbians first appealed to many participants and continued to alienate heterosexual women and marginalize bisexual women. Presenting gendered behavior as essentialist or enduring simultaneously mobilized women, supported woman-only culture, and foreclosed possibilities for coalition work that recognized diversity in gender. Incompatible desires to eliminate gender or to exalt femaleness and irreconcilable tensions between a focus on women's sexual autonomy and wariness of sexuality in the face of male violence exploded into the feminist sex wars. A common difficulty in attempts to determine what aspects fit under sexism was the inclination toward binary divisions rather than considering that degrees of privilege and oppression existed within the same individuals.

Information about sexism and heterosexism permeated the conferences, from the welcome material to presentations and informal discussions. Califia presentations took patriarchy as the root of all oppressions and linked sexism to homophobia. Murphy addressed the lesbian-straight split, which had continued to develop after its inception at NOW in 1969.[2] For newcomers, Murphy offered morning discussion sessions that introduced feminist concepts. Women who formed the first feminist antiporn groups supplemented the sexism presentation. With these perspectives, Califia became part of the founding of rape crisis services and recruitment for protests against pornography, as well as an early site for tensions over appropriate expression of women's sexuality.

READINESS FOR (LESBIAN) FEMINISM 101

Collective members knew that participants would arrive at camp with varied levels of feminist training, so their welcome packet asked women to gain equivalent basics: "The Califia Community Collective suggests that preparation for Califia include reading any book on this list that you haven't yet read." The 1978 list included Elinor Flexnor's classic work on women's suffrage and turn-of-the-century rights, *Century of Struggle*. Flexnor had been part of the Old Left, and *Century of Struggle* introduced her framework of gender/race/class analysis to later feminists. Most of the reading list had early to mid-1970s feminist works that introduced four broad themes. Kate Millett and Anne Koedt's works explained sexism and heterosexism while Del Martin and Phyllis Lyon and Dolores Klaich's books assessed attitudes toward lesbians. Vivian Gornick and Barbara Moran and Adrienne Rich exposed the patriarchal underpinnings of childbearing and motherhood. Toni Cade and Gerda Lerner's foundational collections showed the importance of black women to women's history and society.[3] By 1980, the "Recommended Reading List" had grown from nine works to more than forty-four; more than half the list combined sexism with minority women's experiences of racism.[4] Genres ranged from poetry, short stories, and Marge Piercy's science fiction to autobiography, literary criticism, sociology, and history.

Having pointed attendees to formative feminist works, collective members rotated giving the main presentation on sexism. Murphy often presided from 1976 through 1983 and facilitated a daily breakfast discussion called "the Feminist Primer." The presentation focused on historical and contemporary manifestations of sexism and was called either "Misogyny and the Oppression of Women," or "Overview: From Oppression to Power:♀'s

History." According to Irene Weiss, "it was really Feminism 101" where her "companion lover," Murphy, "talked about how women are *oppressed* and how they *have* been oppressed institutionally and personally. And she spoke a *great* deal from *personal* experience." Murphy and other present- ers' accessible styles highlighted ways in which male superiority and sex- ism stunted women's lives and asked women to envision what they wanted to be.[5] Founder Betty Brooks expressed this solidarity as "the necessity for SISTERHOOD." She invoked a term espoused by Robin Morgan's 1970 *Sisterhood Is Powerful*, which stemmed from the consciousness-raising (CR) goal of constituting women as feminist agents able to oppose patriarchal oppression.[6]

Alice Myers recalled that the Feminist Primer "let people who were first- timers explore ideas, explore reactions, let them talk out whatever situations they were undergoing, and let them know about what it means to be a fem- inist."[7] They learned vocabulary like "patriarchy," "privilege," and "pro- cess" as well as etiquette such as "speaking one at a time and not interrupt- ing with comments of sympathy, support, or disagreement."[8] Betty Jetter remembered the Feminist Primer was wildly popular both at Califia and at discussion groups held at Murphy and Weiss's home. She estimated that the Feminist Primer attracted twenty to thirty women each morning.[9] Al- though Karen Merry had called herself a feminist since she started reading the first issues of *Ms. Magazine* in 1972, the give-and-take over breakfast helped her to integrate into the lesbian community and led her to see Mur- phy as the primary force at Califia.[10]

RESISTANCE TO LESBIAN FEMINISM
AND ITS CONSEQUENCES

The sexism presentations also elicited vehement disagreements, which were indicative of levels of feminist understanding, differing feminist ideologies, and the theories' capacities for alliance-building. Dissenters gave anecdotal counter-examples of the wonderful men in their lives. Collective members, armed with statistics on violence and discrimination against women as well as participants' testimony, would then "explore with the community what it means that a program on the woman-hating behavior of men becomes a program on man-hating in the minds of some women."[11]

The resistance likely stemmed not only from lack of familiarity with sex- ism as a structural concept, but from Murphy and others' promotion of lesbian feminism as true feminism. Murphy's 1976 mimeographed "Les- bianism as a Special Issue" positioned lesbian feminism as "the ultimate solution." Using principles from the body of lesbian feminist theory that started with the Lavender Menaces' 1970 "Woman-Identified Woman," Murphy proclaimed:

> Women loving women is the ultimate solution to living in the patriarchy. As long as women continue to give their sexual and emotional energy to men, men will continue to have power over us. . . . Only by most women withdrawing from the society built on the bodies, brains and blood of women can that society be brought down. Only without us, too, will men be able to recognize the personal limitations of their lives and have the will to change them. By continuing to live with, to love, and to support men, women collaborate with the enemy and contribute to the strength of the patriarchy which oppresses us all.[12]

The tract she circulated reiterated the main idea of "Woman-Identified Woman," that lesbians were vanguard feminists when they directed their emotional energy solely to females and that men retained power by keeping women's energies focused on men. From this viewpoint, any women who supported men collaborated in the oppression of women. Murphy took a further step by arguing that separatism would benefit men by encouraging them to address their dependence.

Collective members' critiques against heterosexuality packaged lesbian identification as a choice for self-exploration and solidarity against patriarchal norms and sought to bust antilesbian myths. They called lesbianism a "sexual preference" rather than a fixed "sexual orientation." This ideology held that gender identity was fixed but sexuality was not; women could choose lesbianism as part of their feminism. Divided into small groups based on whether they currently identified as "lesbian" or "nonlesbian," participants discussed the question "What was your reaction when you first realized that lesbianism had some relationship to your life?" Decentering the norm by calling heterosexuality "nonlesbian" and assuming lesbianism was related to every woman's life prodded women to rethink dominant assumptions. Presenters asked, "What myths and stereotypes about lesbians do you know, and what effect did they have upon that realization?" For example, L.A.'s *The Lesbian Tide* had joined national gay and lesbian protest in condemning NBC's 1974 *Police Woman* episode, "Flowers of Evil," and televised movie, *Born Innocent*, for portraying lesbians as butch and femme murderers who robbed vulnerable nursing home residents or as parts of girl gangs that sadistically raped other girls.[13]

After asking women to be conscious of the problems that societal sexism and heterosexism caused, a Lavender Horizons slide show further reinterpreted received wisdom. "Women Loving Women" humorously reread the Judeo-Christian creation story, with "Eve and Lilith walking hand in hand in the Garden of Eden while an apprehensive god and Adam watch."[14] Eve and Lilith withdrew their energy from patriarchy, and their hand-holding hinted at woman-identified lesbianism as a subversive alternative to the male-dominant/female-submissive reproductive relationship Genesis featured.

Attention to Califia participants' sexual preference downgraded both heterosexual and bisexual feminists' status while calling on them for understanding and support of lesbian feminism. Nationwide, many 1970s–1980s feminists dismissed bisexuality as a transitional stage that retained heterosexual privilege. Murphy spoke against bisexuality. She later wrote condemningly that bisexual women were the only true heterosexual women because, rather than unthinkingly following mandates to be heterosexual, they had experienced sexual attraction to women and chose to continue having sex with men.[15] In that climate, Elsa Fisher consciously chose lesbian identity for acceptance:

> I'm 100% sexually bisexual. I *chose* to be a lesbian. And I *chose* to be a lesbian because I didn't have a choice at the time [laugh] because the community was so *male*-hating at that time that I *couldn't* have been bisexual and have been *accepted in* the women's community. I said, "*Hey*! If I can have an emotional relationship as well as a *physical* one, no *contest*!"[16]

Nonetheless, Jane Bernstein remembered bisexual workshops at Califia and concluded that married women who found lesbian relationships at camp and then returned to dating men must have been bi.

Lesbian feminists' characterization of lesbianism as a superior choice differentiated them from less radical gay males who asserted they were born gay. Karen Merry addressed the stakes:

> I *very* strongly have *always* felt that I *chose* to be a lesbian. . . . But I got pretty upset in these last years when the *boys* were all saying . . . you were *born* this way 'cause I think, I've always thought of it as sort of a little bit of a *cop-out*. "I can't help it. I was *born* this way." I say, "*Screw* that. I'm *choosing* this. . . . This is a *strong* lifestyle. I defy anybody to tell me I can't *be* who I *am*."[17]

Merry's position refuses to let detractors define lesbianism. One can frame homosexual identity as positive or negative whether one claims it is inborn, chosen or combines elements one can and cannot control. Religious conservatives have called homosexuality a dissolute "lifestyle" from which gays and lesbians should repent or be punished with exclusions from the body politic. When believing homosexuality is inborn, extreme homophobes have advocated confining or killing gay people.

Califia women's view that women could choose lesbianism as a strong, fulfilling lifestyle reflected lesbian feminist thinking nationwide. Alix Dobkin popularized the sentiment in her song, "Gay Head" in 1973:

> *I heard Cheryl and Mary say*
> *There are two kinds of people in the world today*
> *One or the other*
> *A person must be*
> *The men are them and*
> *The women are we!*
> *They agree it's a pleasure to be a*
>
> Chorus
> *Lesbian. Lesbian*
> *Let's be in no man's land*
> *Lesbian. Lesbian*
> *Any woman can be a Lesbian*

The song contrasts male-dominated society's "*king*dom" and "the *his*tory of *man*kind" with women who are indifferent to men. Dobkin became the most vocal proponent of lesbian feminism in the musical genre, women's music, which developed to contest masculinist priorities in the music industry.[18]

Collective memory of lesbianism as a superior choice has dimmed since the advent of the AIDS pandemic when spokespeople for gay and lesbian rights have typically championed fixed identity based on much-sought-after biological determinants. Some gay men and lesbians have argued that they would never have chosen a condition that included such discrimination. Lesbian feminists, in stark contrast, have championed choosing an oppositional identity while seeking the destruction of the dominant structures that privilege heterosexuality. A contemporary belief in sexual orientation as genetic destiny correlates with a desire for inclusion within dominant structures. Simultaneously, however, studies correlating hypothalamus size or other bodily variation with homosexuality have provoked questions from prospective parents as to whether they can screen against homosexuality in a fetus.

In a context where feminists remained polarized about sexual orientation, personal networks and venues for advertising Califia inadvertently marked the camps as a lesbian space. Murphy recorded that about 20 percent of the attendees at the camps were heterosexual and that usually one or two were so uncomfortable that they left by the afternoon of the first day. To convert discomfort into CR, heterosexual collective members at the first evening's "getting acquainted exercises" came out as straight. They reassured heterosexual participants at the Late Night Conversation that they were not alone, redefined their discomfort as "a temporary loss of heterosexual privilege," and encouraged identification with lesbians through the temporary feeling of minority-group status.[19] Throughout the week, Murphy tried to forge ties between straight and lesbian women. It was a balancing act to invoke the lesbian feminist theory that had furthered the lesbian-straight split while reaching out to heterosexual women.

"Woman identification" considered men, anything deemed masculine, and heterosexuality to be patriarchal and inferior. From this position, lesbian feminists criticized heterosexual women as "male-identified" and sometimes repeated misunderstandings that butches and femmes simply imitated heterosexuality through their gender presentations and division of labor. Lesbian feminism could constrain the variety of acceptable female gender presentation and expression of desire for women.[20] In practice, women who already identified as butches when they came to Califia found ways to blend butch with feminist and spoke of themselves as butches whose gender identity was "modified" by feminism.[21] It was tricky to balance between ideals that women assert competence beyond traditionally female-assigned tasks and negative stereotypes of butches as aggressive and overbearing.

Women who joined feminist social movement spaces in the 1970s encountered "androgyny" as an idealized look that rejected mainstream markers of femininity and adopted some styles that had previously been commonly associated with men's wear. Murphy continued to advocate such a look as part of lesbian feminist education in her "Lesbianic Logic" column for *Lesbian News*, which ran from August 1982 through June 1991. In "Pretty in Pink," she denounced "lipstick lesbians" and other feminine appearance as part of heteropatriarchal values:

> "woman" is a role all female human beings are required to perform regardless of our age, race, ethnicity, religion, nationality, class, caste, degree of servitude or sexual preference. The role is to be the second, the subordinate sex, defined in our person and our attributes and our activities. . . . This includes . . . looking the way [men] think their women should look.

Murphy claimed that make-up and high heels were to please men, to portray women as frivolous sex objects, and to fund misogynist fashion and diet industries. Murphy admitted that transgressing gender norms was not easy; she had trouble giving up make-up and razors. Nonetheless, lesbians who conformed "pass as heterosexual." She did "not believe that feeling free to wear the visible shackles of our oppression has anything to do with our liberation, as long as most of our sisters do not feel free to wear anything else." She criticized American marketing of hyper-individualism or "personal freedom" as a myth "that has co-opted and diluted every movement for social change in this country including ours."[22] Instead, constraining one's appearance was a necessary counter to societal repression.

Murphy's criticism of consumer culture co-opting social movements was insightful, but women balked at restricting themselves in response. Women who saw themselves as redeploying make-up and fashion in relation to loving women or who did not want to alienate heterosexual feminists with a litmus test contested these teachings within and outside Califia. Latina lesbian Marilynn Cruz Rodriguez, for example, compared Murphy's dress-code demands to colonizing nuns and linked her own use of make-up to a precolonization tradition of Native Americans painting themselves. Cruz Rodriguez argued the lesbian feminist look was white and assimilating herself to it was akin to cultural erasure. When she cut her hair, she lost "a warm cultural friend." When she wore tennis shoes instead of high heels, she "lost [her] zapatiado which gave [her] the rhythm for [her] navigation through this world." Cruz Rodriguez admonished Murphy to ask and listen rather than make culturally insensitive judgments.[23] The personal-is-political method that Murphy used in her column led to criticism that she was condescending and judgmental. Readers who took Murphy's personalized introductions personally, felt attacked, and counterattacked. The personalized nature of the column made for engaging storytelling, but in the end it replicated the dynamics of contestation at Califia, which reshaped differences of opinion as personal affronts.

Given that women continued to come to Califia with variations of feminism that did not prioritize lesbianism or with little knowledge of feminism, some continued to dub the assessments of patriarchy "man-hating." Betty Jetter developed a popular talk called "Man-Hating as Taboo" after the first couple of years of Califia to tackle this problem. In her previous experience leading CR groups for NOW, Jetter encountered women who had been abused or neglected by their fathers or both parents but solely blamed their mothers. She complained, "And always the anger was directed at mothers and the men did not have to take responsibility." Jetter saw women redirect their hostilities from men who behaved badly to women and concluded that, in doing so women succumbed to a strong imperative in American society against man-hating and colluded in their own oppression. Jetter gave the "Man-Hating as Taboo" spiel as part of the collective presentation and presented it at NOW, colleges, seminars, and in people's homes.[24] "Man-Hating as Taboo" encapsulated attacks on feminism and feminist counterattacks. The taboo was revealed when antifeminists and those unschooled in feminism slung the label "man-hating" at women who criticized men's bad behavior.

On the other hand, feminist rage at the prevalence of sexism often blurred the distinction between loathing actions and hating persons or categories of people. Having a target for their anger mobilized women, but they had to counter the man-hating charge for feminism to be viable in a world of women who cared about men. Califia was part of the early development of education against discrimination that countered attempts to derail the topic at hand or decontextualize the institutional support for sexism through charges of reverse discrimination.

"TAKE YOUR POWER!"

Antifeminists have claimed that 1970s feminism was about victimhood, but Califia's training was indicative of how 1970s feminism was anything but an "identity of powerlessness."[25] Feminist legal work to redress injustice and entrance into formerly male-dominated jobs were all active assertions of power. Josy Catoggio quoted Brooks: "*Take* your *power*! Don't tell me I'm withholding it from you. You take it. I'm not keeping you from anything. You just *do* it."[26] Brooks prepared hundreds of individual women to assert themselves. Nonhierarchical consensus structure encouraged women to develop persuasive speaking skills. Jetter remembered that Brooks's first task for women in her self-defense training was to scream. When Jetter asked her daughters whether they could scream, their noise drove her from the room, and she felt so successful in raising them. Every summer's camps rang out with women yelling "No!" or screaming loudly from the diaphragm, which Brooks called the "ovarian yell." Women carried their training for life. Jetter followed the Brooks training step by step to teach three self-defense courses. She taught women to stomp an attacker's instep if he grabbed them from behind. They practiced front kicks to hyper-extend the knee against a frontal assault or to attack the windpipe and face. Most of all, self-defense training taught women they got to decide how to respond.[27] Muriel Fisher relied on the "ovarian yell" in her sixties or seventies. A young man split her from her friend with his bicycle on the pretense of asking for a cigarette. When he grabbed the petit-point stitch purse Fisher's mother had made, Fisher resisted giving up the heirloom. The "kid" pushed over her friend. Fisher recalled:

> I gave an *ovarian* yell from the depths of my belly just as Betty Brooks had taught me. And from Golden Hills they could have heard it in North Park, you know, in the next community. And that kid took off like a rabbit. And *I* held onto my mother's purse. We had the neighbors out by that time, and the police shortly thereafter and blah blah blah. But I will *never* forget that *ovarian yell.* [laugh][28]

By 1979, Brooks was supplementing individual training with collective action. She introduced Support, Education, and Action (SEA) groups to organize women based on geography or special interests, so they could make concrete plans for implementing their Califia training. Carol Albright's SEA formed the San Fernando Valley Rape Crisis Service in 1980 to address a local need. Albright remembered that a devastating French-Canadian film about rape screened at camp sparked the discussion.

> [O]ur *group* was [composed of] women of the San Fernando Valley, and we started talking about it. I mean, there was a lot of *anger* and . . . I mean anger is a *great* motivator. And there was also a lot of *sadness.* And there were women obviously who had been assaulted and abused as children in that group. And so we talked about [creating a rape crisis center] as a possibility.[29]

Califia women acted from personal experience and built on networking that the Los Angeles Commission on Assaults Against Women (1973) and the 1979 revitalization of the Southern California Rape Hotline Alliance (1975) laid. Hotlines existed at Pasadena's YWCA (1974), East L.A.'s Latina-run bilingual service (1976), and the Pacific-Asian Family's multilingual call center (1978), but the Valley and traditionally African American areas lacked services until 1980 and 1984, respectively.[30] Kal Kalivoda was involved in creating the safe space supportively to listen to Valley women as they dealt with the trauma of rape. The center hand-picked forty women to staff it at the end of eight or nine weeks of weekly training sessions that included group therapy about past experiences with molestation and other hardships. The rape crisis center integrated concepts women learned at Califia and from the Radical Feminist Therapy Collective to stress personal experience and support over expert advice, sometimes passing over trained therapists in favor of women without professional counseling credentials.[31] Califia women worked with a community mental health center to staff a twenty-four-hour hotline. They challenged established authorities by running training sessions for police officers, hospital staff, and community members, so that service providers served rape victims more compassionately. Because the Valley hotline was avowedly feminist and dominated by white lesbians, its style conflicted with Latina East L.A. staffers and later African American hotlines that had ties to the South Central chapter of the Southern Christian Leadership Conference and city attorney's office or the Compton YWCA. Within the antirape movement nationally, Latina and black staffers felt alienated by unfamiliar political vocabulary, confrontational style, and informal attire among white rape crisis activists. Although the Valley collective initially got Department of Social Services funding, when California's Office of Criminal Justice Planning took over funding and increased requirements, the Valley did not accommodate. Other area rape centers capitulated to state conditions that services have a hierarchal structure, collect racial data, and mandate victims to report their rapes to the police in accordance with Law Enforcement Assistance Administration requirements. The Valley services retained their radical feminist perspective and lasted until 1986 as a collective that left reporting to victims' discretion and refused to apply for state money.[32]

SPEAKING OUT AGAINST A CULTURE OF MALE VIOLENCE AND CONTRIBUTING TO THE SEX WARS

Organizing that started with private or public self-disclosure was fundamental to politicizing the personal. Feminists spoke out about intimate violence for women's autonomy. The New York Radical Feminists started the first public speak-out on rape in 1971 along with a conference that summarized central feminist thinking on rape: society blamed victims of rape, accused them of lying, and expected higher standards of proof in rape cases than for other felonies.[33] The same year, Bay Area Women Against Rape in northern California created the first antirape groups, and the first feminist women's health center opened in Los Angeles. Women in major cities held similar speak-outs and formed their own rape crisis centers, health clinics, and counseling.[34] CR encouraged women to reveal abuse publically as they allied and planned with other feminists. Twelve out of thirty-two narrators (38 percent) volunteered that they and/or other Califia women experienced childhood emotional, verbal, physical abuse, or molestation and/or adult abuse from a husband, boyfriend, or lesbian partner.[35] Poignant stories generated commitments to avoid violence in their own lives and to protect other women.

Advocates of sexual exploration and presentations on violence against women shared space at Califia, but ultimately criticism of men's behavior positioned most Califia women against pornography and consensual kink. California initiated the nationwide debates that became known as "the sex wars." The same year Califia formed, two antipornography organizations started independently of Califia women. Marcia Womongold founded Woman Against Violence Against Women (WAVAW) in L.A. to protest *Snuff*, which falsely claimed to have murdered women for the production of the film.[36] Women Against Violence in Pornography and Media (WAVPM) coalesced from a 1976 "Violence Against Women" conference in San Francisco. Both groups had East Coast offshoots by 1979.

Two media events brought WAVAW and WAVPM national attention. In June 1976, WAVAW members defaced an Atlantic Records billboard on Sunset Strip that advertised the Rolling Stones' *Black and Blue* album. The billboard depicted a white woman in a ripped white baby-doll dress bound with her hands above her head and her legs spread. She had a dark mark on her cheek and left inner thigh, downcast eyes and an ambiguous open-mouthed expression that could be interpreted as a wanton smile or panting from strain. The "V" of her crotch pointed at the picture of Mick Jagger on the album cover that served as the platform she straddled. The billboard caption read "I'm 'Black and Blue' from the Rolling Stones—and I love it!" (see photograph in this book). Some have argued that the image—also in record stores as a standing display—celebrated consensual kinky sex. The heterosexual juxtaposition between the model and the all-male rock band marketed it for a male audience, but the image was replete with ambiguity. It is easy to interpret the caption as words put in the model's mouth. WAVAW members spray-painted "This is a crime against! women ♀ [*sic*]" on the billboard, called a press conference, and successfully pressured Atlantic Records's West Coast manager to apologize and remove the billboard, which gained them national coverage in *Time*.[37] WAVAW then created a slide show of sexist album covers to marshal support for boycotts. In San Francisco, WAVPM confronted the porn industry in 1977 and rose to Mayor Dianne Feinstein's attention. Due to Feinstein's interest in improving San Francisco's image, she and two area feminists personally contributed to WAVPM. *Hustler* magazine's June 1978 cover picture of a woman in a meat grinder, claiming, "We will no longer treat women like pieces of meat" garnered new recruits and prompted WAVPM to hold a conference that led to the formative antiporn volume, *Take Back the Night*, in 1980.[38]

Slide presentations by WAVAW supplemented the Califia collective's talk early on to raise women's consciousness with powerful images of gendered violence.[39] Their focus on connecting pornography, rape, and general misogyny followed key 1970s feminist authors. Andrea Dworkin became a central antipornography feminist after publishing *Woman Hating* (1974). Likewise, Susan Brownmiller's 1975 *Against Our Will: Men, Women and Rape* ends with a discussion of pornography, followed by testimonies and statistics concerning rape.

The presence of WAVAW at Califia eventually led to overlapping leadership. Dani Adams was a collective member in 1980 and helped lead WAVAW. Her tract, "PORNOGRAPHY = VIOLENCE," recapitulated antipornography feminists' main arguments. Adams first defined pornography to exclude erotica, sex, prostitution, homosexuality, or obscenity. These exclusions seemed to attempt to address the criticism that antiporn feminists allied with social conservatives despite the fact that the conservative program extended from eliminating pornography, media with sexual content, and prostitution to attacking feminism and gay and lesbian rights. Adams defined pornography as "a 'blueprint' for a woman-hating society and it serves as a support system for men who want to hurt women." She listed examples of violent depictions: women and children photographed while "kidnapped and drugged and raped and used for prostitution," women tied up and tortured under the guise that they were consenting masochists, snuff films, and pictures of women being murdered produced for sexual arousal.

In a move common to antiporn feminists, Adams then linked such media production to women's realistic fears for their safety and used statistics about sexual and physical assault:

> approximately 25% of our city's population, 1 out of 2.8 women, will be sexually assaulted or raped in her lifetime, usually under threat of death. And approximately 25% of our population, 60% of our married women, will be battered. And approximately 25% of our little girls will be sexually molested, usually by a member of her family. This epidemic of violence toward women is being virtually ignored.
>
> Educators know that people of all ages learn best by doing; next best by watching what other people do. This knowledge about how we learn is not being applied to pornography.[40]

WAVAW's position that men learned sexist behavior and violence from society and pornographic depictions continued a radical feminist view that dated to 1969 and was popularized by Robin Morgan. In 1975, Morgan concluded, "Pornography is the theory, and rape is the practice."[41]

Over the years, Diane Germain developed and presented a riveting slide show on the commercialization of bodies, which was akin to WAVPM's presentation. She showed how camera angles could eroticize or deprecate women and how advertisers positioned their products in front of women's crotches. She also showed

> children used as sexual objects, women used as objects, like furniture or decoration on a man's arm, . . . fat women looked down upon and ridiculed and humiliated, not even with words, but also with their position—male dominating doctors sitting on a desk talking to a fat woman on a little tiny chair, and she's looking up at him like she's a little girl, which she isn't.[42]

After Germain walked women through interpreting the ways advertisers positioned women, objects, and texts to objectify women or glorify violence against women, most women responded that in the future they would be better able to see the manipulations in advertising that often went unrecognized. For example, even though Bonnie Kaufmann attended only one camp, she remembered a talk on pornography

> made it *so clear* to me that it's *so much* in *advertising*. And I'd never *thought* of it that way. It'd never been pointed *out* to me. And just in *looking* at different *ads*—I remember *that*—I mean, it was *just* so *obvious* to me. Once it was pointed *out*, I really believe that it was *so*. It *was* deliberately there in advertising. It wasn't just *there* because we wanted to *see* it that way. It really was *there*. And I can *still* see things. It really opened my eyes and my consciousness about *so* many things that go on. . . .[43]

Califia's education and groups like WAVAW, WAVPM, and New York's Women Against Pornography trained women to see and interpret sexist images. Where Califia left organizing to the SEA groups or individuals' decision to join WAVAW, the antiporn movement became most famous or notorious for shifting tactics over time from shaming press conferences and boycotts to legislation.

Feminists split over the issue of focusing on porn because pursuing pornographers through city ordinances allied feminists with the rightwingers at a time when conservatives were effectively fighting against feminist and gay and lesbian gains. Antiporn feminists claimed that *Playboy* had "bought off" NOW, the National Women's Political Caucus, National Abortion Rights Action League, and the ACLU Women's Rights Project with contributions. Other feminists raised the alarm that rightwing money to fight porn influenced the antiporn movement.[44] When WAVPM members did not advocate support for birth control and abortion, sex education in schools, legalization of prostitution, or civil rights for gays and lesbians by 1980, their detractors argued WAVPM remained single-issue to work in coalition with groups whose exclusive support for marital reproduction led them to oppose sexual freedoms.[45] In 1983, Dworkin and feminist lawyer Catharine "Kitty" MacKinnon worked for the city of Minneapolis to draft a model ordinance that could amend the municipal civil rights laws to define porn as sex discrimination based on the argument that porn was "central in maintaining and creating inequality." Feminists who opposed Dworkin and MacKinnon's work predicted that the civil law would have a censoring effect because it allowed individuals to sue those who made, sold, distributed, or exhibited porn. An anti–Equal Rights Amendment city council member got the ordinance passed in Indianapolis, Indiana. Feminist lawyer Nan Hunter and law professor Sylvia Law filed an amicus brief for the Feminists Anticensorship Task Force signed by famous feminists like Betty Friedan, Kate Millett, and Adrienne Rich who feared ordinances would ban depictions of rape or lesbian sex that furthered education and art.[46] L.A. County's Board of Supervisors considered a version of the ordinance in 1985 when the U.S. Court of Appeals ruled the Indianapolis ordinance unconstitutional, and another version was defeated in Cambridge, Massachusetts before the Supreme Court declared the strategy unconstitutional in 1986.[47]

Antiporn feminist theory and practices to eliminate sexist images yielded contradictory results: these groups split the feminist movement and aided conservative interests in suppressing feminist discussion, most famously with the WAP boycott of "The Scholar and the Feminist IX: Toward a Politics of Sexuality" conference at Barnard College in 1982 that resulted in administrators confiscating the planning committee's brochure. As Gayle Rubin and Amber Hollibaugh opined,

> RUBIN: "We used to talk about how religion and the state and the family create sexism and promote rape. No one talks about any of these institutions anymore. They've become the good guys!"

> HOLLIBAUGH: "And now pornography creates sexism and violence against women."[48]

At the same time, harnessing women's anger and fear about misogynistic images and real violence against women expanded the base of support for feminism during a crucial period. Ultraconservatives successfully attacked women's right to abortion with the Hyde Amendment in 1976 by preventing Medicaid from funding poor women's abortions. They mounted a victorious campaign that prevented ratification of the ERA in 1982.[49]

THE BOUNDARIES OF ALLIANCES

Given the Rolling Stones billboard image of the bound woman and arguments that she represented consensual kinky sex, antiporn activity dovetailed with opposition to sex that played with power roles, which many feminists condemned as abusively "male-identified." Morgan declared in 1973

> [a] vast difference between [women's] sexuality and that of any patriarchally trained male's—gay or straight. That has, in fact, always been a source of *pride* to the lesbian community, even in its greatest suffering. That the emphasis on genital sexuality, objectification, promiscuity, emotional noninvolvement, and coarse invulnerability, was the *male style*, and that we, as women, placed greater trust in love, sensuality, humor, tenderness, commitment.[50]

Exalting lesbian sexuality as nonpatriarchal fit lesbian feminism's tendency to assert superiority and narrowed the possibilities for sexual experimentation. Anti-kink feminists argued as early as 1975 that "sadomasochism" (SM) was sexist, unhealthy, abusive, and something to which women could not actually consent while U.S. culture was rent by institutionally sanctioned power imbalances. Ti-Grace Atkinson asserted that any feminist, if forced to choose between freedom and sex, would choose freedom and took that as the crucial division between feminism and sexual liberationists.[51]

By the mid-1970s, the presence of a growing minority of self-described lesbian feminists engaging in SM challenged that assertion and opened the way for leather dykes to claim space at Califia amid strong condemnation. L.A. was a hub of SM dykes, including Gayle Rubin and Pat Califia, who had learned from L.A. gay men.[52] *The Lesbian Tide* editor, Jeanne Córdova, kicked off discussion by publishing a transcription of a twelve-woman workshop called "Healthy Questions about Sado-Masochism" at the end of 1976.[53] Córdova set up *The Lesbian Tide* as a sex-positive conduit for information on the formation of discussion groups and new literature about SM.

An immediate denunciation followed by women who produced and distributed women's music through Olivia Records. They contended that feminism's focus on "changing behaviors that were oppressive, and ultimately breaking down power imbalances" was incompatible with SM and that feminism was not simply a catchall term for freedom. Proclaiming that "Lesbians must not perpetuate the idea (or the practice) that sadomasochism is a part of women's sexuality," these women used a problematic analogy:

the male concept of women's "rape fantasies" has provided them with further justification for rape. We also know that, although most women do not fantasize being raped, we encounter women who do and we must analyze that phenomenon. In our analysis, we realized that there is an extreme disparity between the fantasy and the actuality of rape. . . . While we know that women who who [*sic*] are into S&M are not necessarily into rape, we see that there are too many parallels in the actualization of it, such as infliction and acceptance of pain, dominance, and "buying" of powerlessness.[54]

The letter writers recognized a difference between fantasy and reality but then elided the distinction between agreeing to give over control temporarily and sexual assault in a way that implicitly shifted some blame to SM women for men choosing to rape women. Further, they defined SM as a male definition of female sexuality. The *Tide* collective and an anonymous letter in support of the article disputed labeling SM as male-defined.

Feminist proponents of SM related their practices to the recent phenomenon of women taking control and knowledge of their bodies and expressing their sexuality.[55] Daniel Raven, who was part of Los Angeles lesbian circles and attended a Califia conference, reflected back that it was ironic that women were encouraged to own their sexuality rather than be defined by patriarchal norms but "on the *other* hand, there was this, 'We'll define it for you in the lesbian community' in terms of the kind of sexuality you can have. And it basically was very much a woman-on-woman-type thing— gentle, loving, all of that."[56] Whereas participants loved initial sexuality education at Califia, the emergence of SM marked a limit for some women of what was appropriate women's sexuality.

Within *The Lesbian Tide*, writers linked sexual exploration to women's spirituality. They furthered incipient conflict over where SM fit in debates over how to create new feminist norms of behavior and values. Radical therapist Barbara Ruth claimed that "sadomasochism as a liberating practice is only possible for women within a lesbian-feminist context." She defended SM as making manifest the hidden agendas that occurred in all relationships and proposed forming a coven or support group to explore the dimensions of ecstasy.[57] In the same issue's letters to the editor, Z Budapest and Cerridwen Fallingstar debated whether SM was compatible with feminist spirituality. Budapest affirmed that witchcraft worshiped "the capacity in wimmin for pleasure. Any form of pleasure is condoned that harms none and is mutual." She immediately foreclosed the possibility of SM pleasure, however: "Pain is not considered a form of pleasure." Claiming that, historically, women did not engage in bondage with each other, she concluded that SM was "bad magic," whereby the thoughts of fantasy are energized to become fact.[58] Budapest tried to speak authoritatively for the spiritual community, but Priestess Fallingstar dissented, using the same Wiccan principle "an it harm none, do what thou will." She stressed the freedom of those involved to define pleasure for themselves and relayed that "according to lesbians who practice S&M, pain and bondage are a means to an end, and that end is transcendence. It may not be the way I choose to worship Aphrodite, but I do not find it necessary to judge my sisters' sexuality as either 'good' (spiritual) or 'bad' (sinful)."[59] These debates illustrate the interrelations between political feminism and cultural women's spaces and practices. Fallingstar's comment also raises the question of how far feminist spirituality had actually diverged from patriarchal Christian dichotomies of good and evil. Proponents of expanding female sexuality to include SM not only gave as political motives demystifying sexuality and detaching female sexuality from male definitions, but sought to expand concrete women's spaces like support groups and Wiccan covens to include literal practice of sexual expression.

As a space that taught CR, sexual exploration, and alternative culture formation, it may have been inevitable that SM debates came to Califia. SM lesbians sought spaces to express themselves and defend their practices. True to Califia's emphases on open discussion and women teaching what they knew, a few participants at camps, including a collective member, led mini-presentations and workshops to educate on SM and wanted to practice related sexual activities unimpeded by feminist disapproval. By 1980, pro-SM dykes ran up against the formidable opposition of collective members and other Califia leaders. At first SM practitioners confined themselves to secluded areas and encountered little verbal opposition despite some women being "*violently* opposed to sadomasochism."[60] Recognizing that resistance and revulsion existed, a couple of San Diego women held an explanatory workshop.[61] Afterward, Murphy, Weiss, and Jetter vocally argued that SM was unfeminist and subjugating even if play was between women. In 1981, Germain joined Murphy and Weiss as collective members opposed to kink and became more resolute after attending a meeting where she ascertained that white and middle-class women were dominating partners of color or women from working-class backgrounds. Viewing SM through Califia's focus on oppressive power dynamics, Germain labeled "master" and "slave" terms and bondage chains racist and rumors of people dressing as Nazis anti-Semitic. She argued SM reinforced nineteenth-century lies that all women were "natural masochists."[62] Germain prioritized safety for abused women and feminist redress of injustice over sexual liberationist expressions of personal power. As a survivor of an abusive home herself, Germain vehemently rejected the idea of using SM therapeutically to work through past abuse. She saw sex play as trivializing women's real torture, not addressing real power dynamics.[63]

Those who supported open discussion could not stem the tide of opposition that conflated SM with abuse. According to Weiss, power-exchange sex was a "very *dominant* theme" of some Califia camps. She attended some of the workshops that explained SM and believed the opposition and discouragement from most of the collective prevented kink from becoming integrated into Califia as it eventually was at the Michigan Womyn's Music Festival.[64] Raven distinctly remembered Califia was not a place to talk about fantasies or explore sexuality in ways the lesbian community had clearly condemned as "perpetrating more abuse, or allowing it to be perpetrated upon you."[65] Califia was not permanently torn apart by the sex wars in the early 1980s because determined opposition by collective members and vocal leaders like Jetter quashed discussion and isolated SM proponents in contradiction to their policy of free discussion. By 1983 an advertisement for Califia in the *Gayzette* clarified, "The group is not affiliated with any person using the name Califia as her personal name [referring to famous SM writer Pat Califia], nor is the organization a sadomasochism support group as has been occasionally rumored."[66] Throughout the 1980s, debates over SM exploded around Califia throughout L.A., California, and across the nation.[67]

In hindsight, Brooks put these debates in a broader feminist perspective and believed that the sex wars divided feminists' attention from the real issue of male sexual violence. As a sex educator who wanted to fight rape, Brooks distinguished sadomasochism from battery and sexual assault and was never bothered by kink although she dismissed it as a silly luxury.[68] Her sexuality workshops, although unrelated to SM, were sometimes criticized as inappropriate for a space that included children in a "Children's Camp" section.[69] Opposition to SM enforced a limit to Califia women's sexual education, and ended discussion, so that Califia women's energies were not siphoned from fighting actual violence.

A tentative truce in the sex wars is reflected in changing perspectives on SM. Ariana Manov described the divisive trajectory of debates over SM:

> And there was a tremendous division in the L.A. women's movement at
> that time between women, on one hand, who believed that *all* pornography

and *all* bondage/dominance, SM sexuality was *anti*feminist, *anti*woman, *completely* taboo, and *not* even fit for discussion. . . . And then there was *another* group of women who felt like maybe we should at least be *discussing* this. And [then there were] *some* women from Leather and Lace, another [SM] organization, that was saying, "Not only do we *want* to discuss this, it's part of *my* sexuality."[70]

In the late 1980s, Manov used her radical feminist therapy training to facilitate a mediation session at her home. After seeing SM as akin to objectification and violence, Catoggio listened for the first time to "women *speak* from their own *experience* about what they did sexually and what it *meant* to them. And I *got* it." Catoggio heard SM lesbians saying, "What you're *asking* us to do is to *give* up the only way that we *can* get off." In a "click" moment, Catoggio concluded that she had "no right to tell a *woman* that the *only* sex that satisfies her is politically incorrect and she should stop *doing* it." To make that decision for another would demonstrate an inability to trust women to conclude from their own experience what they need. Jetter also came to this position.[71] Rather than a full valuation of women choosing SM as part of their feminist sexuality or at least sexuality separate from and compatible with being feminist, Catoggio and Jetter pitied SM dykes. Their shift is not representative, and other Califia women like Murphy and Germain remained fervently opposed without concession because their feminism trumped kinky sexuality.

In 1984, Gayle Rubin delineated the limits of feminism for a theory of sex and the necessity of recognizing that sexuality is as important a category of analysis as gender.[72] She noted that dominant society only gave moral complexity and the ability to consent to sexual activities already deemed "good." There could be complexity about people's views on married heterosexual sex, but society condemned sodomy, incest between adults, and sadomasochism. In criminal prosecutions, Americans assumed these actions were so disgusting that nobody could willingly perform them.[73] Rubin concluded that gender and sexuality experiences did not exist on fully overlapping planes, and so feminist analysis designed for gender hierarchies could not completely account for the complexities of sexuality. Feminist theory had some power to explain sex, but "as issues become less those of gender and more those of sexuality, feminist analysis becomes misleading and often irrelevant. Feminist thought simply lacks angles of vision, which can fully encompass the social organization of sexuality."[74] One of the hallmarks of a theory of sex for critiquing sexual oppression is a rejection of essentialism, sex negativism, Christian and normalizing psychological categorization of rewarded prescribed sex acts and punished proscribed acts, and the view that only "good" acts have moral complexity.[75] The emotional closeness of sex and ways male violence against women was sexualized prevented many feminists from reassessment that would recognize sexuality as separate but related to gender and equally important.

In the debates over SM at Califia, at the West Coast Women's Music Festival, and on women's land,[76] feminist ideals for sexual liberation collided with visual markers of dominance or hitting that reminded some women of abuse they or their loved ones suffered. Opponents of SM commonly mentioned seeing women lead partners on leashes or walk around with bruises. Women who designed such public scenes did not consider that opponents did not consent to be a party to seeing the displays or their aftereffects. The 1980s were a time when kink practitioners were codifying etiquette, and by the 1990s a dominant rule was that everyone involved should be consenting. At Califia and other sites that Califia narrators attended, those rules were not yet fully established or followed.

Despite tensions between feminism and sexual liberation, American feminists needed allies against backlash when increasingly organized conservative religious Right members attacked feminist and gay gains. In addition to targeting abortion rights and the ERA, New Right members passed homophobic city ordinances and began statewide assaults on the civil rights of pro-gay Americans with California's Proposition 6 in 1978. State Senator John Briggs of the L.A. area sponsored the proposition, which became known as the Briggs Initiative. Proposition 6 defined "family" to exclude gay and lesbian members in order to claim homosexuality was antithetical to state interests in preserving the family unit and continued:

> For these reasons, the State finds a compelling interest in refusing to employ and in terminating the employment of a schoolteacher, a teacher's aide, a school administrator, or a counselor . . . who engages in public homosexual activity and/or public homosexual conduct directed at, or likely to come to the attention of, school children or other school employees. This proscription is essential since such activity and conduct undermines the state's interest in preserving and perpetuating the conjugal family unit.

The Briggs Initiative represented a serious infringement on Americans' freedoms of speech. It defined "public homosexual activity and/or public homosexual conduct" broadly enough that if a heterosexual teacher stated in his home that he supported California's current legal protection of gay adult consensual relationships, and that conversation came to the attention of another employee, he could be fired regardless of his teachers' union contract.[77]

Coalitions of Californians across sexual orientation from feminist, gay, organized labor, and free speech groups as well as teachers' associations, child-care workers, health-care workers, and some churches formed a "No on 6" campaign.[78] Usually Califia did not bring in guest speakers, but during the 1978 voting season, a "No on 6" activist enjoined Califia women to get involved with the group that included queer and straight men to defeat the initiative.[79] Making allowances for political crises reflected how flexible Califia was. Lesbians were important to "No on 6" canvassing because they challenged the false association between homosexuality and pedophilia. Audiences did not believe women molested children. Lesbian speakers could raise the issue that the majority of child molesters were heterosexually identified men and then ask audiences whether they wanted to legislate against heterosexual men having contact with children.[80] Activists benefitted from the fact that Senator Briggs courted homophobic voters to build a base from which to run against Governor Ronald Reagan. Reagan's strong statements against the Briggs Initiative focused on cost of implementation and the potential for children falsely to accuse teachers of homosexuality. When the Briggs Initiative went down in defeat among Democratic and Republican voters, it had the unintended consequences of temporarily uniting a range of progressives and moderates and initiating a public discussion about homosexuality that challenged negative stereotypes.[81]

THE STATUS OF CHILDREN AND AGENTS OF ABUSE

Although feminist spaces were not always equipped for full discussions, sexism education supported women to evaluate patriarchal constraints and mainstream tactics that silenced women. In 1978, Germain entered a concept piece in a women's art show displayed for four weeks at California State University San Diego's (CSUSD) library. The triptych she made about medical, humorous, and derogatory names for women's genitals consisted of large words accompanying identical two-by-two-inch photographs of a triangle of women's pubic hair cropped to exclude hips and navels, so they looked like "fuzzy wine glasses."[82] Germain expected some strong reactions, but nothing like what happened:

> People started to *write* all over them, and they wrote *rotten things* about women and *rotten things* about women's *genitals*. And sometimes they *made* little *poems* about stick a piece of dynamite there and find pieces of this *woman* all over. You know, when it would explode. *Really ugly shit!*

And I *kind* of thought that might *happen*, but I *never* thought it would get as awful as this. Somebody took all of the pubic hairs and like *soap scum* and things like from out of their *drain* in the *bathtub* and, I mean like if you don't *clean* it for a *hundred* years, and *took* it with a *bobby* pin and *stuck* it on *my art* piece. I mean it was *really ugly shit* going up on that *art* piece.[83]

Germain found "much of the graffiti revealed misogyny around fatness, too much hair, and non-blondness of the model. Other remarks were racist and anti-semitic [*sic*]. The worst were references to violence against women and destruction of female bodies."[84] Vandals included a man who identified himself as an English professor, complained, and ripped the panels off the wall. She received a letter speaking for the acting president of CSUSD that, without "wish[ing] to censor or inhibit creativity," disapproved of providing "an outlet for statements that may be *political* rather than artistic in nature,"[85] a distinction that made little sense in the context of 1970s American art.

When Germain announced her intention to present the experience to Califia in 1979 as an example of the intensity of misogyny in society, the controversy that erupted underscored differences between Califia and the university. Califia women understood Germain's piece was significant and consistent with feminist (i.e., political) art. A number of mothers felt the outcry raised such important topics that they wanted to bring their children to the presentation.

Germain opposed having children at a graphic discussion because she feared exposing them to traumatizing new concepts. Women who supported Germain's exclusion of children argued that kids threatened women's sense of safety. Several fat women and women who chose not to have children resisted having children present during intensely emotional discussions about the body because children had been the source of cruel teasing. Kalivoda admitted:

I always had trouble dealing with the children there. I was one of those you read about [in *Learning Our Way*]. I was *not* comfortable around children because I was one of those who was really tormented in childhood and young adulthood by kids; so that was a *real* Califia battle. Wow! It almost tore up the community. But, see, Califia was known for its internal battles in that way. I mean they used to go full circle for the most part. We all came out of it with something. It was a place to exercise.[86]

Women were under extreme pressure in U.S. society not to speak against children. The Califia women who "hated or feared children after years of their own teasing and ridicule" came to the Late Night Conversations to break their silence.[87] Germain paraphrased their arguments:

> "I've been *fat* all my life and I've been *ridiculed*, not only by *adults* but lots of *children*. And I don't even go to the *swimming pool* because I know there's going to be *kids* there. There is *never* a time where there are *no children* at the pool when *I* can go there and feel *safe*, that I can put my very large body in the water or in the sun and not have little kids ridiculing me. I don't *like* little children, and I don't want them around, and they're just *everywhere*." And then we [would] talk about *that*. How *horrible*! Not just *one* woman but several women upset about this. So we said, "Oh, we're not serving these *women*," you know, to give them a *safe space*. We never *thought* of that.[88]

This was one of the strongest assertions that children not only absorbed oppressive values but learned ways to bully other children and adults. After three years of concerns that Califia Community did not do enough children's programming, participants had to navigate between mothers lobbying for their children's education and competing needs of adult women. A protracted debate that continued after the camp led Califia leaders to conclude that although they would seek a coordinator of educational programs for the children, "the children's community existed for the convenience of the mothers, not for its own sake. . . . At Califia, women should not have to sacrifice their needs for privacy and comfort to further the education of children, no matter how worthy the cause of children's education is." Because they could not arrive at consensus, this became one of the collective's few policy decisions.[89]

For that camp, Germain gave the presentation twice: once for women who preferred a child-free space and again for women who wanted to participate along with children. Almost every child attended. Even though Germain tried to tone down the presentation at which children were present, she found the effect on the children and adults startling:

> And little *kids* said, "I heard about a time when there were Jews in concentration camps and they . . . this and this and this happened to women's bodies. That they did *torture* on them and that they did *experiments* on them." And I said, "Oh, my *God*. This little *kid* has been *carrying around* those *horrible* thoughts all by *herself* all this time." And we thought, "Well, she doesn't know. They don't know." They *do* know. Other little kids said things about genitals and attacking and, geez, so they knew about *torture* and everything.[90]

Adults realized that they could not shelter children. They provided a supportive environment in which children could unburden themselves and discuss violence against women that they knew about with adults who comforted them. It was a draining but powerful experience that radically altered views on appropriate discussion with children. In the same session that prioritized women over children, Califia tied together three levels of helping children. They had funneled women into groups dedicated to combating violence, educated children in feminism, and created a space to address children's fears.

The discussions that eventually distinguished between educating children and protecting women were part of a long, painstaking process to reevaluate sources of harm and categories of people needing protection. Hundreds of years of social mores had portrayed women and children as weaker than men. New Left movements had condemned organized violence against minorities, individual fighting, and war in favor of nonviolent resistance and/or had urged oppressed groups to train themselves to defend against subjugation. Feminist opposition to male violence against women and children took the forms of educating society on the breadth of the problem, seeking legislation and law enforcement, creating shelters and other spaces for safety and options, and teaching women self-defense. In 1980, when feminists were still pushing dominant society to come to grips with the prevalence of male abuse of women and children, most feminists resisted addressing women's violence against other women. Opinion polls in the 1970s found that 25 percent of American adults who were sampled approved of husband-wife battles and that high formal education correlated *with* ready acceptance of marital violence.[91] Such fights were considered private matters with which people outside the couple should not interfere. *Ladies' Home Journal* ran articles in 1980 that claimed, "all good relationships would be punctuated by 'rip-roaring fights'" and praised a husband for shoving his irate wife outside and locking the door.[92] At least part of the lesbian feminist goal of choosing woman-identification as a sexual preference was to pull women out of harm's way by decreasing their contact with men. Lesbian feminists like Adrienne Rich in the 1980s said societal heterosexism heavily determined the social construction of sexual orientation to force women into unexamined heterosexual compliance.[93] At Califia, demonstrating lesbian feminist options led some women to reject the sexism and violence in heterosexual society in favor of political and romantic lives with other women.

Woman-on-woman violence was another taboo that feminists began to address in the 1980s. Raven, who volunteered at the Gay Community Service Center in L.A., remembered that at that time the center had no workshops about domestic violence because there was widespread denial that lesbians could batter. Walking away from patriarchal life meant that

> we were all *sisters* and *loved* and *respected* each other. . . . [W]e did not want to admit to these types of issues in our own community [pause] even to ourselves. We certainly didn't want them having been revealed to the *straight* people that we had these issues. Also at that time . . . when [heterosexuals] saw two dykes going at it, they just blew it off anyway.[94]

Since his sex-change transition, Raven retained sympathy about violence against women while recognizing that battering crosses genders and other identity factors. Lesbian feminists, whose members found it relatively easy to understand and condemn men's violence against women and children, were reluctant to believe that women could be violent toward lesbian partners in part because they attributed male violence to essential biology and forms of socializing they held were unique to males.[95]

Jetter revealed the complexities of relationship violence within a women's community. She had a three-year partnership with another Califia participant during which she experienced relationship violence. Several times, Jetter left the woman, who went to "all her [the woman's] friends" out of emotional distress and loneliness. Jetter, in contrast, did not talk about their problems until much later, at which point friends were supportive. During the intermittent break-ups, however, she "felt *guilty* having to have the *community* take care of this woman." Still perplexed at why she did not leave permanently sooner in the relationship, Jetter related that the end of their relationship did not come until her partner left her. Although she asserted that "there *certainly* were a lot of women who were violent with other women," and she remembered hearing discussions about lesbian battering later at the West Coast Women's Music and Comedy Festival, she did not remember the issue coming up at Califia.[96]

Raven's insistence that discussion was taboo and Jetter's brief reflection on her relationship fit a pattern of silence and lack of accountability for battering among lesbians in the 1970s and 1980s. Glorification of woman-identification, lesbian couples sharing friends and limited social circles, and justified fear that homophobic people would use same-gender violence against lesbians and against feminist calls for societal reform contributed to silence about women's capacity to abuse other women.[97]

California sources illustrate the conceptual steps that lesbian feminists took to recognize lesbian battering. Their first discussions frequently promoted the stereotype that the phenomenon was isolated to working-class "old gays."[98] It was not until the early 1980s that lesbian feminists started to discuss the reality of battering within their local communities and at women's events.[99] As executive director of the Southern California Coalition on Battered Women, Kerry Lobel's 1982 article in *The Lesbian News* reprinted four myths and realities about lesbian battering written by Barbara Hart, vice president for communications with the National Coalition against Domestic Violence (NCADV) and a founder of its Lesbian Task Force. These points concluded that battering cut across feminist and nonfeminist lesbian relationships and that denial of reality would not achieve "dreams of a peaceful, loving women's community." Hart posited reasons that lesbians would be more likely than heterosexual women not to recognize themselves as victims and reasons that lesbian victims could fear seeking help more than did heterosexual women.[100] This cover story both introduced the issue and decried the rise of conservative fiscal policies that undercut funding for a growing battered-women's movement.

Despite decreases in funding, a few shelters nationwide expanded their outreach to lesbians. Lesbians were disproportionately active in providing services to heterosexual battered women by forming and staffing rape crisis hotlines and domestic violence shelters. Ironically, homophobia and heterosexism within shelters and from funders increasingly kept staffers closeted and made it difficult for battered lesbians to feel safe using these services.[101] In a few cases, shelter staff gave presentations and left flyers in lesbian-identified and feminist spaces specifically to inform lesbians that they could find crisis hotline operators, safe homes, transportation, legal help, and support groups.[102] Such education moved to the national level after 1983 as the Lesbian Task Force of NCADV raised awareness.[103] During the early 1980s, battered lesbians and sympathetic shelter staff began to compare heterosexual male violence against women to lesbian battering. They demanded that lesbians hold batterers accountable rather than shun or isolate the victims of abuse.[104]

"PATRIARCHY MADE SIMPLE" AND U.S. TERRORISM

As Califia camps continued into the mid-1980s, Jetter filled an important role in conveying antisexist, prolesbian teaching that stressed social construction and political choice as means for feminist empowerment. She officially joined the collective in 1984, after Brooks, Murphy, and Weiss had left. Her participation session about "Patriarchy Made Simple" analyzed gendered language as binary oppositions and appealed to women to align with feminist politics.[105]

Jetter's sessions remained vivid for a fifth of interviewed participants.[106] She asked attendees to shout out stereotypically masculine and feminine characteristics while she wrote them on a big chalkboard. Associations with strength and leadership tended to accumulate on the masculine side.[107] The whole group then deconstructed the lists by considering how they already had positive traits associated with masculinity. In another list exercise, Jetter solicited all of the derogatory names for women and men. Kalivoda remembered the impact of this exercise:

> She wrote small. . . . And the women's list would get longer and longer until there was no black space on the board when the men's list kinda stopped. Talk about *impact*. . . . because you don't even *realize*. And you have to take it in from the time you walked across the ash you know. You don't *realize*. And that's the kind of impact that the sexism stuff had. And yeah women knew some of this stuff, but . . . a lot of these women that attend[ed], you know, they had ten percent awareness up here, but the rest they accepted as a natural part of life until we started talking about this stuff. And with that many women in the groups all kinds of stuff came up.[108]

Central was Jetter's assessment that language shapes norms of thinking and behavior. Since patriarchal power perpetuated dualistic language, feminists needed to empower themselves by creating language to change reality and counter social conditioning.

Jetter led women to deconstruct how meanings were socially formed through language, enforced, and accepted. She engaged in a practical application of poststructuralist cultural studies and literary criticism toward a political goal. Kathy Wolfe videotaped one of these presentations at a Califia "Autumn Celebration of Women's Culture" held Thanksgiving weekend 1985. Using national and personal examples of leaders' power, Jetter argued that "reality" is a community consensus based on "the people who actually have power to make things happen." Reagan's use of the word "peace" to mean sending the U.S. military into Lebanon redefined the word to include violence, and Americans who repeated his interpretation of military action in Lebanon as "defending the peace" complied in enforcing a new meaning for the word. Jetter asserted that when people adopt leaders' terms, they extend the power to change language to those leaders.

> What we had done was acknowledge that this person had the power to change our language. And that's how language is created. One of the

things that women have to do, feminist women in particular, in order to empower ourselves, is to start to create language that is empowering to us. I could do a talk on sexist language as well and show where our language is especially degrading to women or making women invisible or that sort of thing. Our language also creates our reality for us as well.[109]

Turning to social enforcement, she described male bonding at length as a regulatory device to which men and women acquiesce that keeps them in their roles through fear of ridicule, ostracism, or violence. This model led the audience to discuss gang rape, incest, battery, objectification of women through pornography, sexual harassment, control of women's reproduction, and economic deprivation.[110] Jetter labeled crimes against women "terrorist activities," tightly linking "male bonding" to a term that was loaded with political connotations stemming from the Iran hostage crisis in 1979 and successful anti-American terrorism during Reagan's presidency. Jetter denounced all men as active participants in terrorist activities or passive collaborators who did not marshal the courage to stop male terrorists. Men benefited by getting access to money, freedom of movement, and leadership even though their behavior was constrained by pressure to purge anything "feminine" from themselves. Many women assisted terrorism by bolstering men and excusing their bad behavior instead of holding them responsible for male-perpetrated atrocities. After years of Jetter's "Man-Hating as Taboo" workshop, her analysis of gender terrorism met a receptive audience. Jetter compiled the strategies status quo–defending women used to derail presentations about men's bad behavior. She was part of an incipient move on the part of diversity trainers to reveal derailing techniques such as charging reverse discrimination, dismissing criticism, or attacking the presenters' tone to discredit them.

In the decade of Califia Community conferences, women adopted a combination of beliefs regarding sexism and sexual orientation. Califia's message that women could take back power to defend themselves and reshape society despite the prevalence of violence that swirled around them was typical of feminism of the time. Lesbian feminism also argued that women could choose lesbianism as a way of life superior to heterosexuality. Murphy started the antisexism presentations by arguing that when women focused their energy on other women, it would force men into positive change. After the idea that people labeled male at birth were irrevocably misogynistic had expanded, Jetter portrayed men as terrorists or collaborators in the war against women. Califia was part of the period's recruiting of "an army of lovers" that optimistically believed woman-identification would revolutionize the world and hold the line for women's safety and security. The messages expressed tensions within the movement over the degree to which feminists could raise a new generation of antisexist Americans. The movement was key to institution building that supported women who had been raped and battered and was understandably slow to fully examine women's violence toward women. A legitimate siege mentality led many to prioritize safety and ideology above sexual liberation, which produced strange political bedfellows, fragile alliances, and fallout.

Cabin at de Benneville Pines. Courtesy of the archives of Camp de Benneville Pines.

Lodge at de Benneville Pines campsite. Courtesy of the archives of Camp de Benneville Pines.

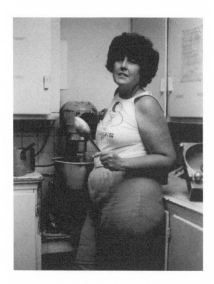

Marilyn Murphy wearing a Sagaris shirt in a Califia Community camp kitchen. Courtesy of Betty Jetter. Photo from Betty Jetter's collection.

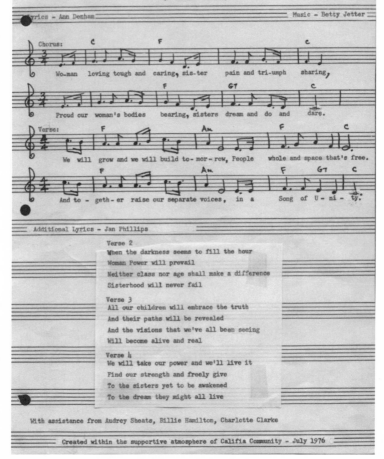

"Song of Unity: A Woman's Anthem." Ann Denham and Jan Phillips wrote the lyrics, and Betty Jetter set them to music in honor of the first Califia Community camp in July 1976. Courtesy of Betty Jetter. Photo from Betty Jetter's collection.

Billboard advertising the Rolling Stones album *Black and Blue*, which WAVAW members protested by adding graffiti to the bottom that read, "This is a crime against! women ♀." Courtesy of Northeastern University Libraries, Archives, and Special Collections Department.

The beginning of a class presentation when participants listened to a speaker with working-class experience. Courtesy of Betty Jetter. Photo from Betty Jetter's collection.

Copy of a Califia camp schedule. Participants could add workshops they wanted to teach in open slots around the preplanned times for registration, meals and clean-up, self-defense and other exercise, the feminist primer, main presentations, the community meeting, late-night conversation, a group picture, entertainment, and closing ceremonies. Courtesy of Diane F. Germain.

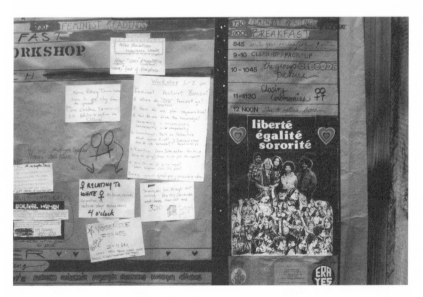

The continuation of a Califia camp schedule. Courtesy of Diane F. Germain.

Banquet setup for closing ceremonies. Courtesy of Diane F. Germain.

Founders and collective members moderated at the closing ceremonies. Left to right: a founder, Marilyn Murphy, Irene Weiss. Courtesy of Diane F. Germain.

Mealtime at Califia Community. Courtesy of Betty Jetter. Photo from Betty Jetter's collection.

María Dolores Díaz as she danced with her then-partner at the Califia dance. Courtesy of Irene Weiss.

Yolanda Retter Vargas at camp. Photo by Jane Bernstein. Courtesy of the June L. Mazer Lesbian Archive.

Diane F. Germain at camp with doris davenport and davenport's lover at the time, Norma Esfeld (aka Amrita Yachana). Courtesy of Irene R. Weiss.

Diane F. Germain at closing ceremonies. Courtesy of Diane F. Germain.

An example of the Califia Community group photographs taken for each camp. Participation in the photograph was optional. Courtesy of Betty Jetter. Photo from Betty Jetter's collection.

CHAPTER 4

CHANNELING CLASS RESENTMENTS

RADICAL LESBIAN FEMINISTS TAUGHT THAT patriarchy was an over-arching structure with many negative consequences. These feminist teachings tapped into women's personal experiences to encourage them to organize instead of feeling passively victimized. Personalizing patriarchy was a springboard from which women nationwide joined or created projects to combat violence against women and children, alleviate other forms of sexism, and address homophobia. Advocating structural changes by targeting pornography, prostitution, and media depictions pitted feminists against each other over women's sexual autonomy, censorship, and working within sexist government systems or with conservatives. Simultaneously, the bonds facilitated by "personal is political" consciousness-raising fostered an array of forms of intimacy among women. Califia's analysis of classism personalized class-based values that correlated with Americans' class of origin in order to help women work together across class differences. Unlike the lessons on patriarchy, the class presentations did not steadily connect people's experience to a critique of capitalism or result in projects that united Califia women with Americans who worked for socioeconomic structural changes.

Liberal criticisms of class inequality had gained traction since the 1960s, and a minority of feminists developed socialist feminist theory of patriarchal capitalism based on their experience in the New Left. This chapter argues that Califia, in contrast, was representative of CR that analyzed interpersonal dynamics based on class, a method famously popularized by the writings of the Furies. This method avoided persistent mainstream slurs that feminists were "communist" and "un-American," a New Left organizational history of factionalization, and feminist concerns about socialist infiltration of other groups. A significant consequence of avoiding broader efforts at redressing class hierarchy was that, by and large, attendees did not join area campaigns for welfare rights, labor reform, or other types of economic justice in response to their participation in Califia, as they often did as a result of teachings about patriarchy. Instead, they addressed working-class feminist pain and irritation at downward mobility while they called for middle-class women to reform their practices.

It is important to comprehend the long-standing anticommunism in the United States as a context against which New Left and socialist feminist members theorized. By looking at the ways Califia women broke with anti-capitalist criticism and understanding the impact of economic policies in the 1980s, this chapter addresses the challenges for 1970s and 1980s feminists. Events in southern California, national politics, and feminist interactions with socialist groups affected choices on how to characterize class differences. The Califia programs on class illustrate wariness about socialist feminism, limits of radical feminism, and the ways multicultural feminism's inclusion of class hierarchy and anticapitalist critique sometimes remained muted in all-women spaces.

CLASS CONTEXT AND ANTICOMMUNISM

Southern California was a base both for a leading feminist analysis of capitalism before World War II and for strong postwar anticommunism. The Marxist feminist ideas of Mary Inman (born Ida May Inman in 1894) permeated the Communist Party of the USA (CPUSA) by 1948, while the anticommunist career of Richard Nixon that predated McCarthyism drew support from the same regional values that made Orange County a seedbed for the militantly anticommunist John Birch Society and then the New Right.

Inman's relationship to the CPUSA was fraught, and the incomplete influence of her Marxist-feminist analysis on later feminists is significant to understanding options in the 1970s and 1980s. Although socialist feminists rediscovered and embraced Inman, separatist feminists shared some of Inman's perspectives without adopting her anticapitalist solutions.

Unlike later radical feminists' work, Inman's activism started with socialism and trade union organizing when she joined Eugene V. Debs's Socialist Party at age sixteen. By 1940 she had settled in Los Angeles and published *In Women's Defense* under the penname Mary Inman. Inman's writing built on Charlotte Perkins Gilman's communal living proposal for educating nonsexist children and giving women fulfilling work. Inman argued that the denigration of housework was the source of women's oppression. She believed domestic and reproductive labor were types of productive work akin to the wage-earning employment men did. Inman followed

Gilman in claiming that a long-term solution to the drudgery of housework was communal living where women shared child care, cooking, and cleaning to free time for them to pursue other interests. Before this proposed socialist utopia materialized, Inman thought, housewives should unionize and demand wages. *In Women's Defense* went through three printings in 1940 and was well received on the West Coast among leftists, the YWCA, and other women's groups. Inman taught courses at the Workers' School in Los Angeles about women's status under capitalism and spoke at progressive events in southern California.

She ran afoul of CPUSA leaders by considering housework part of the production of goods. The CPUSA position had developed from Friedrich Engels's *Origin of the Family, Private Property and the State.* Engels and Karl Marx had argued that the monogamous nuclear family arose to pass on private property. Engels theorized further that industrialized capitalism divorced the production of goods from the home and oppressed women by separating them from wage work and relegating them to the family sphere of home and childrearing. CPUSA leaders feared that Inman's glorification of housework as holding economic value would support conservative Americans' goals of forcing women to remain at home. The leaders also found Inman divisive because she resorted to personal attacks when questioned about her position.

Nonetheless, Inman had lasting impacts for the CPUSA and feminism. The CPUSA adopted her explanation for working-class men's oppressive beliefs: ruling-class Americans legitimized and publicized sexism and racism, so that all levels of society adopted oppressive views, which deflected working-class men's attention to racial and gender issues and positioned them as a buffer between women and the more powerful oppressors that minorities had in common. Inman also exposed the linguistic imbalance of sexism through a list of ninety-nine derogatory names for women and children she compared with a much shorter list for men (not unlike the lists Jetter independently had participants create). She decried wife beating, prostitution, and an overemphasis on beauty for women, and all of these ideas permeated the CPUSA by 1948.[1]

Inman is important because her ideas for blending women's emancipation with class reform circulated nationwide before rabid Cold War anticommunism and were picked up again in the 1970s when feminists tapped her to give talks and increased her public stature. Post-war anticommunism eclipsed Inman's celebrity but could not obliterate analyses of women and class. For example, at the height of McCarthyism, Selma James dispersed her pamphlet, "A Woman's Place," across L.A. and the United States analyzing the tensions working-class women felt over being responsible for housework while also needing to work within capitalism.[2] Women who affiliated with the CPUSA in the 1940s and 1950s brought the analysis of gender, class, and race into feminism. Throughout the twentieth century, though, the audience for socialist feminism was limited. When socialist feminists refocused interest on Inman, her effect in the 1970s seems to have centered on spaces socialist feminists carved out.

Deep-seated national opposition to anything that could be labeled communist or socialist may have been insurmountable for training a diverse group of women from mainstream backgrounds to understand structural class hierarchy. Starting in 1946, politicians used anticommunist stances to advance, and anticommunism was connected to the antifeminist postwar goal of returning American women to unpaid domestic work. In 1946, Richard Nixon started his political career from southern California by red-baiting his New Deal opponent for state Congress despite the fact that Democrat Jerry Voorhees had served on the anticommunist predecessor to the House Un-American Activities Committee (HUAC). The following year, Ferdinand Lundberg and Marynia Farnham's 1947 *Modern Woman: The Lost Sex* built on government and business propaganda. *Modern Woman* urged women to remain housewives who did not harm their husband's egos, neglect their children, and ruin their marriages by "competing" with their husbands through wage work. *Modern Woman* claimed Kremlin-deployed agents encouraged feminism among American women to disrupt U.S. society to the advantage of the USSR.[3] Meanwhile, Nixon gained national attention by serving on HUAC, prosecuting Alger Hiss as a spy for the Soviets, and pursuing the case after several HUAC members had dropped it. Nixon again successfully employed red-baiting the year conflict in Korea made anticommunism a nationwide issue. In his 1950 Senate race, Nixon beat liberal Democrat and three-time Representative, Helen Gahagan Douglas, after they traded insults that he was "Tricky Dick" and she was "pink right down to her underwear."[4] From there he rocketed to Vice President in 1952 and later won the presidency in 1968.

In the late 1940s through the 1960s, California conservatives promoted a privatized and circumscribed sense of responsibility and decried liberalism as fostering an authoritarian state that quashed personal rights. Their rhetoric hid the fact that California's economy was dependent on huge federal defense subsidies. Between 1946 and 1965, 62 percent of the federal budget went to defense, and the Sunbelt and West saw most of this money. Southern California became the largest military-industrial complex, getting twice as many defense dollars and any other state. The over $50 billion that poured into California between 1950 and 1960 paid the wages of military contractors and civilians whose businesses supported a massive population boom. Despite the fact that Californians depended on big government, anticommunism led many southern Californians to reject any type of collectivism and decry government intervention.[5] California conservatives mirrored the Right in the rest of the nation in their antiunionism, preservation of discrimination in housing, and desire to end the income tax, and culminated in Ronald Reagan's gubernatorial proposal that the state solicit business and industry to run former state offices.

Reagan developed politically in this climate but came to characterize a New Right or neoliberalism, with policies that rewarded big business and the wealthy at the expense of poor and middle-class Americans. He worked with the FBI during the McCarthy campaign by testifying against people in Hollywood's motion picture industry who were accused of communist sympathies. When he married Nancy Davis, his father-in-law's conservative activism influenced him. Reagan became a General Electric spokesman in 1952, giving hundreds of speeches on foreign communist threats and the dangers of domestic socialism.[6] Receptivity to anticommunism led Orange County to become a stronghold for the ultraconservative anticommunist John Birch Society from 1958 through the mid-1960s. Birchers set up bookstores and billboards and honeycombed the staffing of conservative political campaigns on the county level up to the 1964 Barry Goldwater presidential run. Reagan, who was never a Bircher, stumped for Goldwater against "welfarism," bureaucracy, and usurpation of individual freedom. Although Goldwater's campaign was doomed by his image as an extremist who might use nuclear weapons, he won all southern California counties except Santa Barbara.

Within this Cold War political context, California represented national division over how to support business interests, continue economic growth, alleviate poverty, and protect citizens against the excesses of capitalism. During Democrat Pat Brown's governorship (1959–1967), California's Congress instituted protections for consumers, fair employment legislation, and a master plan for higher education that created one of the largest populations of formally educated Americans in the country.[7] At the same time, California had deep pockets of urban and rural poverty. Michael Harrington's 1962 exposé on American poverty in *The Other America: Poverty in the United States*, gained the attention of the Kennedy administration and influenced Lyndon Johnson's War on Poverty. Young Americans interested in expanding representative democracy to disenfranchised African Americans and adults under age twenty-one rallied for change, especially as military conflict in Vietnam increased the danger that young men would be drafted.

On the other side, Reagan ran for governor in 1966 attacking the student free speech movement, "sexual perversions" at Berkeley, "welfare cheats," antiwar protestors, and Watts rioters who protested police brutality and poverty.[8] The conservative New Right movement, with its Sunbelt stronghold, capitalized on the prevalence of anticommunist sentiment and the ease with which the communist label could be affixed to political opponents as diverse as unionists, homosexuals, civil rights proponents, and politicians who favored social programs beyond Social Security.

Although Reagan would become the face of the New Right, his governorship seemed out of step with national activism. Due to liberal politicians' support of the Vietnam War, socialist anti-imperialism held appeal for those who did not want to "sell out the Third World" and peaked during the late 1960s to mid-1970s.[9] Socialist feminists formed seventeen women's liberation unions in major cities from New York to Oregon with six in California. This version of feminism drew a small minority of American women compared to liberal or radical feminism; local core activists numbered seven to two hundred, while their mailing lists sometimes included nine hundred women. Usually the civil rights movement, antiwar organizing, and Students for a Democratic Society politicized these mostly white, middle-class, college-educated, childless women in their mid to late twenties. Their unions lasted an average of four years and, with the exception of Baltimore's, had all disbanded by the end of 1977. Historian Karen Hansen has argued that women's liberation union members theorized and published with New Left members as their primary audience rather than other feminists. Socialist feminists tried to develop a comprehensive theory of oppression that could cure all sources of exploitation concurrently. They criticized themselves for lacking the appealing personal aspect that was central to radical feminism and for being slow to develop concrete projects that could showcase socialist feminist theory of capitalist patriarchy to distinguish themselves from other feminists. Projects to organize and include poor women provided valuable services but entailed problems with the organizers not coming from the constituencies they sought to organize. Due, in part, to directing attention to New Left members, groups with competing Marxist emphases tried to take over socialist feminist unions, which diverted energy from concrete projects. The collapse of these unions by 1977 was part of the decline of the New Left after the end of the Vietnam War. It was very difficult to remake the Democratic Left with concrete plans simultaneously to fight capitalism, sexism, homophobia, racism, and imperialism.[10] Barbara Epstein argued that as the New Right gained ground, socialist feminists were best equipped to find places in academia because they were more likely to hold graduate degrees and have backgrounds in "an intellectual wing of the women's movement."[11]

That said, before 1977, socialist feminists had a physical presence in L.A. and space within the feminist press. Socialist feminists dominated the Los Angeles Women's Center in 1970, formed a Socialist Feminist Network, and overlapped with feminist lesbians by seeing lesbianism as a solution to "sleeping with the enemy."[12] The newspaper *Sisters* publicized important socialist feminist work from across the country and printed articles that L.A. feminists created.[13] These topics, however, became less frequent contributions to the feminist press after the mid-1970s.

By the time Jerry Brown took the governorship in 1975, the dynamics of activism, campus life, and urban poverty had changed in competing ways. Some of the goals of activists had become mainstream: eighteen-year-olds could vote, the military had initiated withdrawal from Vietnam, and federal contractors, including universities, had to implement steps not to discriminate by race, color, religion, sex, or national origin in hiring and pay decisions. Scholars also characterize activism as starting to wane on and off campuses. Affirmative action encouraged more students of color at universities, but California's congress had legislated that its universities would no longer be tuition-free to in-state students, a previous policy that had opened the California system to first-generation students from working-class and poor backgrounds. Urban poor had benefitted from welfare rights organizing and Great Society programs such as food stamps, but the number of urban poor people and size of African American ghettos, Latino barrios, and white or racially mixed slums in which they lived expanded more rapidly than overall population growth. Between 1970 and 1990, economic structural changes would most harm those who had less education and fewer job skills, so that the poorest twentieth of Americans saw a real-dollar decline in their incomes.[14]

National economic and political context from the mid-1970s through the 1980s is crucial because feminist organizing did not end with Vietnam or the inauguration of Reagan although neoliberal policies impeded social justice work.

RELIANCE ON WORKING-CLASS EXPERIENCE

In the context of these mixed societal results, the Califia introduction to the class presentation carefully denied anticapitalism while addressing countercultural glorification of the underprivileged. Ahshe Green had given a talk about class at Sagaris, where she used personal stories to construct a riveting account of how women could examine the values, attitudes, and behaviors they learned as children in order to retain useful ones and reject those that offended others or were no longer appropriate. When Green relocated to San Diego, Califia founders Brooks, Murphy, and Jodie Timms were already aware of how powerful her presentation was. Green presented at the first two years of Califia. A collective member touted those with working-class backgrounds as "the backbone not only of [the] human race, but America." Noting that a myth of class equality prevented people from knowing "where they fit in a class spectrum," the introducer concluded, "And so, usually when you mention class, people think, 'Now we're going to have a discussion on Communism.' Well, this is not going to be a discussion on Communism, Marxism, or Socialism at all." Instead, the group got the experience of Green and the collective members from working-class backgrounds: Mary Glavin, Sue Dunne, Murphy, and Timms.[15]

Green and others at Califia prioritized attitudinal similarities and differences in keeping with the radical feminist goal of changing perceptions. Scant attention was given to leftist class theory. Manov remembered no formal links drawn between personal experience and institutional class hierarchy or structural reproduction of class. Although she came out of the New Left, she and others did not represent their groups or talk about class analysis in the larger sense at Califia.[16] Socialist feminism might have received a chilly reception. There was a history of socialist groups trying to take over other New Left or feminist organizations. Califia leaders like Jetter had experienced socialist men in NOW directing women to introduce a socialist agenda.[17] Jetter remembered never discussing Marxist theory at Califia and learned what little she knew from a slim volume a woman loaned her in another group. At Califia she first recognized that her Sicilian immigrant grandfather's job as a ditch digger would be considered working class.[18] From childhood, Murphy's understanding of poverty was shaped by her union father. At Califia, however, she too fell back on a personal history of deprivation and class-based shame rather than her memories of walking a picket line at age ten with her father and all the times he was fired for criticizing oppressive work, supporting a coworker against a supervisor, or organizing a strike.[19] Jettisoning union rhetoric minimized or bypassed sectarian politics and validated individuals' experiential contributions. In contrast, the most famous socialist feminist union, the Chicago Women's Liberation Union, was rent five times by attempted sectarian takeovers and folded in its eighth year just after voting to expel a faction. Equally importantly, California union power had dissolved by the end of the first year of Califia, so women new to feminism were less likely to become educated in socialist feminism in the L.A. community.[20]

Green split society into a minuscule percentage who owned and controlled the majority of property, middle-class people who organized things, and working-class people who did the labor. Because the middle class were put in charge of hostile workers and looked down on by the elite, to whose position they aspired, the middle class found it important to "be nice" in order to play down hostility.[21] Green constructed a set of classed generalities that resonated with her audience.[22] While upper-class and working-class people believed they got ahead through luck such as the family into which they were born, middle-class people touted "hard work." Neither elites nor the poor needed to be liked as much as did middle-class managers, and so both displayed higher degrees of eccentricity compared to middle-class norms of behavior. The rich could marry for money, and laborers in perilous economic situations depended on spouses for survival, but the middle class developed a romantic ideal. Historians of sexuality have supported the argument that middle-class Europeans spread the ideal of romantic love. Thus, Green argued that for diametrically opposite reasons commonalities between the upper class and working class distinguished them from the middle class and heightened class conflict.

By fleshing out points with personal anecdotes, Green paralleled other feminist efforts to analyze the personal as politically instructive. Illustrating ways of showing support, Green related a story about having an unwanted pregnancy to argue that working-class people valued material support over verbal support because survival depended on concrete aid. She first disarmed her audience by noting, "This is all tricky 'cause I was a lesbian for a few years before I had gotten pregnant, and this was a few years ago. And it's always tricky when lesbians get pregnant [laugh]. Raises a lot of issues in the community [audience laughs]." She recalled how close she and her middle-class roommate were, how the woman worked in a lab and could have tested a urine sample for pregnancy, but, instead, gave copious verbal support about "what a drag" it must be to be pregnant. After numerous days in bed with nausea, a working-class acquaintance dropped by, surveyed the situation, and reminded Green that she could get a urine test from a feminist clinic. Green concluded:

> It's a funny thing about working-class women and health, you know. We don't know a whole lot about our own health. Like if you're sufferin' . . .
> I'll find out about health. But if I'm sick, you just, you go to the doc-

tor when you're really really sick, you don't go for yearly checkups or something. So if you're sick you just try to ignore it, and if nothin' happens when you ignore it, then you try to play it down, but you don't think a[bout] goin' to the doctor. And even if [I] get it together to know that I'm pregnant and I needed a test . . . I didn't know what to do. And I knew what to do kind of because I was middle class by then, or upwardly mobile, but I forgot. . . . I go into my old ways when I'm in a crisis. And I just didn't remember that you can just look in a newspaper and get a clinic. But the working-class woman that walked in the house wasn't even a close friend, and she thought of it for me. And it wasn't no trouble, I mean it only took her five minutes. And, then I got fixed up, got an abortion, I was all set.

In Green's interpretation of her inability to act, class background had lasting effects that overrode class mobility. She concluded from many of the cross-class conflicts she related that women from different classes simply needed the awareness to make allowances for what women around them needed or to ask directly for what they wanted.

In a story about her upward mobility and her roommate's downward mobility, Green pointed out that cross-class aspirations could provide both parties with skills but could also cause tensions over conflicting goals.[23] Her roommate's disparagement of formal education as "whitey's game" clashed with Green's struggle to attain higher education and her drive to master vocabulary, argumentation, and abstract concepts. Later Weiss would agree about the value placed on college education: "poor and working class Dykes often think of a college degree as a kind of union card. We think it means that we will always be able to find work (above minimum wage) and therefore it is our ticket out of poverty."[24] Green noted that behaviors she saw as working class and her roommate wanted to cultivate—passion, expressiveness, and disregard for others' opinions—Green no longer fully valued. The key was to be conscious of class attributes, so that one could choose what was appropriate to the situation.[25]

This was a point first published by The Furies. Twelve lesbians from different classes who lived together as the Furies Collective in Washington D.C. wrote significant analysis during the collective's existence between the summer of 1971 and spring 1972. A key difference between the Furies' publishing and Califia camps was that Califia actively engaged more than two thousand women in CR about their class-based attitudes and created a space where at least one hundred women at a time lived out those dynamics together for a week.

Working-class feminists balked at the downward mobility made chic by the 1960s and 1970s youth culture. They saw middle-class youth playing at poverty as embracing what, to working-class Americans, had been marks of deprivation and shame. Class tensions exposed during the 1960s generated new feminist theory, which argued that class awareness and a commitment to purging classist behavior from oneself preceded class struggle. Furies members, Rita Mae Brown and Tasha Petersen, especially decried the classist assertions that downward mobility would remove class differences, saying that made a mockery of working-class lives by temporarily adopting a lifestyle while retaining middle-class attitudes and behavior. They argued class went beyond Marx's relationship to means of production, and instead, fundamentally involved the assumptions and behaviors formed in childhood.[26] Brown and Charlotte Bunch both participated as lecturers at Sagaris as well as having published ten volumes of *The Furies* newsletter and essays reprinted as *Class and Feminism*.[27]

Although Green advised women to choose behaviors that were appropriate to their current conditions, some of her distinctions favored working-class values and paralleled leftist and feminist critiques of U.S. society. Green contrasted support from working-class neighbors or extended family with the insular and unsupportive dynamics of nuclear families. She criticized the middle-class myth that one would always be happy as preventing women from seeking the necessary discomfort of CR. She mirrored trends among social historians that glorified immigrant communities and attributed the source of middle-class neuroses to postwar suburbanization. Green was ahead of a curve that compared the directness of physical violence to verbal manipulation and covert power plays. While she had rejected physical violence, she felt that characteristically middle-class backstabbing was equally violent.[28] When Phyllis Chesler published *Woman's Inhumanity to Woman* in 2001, many feminists decried her critique of gendered patterns of violence, not ready to acknowledge that women could rival men in abusiveness.

Like other feminist activists, Green privileged support for activism over navel-gazing therapy. The value CR put on showing that women's problems were based on institutional oppression, rather than personal failing in conjunction with psychiatric abuse of women, led some feminists to be highly critical of normalizing therapeutic techniques. In the broader Califia setting, Murphy and Weiss echoed Green's prioritization of activism over therapy. Murphy opposed therapy's attempts to focus on individual responsibility and take the edge off women's anger rather than facilitate collective action. She remembered losing most of the female friends with whom she had discussed books and ideas in Oklahoma in the late 1950s to mid-1960s because they "were victims of psychiatrists and electric shock treatment, efforts to 'normalize' them, to help them adjust to their role as wives and mothers."[29] Weiss felt that 12-step programs became a way of life for some women and diverted them from the types of CR and coalition work for activism that Califia sought.[30]

The classism presentation pressed women from middle-class families to intervene on behalf of women from poorer backgrounds instead of trying to enforce middle-class ways. Those who had middle-class training in money management, negotiating verbal manipulation, and formal education could help working-class women who lacked those skills. Exhorting women to adopt behaviors their experience taught them were unsuccessful, however, would be ineffective. For example, if one's experience was that the next crisis would always eat up the savings, why save and postpone joy? Instead, middle-class women could be allies by sticking up for working-class women when other middle-class authorities tried to oppress them, by enforcing that middle-class women pay the high end of sliding scales, and by ridding programming of white, middle-class bias.[31]

After the formal presentation, a two-part interactive session demarked the lines between Califia women. Collective members from working-class families created questions over the first few years of Califia to help women determine their own class backgrounds. Women considered the class implications of questions like "Who did the housework in your family—Your mother? You and siblings? A maid? What is your educational level? Who paid for your education? When you were a child, did you have enough underwear and socks? Did you get a regular allowance? Who paid for your first car?"[32] Situating themselves got them ready for Glavin's "The Passing Game." Those who came from working-class backgrounds or poverty were asked, "How did you pass as middle class?" and "What price did you pay for passing?"[33] A collective member began by sharing a personal story.[34] Meanwhile, women from more privileged backgrounds could only say "pass"[35] because they were to remain silent, listen nondefensively to the others' experiences, and learn about the personal effects of institutionalized classism in the United States.

Women who knew or newly discovered that they came from working-class or poor backgrounds found the experience life changing. They grew up when U.S. culture was nearly silent about class hierarchy and promoted widespread identification with the middle class based on consumption. Merry remembered that initially people tittered at the questions and were nervous about the grave pronouncements that people had to stay for the whole discussion. By the end, she was in tears because she finally realized that her years of trying to fit into lesbian clothing norms by buying Birkenstocks and "the right shorts" hid a working-class struggle to survive emotionally and materially. The opportunity to process this flood of information in a break-out session without the middle-class women present helped her to make sense of her past and made her feel strong. She came to pity middle-class people because they had not had the same struggles to get where they were.[36] Merry's conclusion indicates the propensity at Califia for women to divide identities into opposites and to invert inequalities, so that women gained from identifying with less-privileged identities.

Collective members' own working-class backgrounds gave them the expertise and the responsibility to lead the classism presentation. Not only did Green spread her message beyond Califia, other collective members replicated her work. Green published an article that repackaged key points of her class talk as "Ashe Speaks" in *Country Women*'s issue devoted to class.[37] Murphy circulated a paper on distinguishing values by class backgrounds called "Did Your Mother Do Volunteer Work?"[38] By Catoggio's memory, after the 1977 Califia camps, Green abruptly left California to join guru Rajneesh's Oregon compound, and a collective member dropped the classism presentation in Catoggio's lap.[39] Catoggio, an articulate Sagaris planner, seemed the logical choice when the speaker needed working-class credentials. For the camps in 1978 and 1979, Catoggio repeated Green's examples and structure based on the audiotape of Green's presentation. Eventually she adapted it with her own life experience. Twenty years later Catoggio recalled the details of the presentation.[40] After Catoggio left the collective, Murphy often led the presentation into the 1980s.

CLASSES OF IMPACT

Dissections of how survival values were classed and could inadvertently harm activism gave participants memorable resources for dealing with class differences. For example, is honesty about truthfulness or trustworthiness? When survival depends on not telling outsiders things that would lead them to deprive one of resources, deciding whether to give truthful information requires assessing the recipients' good intentions. Murphy related this observation to feminist procedure. She noted that when middle-class feminists insisted on parliamentary rules or consensus methods, working-class feminists with backgrounds of simultaneous conversations and passionate outbursts could feel squelched. They regarded the middle-class idea of rotating speakers as a tactic to suppress dissent while some middle-class feminists saw working-class feminists who spoke out of turn as disorderly. In such a climate of middle-class rule enforcement, working-class women might not trust middle-class ones enough to give them information and work with them.[41] Such an analysis did not privilege one way of operating. Despite being generalizations that would not always hold true, participants already familiar with the class presentation could appreciate these nuances and were not getting these discussions anywhere else. Such a focus on cultural sensitivity has since partially entered classroom teaching and popular culture although classed interpersonal relations remain undertheorized.

The responses from working-class background women who never knew Green but who discovered their backgrounds through Catoggio's vicarious renditions or Murphy's later facilitation remained emotionally powerful, indicating the power of CR for personal understanding. Kal Kalivoda recalled:

> Califia hit me in the gut like a boulder most particularly in the classism issues. . . . I was under the impression that I came from a middle-class family. I mean *everybody* came from a middle-class family. That was a given until I went to Califia. And when they started talking about working class and middle class, it was like being shocked. I had no idea that there were differences. I had no idea that I was considered working class—*lower* working class quite frankly. When I was a little kid if we couldn't scrounge enough meat, my dad went out and shot a couple robins and sparrows, and we *always* had meat on the table. See that was a criterion. You have meat on the table, you've got a meal every day, you're middle class.
> KAL KALIVODA (CALIFIA COMMUNITY PARTICIPANT 1979–1985)[42]

Analogies such as "hit me in the gut like a boulder" reveal the intensity of a "click" moment. The dominant worldview with which these women were raised was false. Families like Kalivoda's followed middle-class norms, such as making meat the center of the meal. They diverged from middle-class expectations about the frequency of meals or where meat came from. They might hunt and dress the kill instead of buying it prepackaged from a butcher shop or supermarket.

Discussions about personal experiences resonated with women in a way that reading abstract class theory did not and allowed them to link their family experiences to a broader history of class struggle. Germain remembered:

> [W]hen I *heard* what we were *talking* about and I *realized* what it was to be *working class*, come from working-class *people*, come from *poor* peo-

ple, come from *grandparents* who worked in a *woolen* mill and *that* part
of American *history* where these *workers* were so *pushed around* and *oppressed.* . . . I mean, it wasn't like I needed to read a *book* about how my
grandmother was abused . . . *coming* from a *people* who spoke another
language.

Speaking *French.* . . . People who speak another *language* are *mis-
treated* . . . and certain *attributes* are given to French-*Canadians* that are
really *mean-hearted* and *insulting.* So, I mean, I could relate to all of that.
And I could relate to being *ashamed* of things in my household—*clothes*
that weren't *good* enough, of going to social events and not knowing how
to *behave* and being really *embarrassed* about things that happened in our
family. . . .

Sometimes it was *global* about the *oppression* of workers; but sometimes
it was *very particular,* about *uncles* that had *bad cheap haircuts,* and somehow growing up to a point where you *realized* that and were *ashamed* of
it. Ah, *relatives* with *bad teeth.* They might have . . . *cavities* that were not
taken care of and actually *showed.* Some of that *humiliation,* some of that
not wanting *certain* friends to come to your *house.* Some of the other *poor*
ones could come to your house because they wouldn't *remark* about some
of the things that were going on there. But growing up to a point where
you *knew* that this one and this one—you didn't want those *nicer,* upper-
class people coming to your house because they would notice right *away*
that there were little rickety-rackety *things* happening [laugh]—furniture or
ways of doing things.[43]

From a basis of considering one's own classed values, it was eye-opening
to recognize that formative experiences continued to influence or disrupt
relationships. Bencangey summarized the class presentation's effect: "When
I got there, the classism presentation that I went to blew me away in that I
had never thought of myself as working class or that what class I had come
from would still be influencing the way that I thought."[44]

The presentation heightened awareness about scarcity when unexamined
habits continued class-based behaviors that were not necessarily appropriate to new conditions. Examples of middle-class women casually neglecting
to return borrowed items struck a nerve. Food and money were constant
sources of anxiety for many participants who had grown up with scarcity.
When Murphy objected to Brooks taking some of her piece of cake, her
friend's assurance that "there's plenty more cake in the kitchen" did not
mesh with the childhood experience of Murphy and other women at the
table. Some women at the campgrounds were so anxious that the food
would run out that they cut in line. When middle-class participants com-

plained about their rudeness, Germain argued that their behavior could be an inappropriate holdover from childhoods of actually not having enough food and battling with siblings to get more.[45] While middle-class collective members were confident that Califia would always stay in the black, working-class leaders fretted partly because they knew the shame of needing to borrow money.[46]

Middle-class participants' responses were divided between recognizing they obtained heightened awareness and feeling defensive. In an attempt to guide middle-class women toward an equitable use of their energy and resources, Califia asked women with disposable income to consider sharing their prosperity by donating money for organizing the camps and by subsidizing the fees of currently poor women so that they could attend the camps.[47] Weiss, who held a nursing position, recalled that when Murphy told her about Califia early in their friendship, Weiss said, "I'd like to go, but I was working and I could only go for half a week. Was there a half-week rate? And [Murphy] said, 'You can afford to pay for the whole week whether you come or not, and some other woman can *benefit* by your extra money.'" Weiss counted that as the beginning of her *true* feminist education: "the statement just resonated with" her.[48] Usually ten to twelve women donated money to cover fees for women too poor to pay the low end of Califia's sliding scale. This way, Califia made feminism accessible to as many women as possible.

While Weiss had risen from a background with deprivation, acknowledging class divisions was harder for many from middle-class families. During the first year of Califia, the classism presentation created a rift that took the rest of the week at camp to heal. Women did not want to be cast as part of an oppressive group. Why spend so much time on what divided them? Why did working-class women get to caucus by themselves? Feminists who had divorced themselves from their families of origin and embraced class analysis identified with the working class and were brought up short when they realized that the focus on class background forming one's views excluded them from the working-class caucus, while currently middle-class participants could join it. Forrest summarized, "So the downwardly mobile women would get booted out, and they'd get really pissed off about it."[49]

The Furies had warned about middle-class reactions—denial of class privilege and power from supporting an oppressive system, downward mobility and romanticizing or patronizing the poor, paralysis from guilt and fear, retreat in confusion, labeling the issue divisive to prevent discussion, or a red herring dismissal of some working-class women as class opportunists using issues for personal gain.[50] The Furies also suppressed middle-class women like Joan E. Biren by pressuring her not to use the verbal articulate-ness others associated with the middle class. The group broke up, in part, over class tensions.

Germain remembered women continued to try to derail the passing game by objecting that the poverty of others was not their fault and that they had important things to say. Other working-class narrators also complained that middle-class women had trouble holding their tongues. What began with laughs and receptivity turned to resistance, but a number of middle-class narrators believed that despite the emotion and sense of exclusion, it was imperative to recognize that they were not all the same.[51] Women of color narrators, especially, remembered the class discussions as less "volatile" than discussions about race. Women from working-class backgrounds were in the audience ready to support presenters with their own experiences whereas the race presentation developed in such a way that women of color presenters did not have participants of color to support them at the presentations.[52]

Disagreements over distribution of the work at the camps and in the collective indicated that Califia women saw classed behaviors as intertwined with other factors like lesbianism, race, and experience in feminism. Everyone at camp was to do two hours of kitchen work and two hours of childcare. Barbara Forrest stressed, "None of the middle-class white women *ever* worked in childcare on a volunteer basis." She revised that to say that, unless the women were mothers or in education, their class values precluded taking on childcare themselves. Another interpretation would be that sexual orientation drove nonparticipation. Child-free lesbians may have wanted to maintain their choice not to care for children. Participants could double up on some forms of work to the exclusion of others. In contrast to the stereotypical view of middle-class volunteerism Murphy put forward in her presentation and writing, Forrest saw Califia's organizers as dominated by working-class women and criticized the high-paid therapists and lawyers who were reluctant to donate time. Likewise, Otero remembered that wealthier Latinas missed shifts at Lesbianas Unidas camps in the 1980s, which were modeled on Califia. She characterized the class split between Latinas as "higher class Latinas . . . who felt like . . . they should be serviced. Whereas the working-class women said, 'Yes, we're willing to be part of this and *work*.'"[53] Brooks, a target based on her continuous middle-class status, noted wryly that volunteer-run groups on shoestring budgets "need middle-class women who will give of their lives."[54] Anna Maria Soto, however, criticized her comember of the collective, Brooks, as unwilling to do the mundane work and attributed that to Brooks having been involved with feminist work for so much longer than other collective members.

Despite tensions, some found the class workshop freeing because it explained and helped diffuse or avoid conflicts. Elsa Fisher repeated three times that nothing changed her life like the class presentation. She went from believing that there was "no such thing as classism" and that everybody could do whatever he or she pleased to recognizing that her judgmental certainty of what was right and her money-management skills were products of an upper-middle-class upbringing. She felt freed to let go of her judgments.[55] Manov praised the presentation and "fishbowl" observation of working-class experience as "brilliant" and said it made a "tremendous impact" on her. She remembered specific Passing Game questions and how validating it was for working-class women, who sometimes burst into tears at finding others who shared their experiences. She also recalled, however, that middle-class women chafed at remaining quiet because they had suffered alienation and isolation as middle-class women, which went unaddressed.[56]

Middle-class leaders developed a component for more privileged Califia women, so they would have space to talk and could confront working-class organizers' evaluation that middle-class participants did not do enough. Lillian West recalled that "middle-class women were really uncomfortable, and how loving some of the middle-class women were as far as attending to those women, and trying to explain to them on a sideline and tell them not to take it so personal."[57] In 1982, Jan Hines and Suzanne Beford formalized a break-out session for middle-class women. They assured their group members that they did not need to feel guilty about being born into the middle class but that there was work to be done.[58]

Unfortunately, a focus on class background privileged those from working-class backgrounds against women from more wealth without considering how upwardly mobile women benefited within the heterosexist class system of the United States. Bencangey could tell her companion to shut up during the Passing Game because women from less-affluent backgrounds reaped authority within that space. Otero dismissed the importance of the class presentation, substituting heterosexual privilege. She noted that a number of white women she met may have come from poorer backgrounds like her Mexican-American family, but they married, gained divorce settlements, sent children to private school, lived in Michael Jackson's neighborhood, and bought expensive recreational vehicles. When she was "barely making it," literally living in servants' quarters or a studio apartment that rattled whenever a train went by, she had little patience for protestations from currently middle-class women that they had suffered.[59]

One narrator criticized the presentation as ethnocentric although some working-class Latinas found it powerful. María Dolores Díaz grew up in an upwardly mobile Honduran family. She found the classism presentations and discussion too centered on U.S. life. Grouped for discussion with a white upper-class woman who refused to talk to her, Díaz was struck by the American assumptions that women of color would be working class or receiving welfare.[60] Class privilege did not necessarily translate well from one country to another. For college-bound Chicanas like Soto, however, Califia explained the discomfort she felt at college around class and racial differences when those issues were not addressed in classes.[61] Because Califia presenters used a personal framework to understand American life, they were careful to point out that they only represented urban working-class experience or that their understanding of extended family connections was filtered through Sicilian immigrant experience.[62] This model fit many people well in the beginning but was stretched to its limits in the 1980s to accommodate growing numbers of women from dire poverty.

FEMINIST CLASS CONSCIOUSNESS
AMID THE FEMINIZATION OF POVERTY

Although Califia's camps became a model for groups like Lesbianas Unidas, class-based CR did not translate directly into activism beyond the ways individual women carried their heightened consciousnesses into their work relationships, activism groups, friendships, and partnerships. Pam Chavez Hutson was representative in considering Califia important because she learned there to try to understand perspectives with which she did not identify.[63] This was Califia's goal; leaders sought to hone participants' understanding to reform interpersonal relations so that their relationships would not explode based on unexamined class differences.

Like the other presentations, the classism training incorporated new attendees into a common Califia value system but also needed revisions to hold long-time participants' interest and to reflect changing societal conditions. A major trend over the 1970s and 1980s was the way poverty became "a female problem." Diana Pearce assessed in her foundational "The Feminization of Poverty" why women were two-thirds of America's 15 million poor over sixteen years old and 70 percent of impoverished elders by 1976. Women who headed families because of divorce, nonmarriage, and widowhood were especially vulnerable. Most women worked in gender-segregated fields, and over half of those occupations paid poverty-level wages. Part-time work tended to confer lower hourly wages and benefits. Half of women whose ex-husbands were required to pay child support got no money from their exes and another 28 percent did not receive full support. When women had to turn to welfare, declining benefits and states' right to pay less than states determined was the minimum needed relief, left women's incomes between 40 and 70 percent of the national poverty level. Even when women entered the "Work Incentive Program" part of welfare, they usually could not become economically independent because the fields for which the WIN program trained women tended to pay poverty-level wages.[64] Overall, even women with employed husbands suffered in the 1970s and 1980s. Inflation, combined with a stagnant economy from 1973 to 1979, decreased discretionary income per worker by 16 percent. Families and individuals coped by increasing their consumer debt and/or trading leisure time for more paid labor, sometimes necessitating higher expenses for childcare and prepared meals. Most new jobs created in the 1970s were low-paying service work without good advancement.[65] From the 1950s through the 1970s a wage gap between men and women was based on a combination of discrimination and gender-segregated jobs. In the 1980s, poverty rose across the United States and constituted 11 to 15 percent of the population by the conservative estimates of the federal poverty line. In the U.S. Census, statistics for poverty among African Americans, Latinos, and female-headed households were more than double the national average, ranging from 25 to 40 percent.[66]

African American women in L.A.'s Watts neighborhood and Mexican American women in East L.A. started organizing for the rights of women on welfare before the term "feminization of poverty" existed, so both welfare rights and the declining unions were recognizable movements to join. Johnnie Tillmon initiated Aid to Needy Children—Mothers Anonymous with other Watts-area mothers in 1961 because social workers assigned to welfare recipients did not inform them of their legal rights. She later helped lead the National Welfare Rights Organization (NWRO). Although Tillmon did not initially label herself "feminist," her work for welfare reform prioritized women's autonomy and advancement. In 1972 she connected oppressions from being a woman, black, poor, fat, and middle-aged in "Welfare is a Women's Issue," which she published in the first issue of *Ms. Magazine*. Tillmon considered welfare to be like "a super-sexist marriage," and *Ms.* gave her experience-based stance publicity among feminists.[67]

In 1967, Alicia Escalante's own experience and attendance at the L.A. chapter of NWRO were catalysts for expanding L.A.'s welfare rights to Mexican Americans. Escalante grew up in poverty and saw a welfare social worker's prejudice against her mother. ANC—Mothers led the chapter meeting of NWRO she attended, and the combination of personal views and organizing spurred Escalante to help found the East Los Angeles Welfare Rights Organization (ELAWRO). Like NWRO, ELAWRO informed welfare recipients of their rights, but ELAWRO separated from NWRO to emphasize specific needs within Chicano communities such as Spanish-language forms and bilingual social workers. They documented discrepancies among policies at the local, state, and federal levels and lobbied politicians. Members of ELAWRO succeeded in getting staffing changes that included hiring bicultural welfare recipients for entry positions and enhancing cultural competence among the social workers.[68]

Increasing numbers of women from or in poverty attended Califia at a moment when welfare rights work was well-established, but Pearce and other feminists were just beginning to explain the "feminization of poverty." Through their description of classes, collective members combated internalized views that poor people deserved poverty due to personal failings. Califia women, however, did not have enough poor women's experience to develop useful generalizations about poverty-class values and behaviors or to motivate participants to connect to L.A.'s welfare rights activism.

Women who grew up extremely poor or were currently poor may not have benefited as much from the Califia presentations as working-class background women did. Since attendees did not have enough experiences to draw broad conclusions, Califia leaders included assessments of systemic poverty. These assessments tried to make sense of the effects recession, shifting the burden of income tax to the nonwealthy, and simultaneous cuts in social programs like welfare had on women. Califia introduced a few written sources such as the Southern California Interfaith Hunger Coalition's "Welfare—Myths & Facts" to counter Reagan-era scapegoating of welfare recipients as the cause of national economic recession.[69] An increase in Califia women from middle-class backgrounds who were currently on welfare revived tensions over downward mobility that, in this case, they had not chosen. Forrest considered women who were impoverished by economic recession or other circumstances to be "totally in denial" about how long they would struggle.[70] Break-out sessions continued to be based on one's upbringing and put them with the middle class.

For a number of reasons, Califia women framed class difference as upbringing and interpersonal relationships. California and the nation's fervent anticommunism, feminists' fear of sectarian infiltration, the decline of socialist feminist groups outside of universities by 1977, and liberal attention to antipoverty campaigns without Marxist analysis all predisposed Califia women against socialist feminism even when they recognized structural aspects to poverty.

The classism presentation could not create a systematic challenge to U.S. class hierarchy, but it was never geared to such a task. By introducing women to the concept that not all Americans were middle class and by differentiating values by class, radical feminist takes on class both prepared women for learning Marxism elsewhere and mitigated against that possibility. They portrayed class values and behaviors as aspects people could learn to choose to fit their situation rather than as fundamentally at odds. To the extent that they knew about socialist feminism, Califia women rejected that model of analysis because they had seen socialist New Left women as pawns of New Left men and were unmoved by theories that lacked emotionally compelling personal emphases. Given that socialist feminism had peaked, waned in popular counterculture, and been preserved primarily within university settings, many Califia women simply did not learn that form of feminism at all. Instead, Califia provided training on class-based values and patterns of relating, which participants could not find elsewhere. In a decade when union membership plummeted, welfare rights groups were beleaguered by neoliberal policies, and the Poor People's campaign of 1968 was a distant memory, the decision of most Califia women not to try to connect with class social justice movements was likely a product both of their focus on gender and sexual orientation and movement retrenching in the face of an onslaught of attacks from the New Right. Collective members, instead, responded to changing conditions in such a way that women could gain respect for people in poverty and working-class positions and address unstated class biases within feminist process. Narrators widely reflected that they have carried their changed consciousnesses into their work and personal lives and are more willing to point out unconscious classism.

CHAPTER 5

ANTIRACISM TO GET UNDER THE SKIN

LIKE THE TRAINING ABOUT CLASS, Califia's presentations on race sought to nurture integrated women's groups that functioned effectively across differences. This chapter argues that Califia founders expressed feminists' concern to teach women to work together and that the development of antiracism trainings represented feminist views on race in the 1970s and 1980s in four main ways. The pedagogy developed from earlier Black Power calls for whites to help other whites unlearn racism; Califia founders developed antiracism as one of the consistent presentations in hopes that white women could become antiracist enough to unite with women of color in sisterhood. Later efforts to raise attendance by women of color challenged the efficacy of initial pedagogy. Women of color teachers provided more complexity, force, and broader antiracist focus, which helped women of color participants at an unintended emotional cost to the teachers. The trajectory from white founding to multicultural leadership became part of the cycle of reincorporating racial inclusion in feminism. The resulting creation of two formative groups and the refashioning of Califia into women of color camps exemplified the increase in feminist antiracist work while mainstream America de-emphasized racism.

If Califia's work on sexism showed the centrality of reclaiming power against male violence for radical and lesbian feminists, and the training on class difference reflected a CR-focused rejection of anticapitalist theory, Califia's antiracism work symbolized the enduring divisiveness of race and racism in 1970s and 1980s America and feminists' prioritization of race as mainstream society de-emphasized racism.

DE FACTO SEGREGATION

Califia collective members had to work hard against decades of segregation and racial tensions to create diversity. Practices that enforced racial segregation in California were national reminders that southern segregation laws were only one method by which to deprive Americans of equal opportunities. New Deal programs that sought to decrease local poverty adopted widespread prejudicial assumptions, and postwar programs built on those biases. For example, the Federal Housing Administration and the GI Bill subsidized home buying in white-only neighborhoods for millions by working with mortgage companies and realties that required racial homogeneity to consider neighborhoods desirable. City officials used federal urban renewal and highway funds after 1956 to facilitate suburbanization of white Americans, to raze poor neighborhoods of color, and to crowd minorities into ghettos. Zoning and the intentional placement of transportation systems and industrial areas created buffers between working-class areas and affluent suburbs. Until 1948, it was legal to bar certain racial and ethnic groups from buying or renting homes or to sell houses with restrictive covenants in the contracts that forbade resale to African Americans, Jewish Americans, or other minorities. Even after the Supreme Court ruled this practice illegal, people continued to use restrictive covenants. Real estate agents also maintained racial homogeneity by refusing to show homes in some neighborhoods to people of color, and developers built with a target race in mind. Neighborhood segregation impeded public school desegregation by tying districts to neighborhoods. Across the country, after the Supreme Court *Brown vs. Board of Education* ruling to desegregate, white-collar suburban families who opposed integration used a color-blind discourse that claimed that merit-based individual effort produced different levels of success and that their children would be disadvantaged by being grouped with low-performing students. Attributing education, salary, and other marks of privilege to merit ignored institutional supports for racism. By the late 1960s and early 1970s, these families were decrying attempts to further school desegregation by busing students out of their neighborhoods.[1]

California Governor Pat Brown had embraced civil rights in 1959 by appointing several black and Latino staffers and signing civil rights measures to guarantee fair employment, access to businesses, public accommodations, and publicly funded housing. In 1963, however, California joined states like Alabama, Georgia, and Mississippi as sites where civil rights activists demonstrated against businesses, government agencies, and segregated housing. Black and white protestors from the National Association for the Advancement of Colored People, Congress on Racial Equality, and Student Nonviolent Coordinating Committee (SNCC) picketed Sheraton hotels, Bank of America branches, federal buildings, city halls, and courthouses, charging discriminatory policies. The California Real Estate Association promoted Proposition 14 in 1964 to overturn a new state law that banned discrimination in the sale or rental of private dwellings. Brown hoped the state law would dismantle ghettos and de facto segregation. He and activists faced a strong lobby and voters who cared more about customary but illegal practices of refusing to sell or rent to minorities than their governor's appeal that there was "no greater victory for social justice and peace in the community" than a vote against Proposition 14. The majority of California voters supported the supposed "right" to discriminate by race in housing on the 1964 ballot.[2] In 1978, when California homeowners felt squeezed by the high property taxes that accompanied the real estate housing boom, their interest in getting better services and lower property taxes ultimately got framed as a politics of race. About two-thirds of the tax relief Proposition 13 provided went to businesses and not homeowners, but promoters convinced Californian homeowners they were in competition with city welfare recipients for scarce government services, and Proposition 13 would somehow prevent "their" tax dollars from going to black and Latino housing projects. National business organizations, New Right activists, and sympathetic politicians used the same rhetoric to redistribute revenues to businesses nationwide at the expense of private citizens of all races.[3]

RACISM IN BLACK AND WHITE

As Califia founders considered the divisions women faced in this context, their 1977 brochure listed race among ten issues to address.[4] The next year's brochure lists among seven goals, "1. To make Califia Community a forum for examining the issues which divide women in hopes that understanding and appreciation will develop, enabling us to work together on the common problems which oppress us"; and "5. To provide an environment in which women of color can dialogue and possibly form coalitions with white women to help strengthen each others' struggles against racism and sexism."[5] Point 5 offered hope for coalition work to interest more women of color in the camps. In its fifth year of operation, Califia distilled the defining impediments to women's unified work for progress down to gender and sexual orientation, class, and race.

Before 1978, the all-white collective members presented antiracism for white participants. They heeded demands from SNCC and the Black Power Movement for aware whites to educate other whites, and this was the most widely supported strategy proposed in antiracist handbooks in the late 1960s through the 1970s.[6] Califia presentations called on whites to take control of their own racism because "the interracial encounter group may often serve as simply another form of exploitation of minorities for white people's purposes. The benefit seems to be greater for whites than for Third World People."[7] As Germain remembered, "white women had to take the responsibility of helping other white women who made racist comments" because women of color should not be continuously put in the position of helping white women out of racism.[8]

Although southern California had high concentrations of Latinas, American Indians, and Asian Americans, manuals of the day focused racism on the oppression of African Americans. Representative of the pre-presentation reading packet was Sara Winter's "Rooting Out Racism." Winter addressed whites' guilt and avoidance of race issues through segregation, emotional detachment, and simply not seeing.[9] Assuring her audience that their internalization of racism as children was not their fault, Winter argued that whites, nonetheless, reaped benefits and had a responsibility to work against racism. She recommended whites analyze stereotypes and fears they experienced in racially mixed situations, listen to "black friends, associates and acquaintances about what they've experienced," engage in "searching out valid information on race and racism" and "interrupting other whites' racist remarks or actions," and influence practices like hires and housing policies or curricula.[10] "Rooting Out Racism" became a template for the antiracism work white Califia women did.[11] Until 1979, the collective was completely white, and the women attending were overwhelmingly white as well. Not only were the presentations on race geared for them, but the attendance of women of color was often due to white women's suggestions that they come.

The permutations of Califia's early racism presentations situated Califia within a changing feminist movement. Initial feminists had been part of the civil rights movement. Black Power, Chicanismo, and the American Indian Movement created racially homogenous liberation movements. Their adherents expressed exasperation at dealing with unintentional racism from white civil rights activists. Many feminists of color organized with other women of their race or ethnicity who shared lived experience as minorities. Sometimes white women's interest in sisterhood eclipsed their concern for desegregation actions. African American feminists and Chicana feminists typically organized separately from white feminists to avoid inconsiderate interpersonal relations and because priorities seemed to differ. White feminists increasingly refocused on racism's negative consequences for all people regardless of race in the 1980s, and Califia was one of the few spots outside the academy where L.A. feminists seriously discussed race from 1976 on. Even so, it took women of color to prod Califia participants into more intensive antiracism work.

FATEFUL RECRUITMENT

Massive changes in the racism presentations and the racial composition of attendees began when a woman who usually gave the racism presentation did not show up. In 1978, feminists María Dolores Díaz (Honduran) and Gloria Rodriquez (Chicana) were among those who attended Califia.[12] The night before the racism presentation, Murphy and Weiss approached Díaz to help substitute. Breaking with the strategy of whites teaching whites about racism, they wondered whether "because she was a woman of color, couldn't she do something."[13] Díaz said that they asked her to read a poem by a woman of color—a simple task for a woman who had earned a doctorate and was then a university professor. Díaz demurred that she would like to read the presentation notes overnight. She approached the other two identifiable women of color and got their support for her plan. The next morning, instead of the planned presentation, Díaz told the story of her involvement to the hundred or so attendees and asked, "Will my sisters of color please come up and be with me?" With a total of five women holding hands, she said, "This is your racism presentation," bowed, and left them to discuss how unspoken racism led to such a white-dominated camp.[14]

In keeping with Califia's stated goals of self-empowerment and practicing the skills needed to direct that power toward changing themselves and the world, Díaz did not simply fill in at the last minute and leave white Califians to contemplate the paucity of self-identified women of color attendees.[15] She organized an integrated caucus and demanded Califia develop a recruiting task force by September 1978 and have three women of color on the collective by July 1979. Díaz and Rodriquez labored to encourage women of color to respond to Califia's call for task force members, to inform area women about Califia, and to raise money to help women of color come to Califia.[16] The inclusion of more women of color dramatically altered the strategies used in antiracism work.

Demands for inclusion and leadership corresponded with a new trend in the wider lesbian feminist movement, which, in turn, had further implications for Califia. In 1978, the short-lived National Lesbian Feminist Organization (NLFO) held a founding conference in nearby Santa Monica. The organizers were Jeanne Córdova (an Irish and Mexican American who did not identify as a woman of color at the time) and a number of her white friends. All but one delegate was white, while the few other women of color were present as observers and staff. Yolanda Retter Vargas, who was doing security, related:

> So, a white woman from Colorado, I believe, stood up and said, "Where are the women of color delegates?" and all hell broke loose. So what wound up happening is any woman of color that was present and wanted to serve in that capacity was recruited as a delegate. And what came out of that that's important is that it was decided that *all* decision-making committees had to be made up of fifty percent women of color. And even though that organization didn't live long enough to carry it out, word got out this has been implemented. And as Mina Robinson, also known as Mina Meyer, who attended that conference, said in an article in *Sister* newspaper, this was the first time that white women had to really *deal* with the issue of color. So, at any rate, there was a *thread* there that connected up to awareness. . . . some of the women who were at that *conference*, who were women of color, helped found the LOC, the Lesbians of Color group.[17]

The NLFO decision is an example of the repeated problem of reincorporating diversity within social justice movements. Retter Vargas noted that word spread; the presence of Díaz and Rodriquez in Lesbians of Color (LOC) and Califia precipitated the formation of tentative connections between these two groups.

Janet Jakobsen analyzed in *Working Alliances and the Politics of Difference* that when movements started out diverse, they often foreclosed that diversity because it was difficult to analyze and work across complex, shifting, interlocking structures of difference. It is clear that previous racial and class justice movements, feminists of color, and working-class feminists contributed to forming feminisms of the 1960s. Feminist theory texts of the 1980s to 1990s sometimes erased minorities' contributions to portray the movement as diversifying in the mid-1980s. The inaccurate tale of a necessary development from white feminism to diversity falsely fails to recognize that there continually remains a danger of reproducing homogeneous groups. It also prevents activists from learning successes and failures in their movements' past.[18] The founding of NLFO and of Califia were moments of predominant racial separation but not the first appeal for representation from people of color. Judith Hole and Ellen Levine put the first call for 50 percent representation on all committees at the National Conference for a New Politics in September 1967 in Chicago. A women's group, which included feminists who would become famous—Jo Freeman, Shulamith Firestone, Naomi Weisstein, and Heather Booth—advanced a resolution that would have required all committees also have 51 percent female representation.[19] At NLFO it was telling that lesbians of color were present as observers or staff. They were looking for like-minded political lesbians, but local dynamics had not produced integrated leadership. NLFO was part of a platform from which lesbians of color launched groups to deal with issues that concerned them.

Based on overlapping membership, Califia and LOC cosponsored a racism/sexism conference at the Women's Building, and throughout 1978 and 1979 area women's organizations asked the Califia collective to do racism workshops, placing Califia on the map of L.A. feminist race work. Through these efforts, white collective members became more skilled at presenting antiracist workshops, and racial diversity at Califia grew.[20] Overlap in membership between Califia and LOC, however small, in addition to recruitment from broader communities of color, had concrete effects. The number of women of color attending and taking leadership positions on Califia's collective or in its antiracism presentations increased. Consciousness and tensions about race and ethnicity issues increased and, ultimately, Califia's geographically and racially based Support, Education, and Action (SEA) groups expanded political spaces for women of color and antiracist work.

As Califia became established, collective members continued outreach and added camps at new locations to enlarge their audience. Raising consciousnesses had funneled women into existing organizations. Brooks wanted women to start their own local activist groups. Camps between 1978 and 1982 broadened the diversity of attendees' race, ethnicity, class, sexual expression, and disability status with important consequences. Califia women were part of creating culturally sensitive education about race, ethnicity, and class. Their struggles and the support services that they set up from incipient SEA groups detail processes for feminism nationally.

INTEGRATING DIFFERENCE

The collective in 1978 was white and predominantly lesbian, but its members increasingly prioritized race at the insistence of Díaz, Rodriquez and their supporters. As Califia changed from recruiting individuals to investing groups of women of color with power on the collective, Califia women showed that radical lesbian feminism fulfilled a need and could accommodate difference but had to expand from challenging heteropatriarchy to a model that better integrated diverse experience on all levels.

Leaders' comfort with a lesbian majority led to resignation over the dwindling numbers of straight feminists who attended while an unexam-

ined whiteness influenced their ability to attract women of color. Narrators generally believed that fewer heterosexual feminists attended after the beginning years, a trend that coincided with fewer established promoters being or remaining married to men.[21] Long-term participants like Germain sought to carve out a space where "lesbians come first." She lamented that discussion of sexism, racism, and classism prevented "talk about *pure lesbianism* and *pure lesbians* and *just us*. And it was *difficult* because people who were in the *antiracism* workshop said, 'That's *racist*,' because I said, '*Lesbians* ought to come *first*.'"[22] Although Germain sometimes fell silent when accused of racism, she continued to maintain that Califia should have done more on "a hundred percent pure lesbianism." In contrast, Lillian West sought Califia as she was coming out because it blended caring women, feminism, and a space to find out what women of color were doing. She believed she was asked onto the collective within months of attending in 1981 because she was African American. West found it challenging to recruit other women of color because a "lot of middle-class women don't have the same issues as women of color."[23]

West's awareness that issues differed based on women's class and race represented a broader shift in trying to consider multiple identity factors at once. Califia was very typical of progressives' compartmentalization of identities. In the 1970s and 1980s, women of color feminists published that race, ethnicity, and class influence sexuality in a "simultaneity of oppression." Cherríe Moraga concluded:

> For if race and class suffer the woman of color as much as her sexual identity, then the Radical Feminist must extend her own "identity" politics to include her "identity" as oppressor as well. (To say nothing of having to acknowledge the fact that there are men who may suffer more than she.)[24]

Asked about multiple oppressions, Retter Vargas said, "We *all* knew the litany. . . . We didn't always know or understand the connections. We often did not take the *time* to *get* the connections so that they weren't not only in our minds, but they were in our practice."[25] Creating separate binary oppositions (women/men, lesbian/heterosexual, working-class/middle-class, blacks/whites) had been a common strategy both for mobilizing constituents and for more privileged minorities to try to understand and build alliances with other minorities through analogies that glossed over ways a potential ally might be part of a group with unearned privilege. As Jakobsen noted, this pedagogy flattens out complexity and cannot "articulate relationships among marginalized persons and groups."[26]

With white experience such an unacknowledged filter for their ideology, collective members initially took flak from the larger L.A. feminist community over being an all-white collective doing antiracism CR in the community.[27] The stark contrast that Díaz drew between five women of color on stage in 1978 and the more than one hundred women in the audience initiated change.[28] She and others successfully pushed for an integrated collective and recruited women of color to the camps. Lesbian and, to a lesser extent, nonlesbian women of color had some interest in attending Califia as a space separate from men if they prioritized being with women over separation from whites.

Changing the composition of the collective was facilitated by its high turnover rate, but the collective had to expand in numbers and sensitivity to retain women of color. From 1975 through 1978, generally eleven white women composed the collective. Five left after the 1978 camps, and the remaining six reached consensus to include four new members, three of whom were black women.[29] In 1980 one African American woman remained active on the collective out of twelve members.[30] Sustained change occurred when three bicultural women and two Chicanas replaced five outgoing members in 1981, making the seventeen-member collective 35 percent women of color.[31] By 1982, Califia's fourteen active collective members were 50 percent women of color as NLFO required.[32] The collective swelled to eighteen in 1983, probably to compensate for distractions in Brooks's, Murphy's, and Weiss's lives, and was one-third women of color.[33] In 1984, five out of sixteen members (31 percent) were women of color.[34]

Small numbers of women of color could shrink further with the day-to-day realities of meetings. Germain recalled the impediments raised by consensus-driven meetings in the midst of L.A.'s sprawl and the shift in tactics used to recruit women of color:

> And so little, pitiful little *steps* were taken. And then there would be a woman of color for a while, and then there would be another woman of color for another while, and they would come and go, and I'm sure they found it *difficult.* . . . And *what* conclusions we came to finally was, if you *want* to have women of color on your *collective*, and you *want* them to *stay* for long periods of time, you *can't* just bring one or two at a time. What you *need* to do is get like *five* women of color and *bring* them on *all at once*, and *now* they feel like they've got a *caucus*. They've got *other people* who understand what's going on rather than one lone black woman or one lone Latina or one lone Asian woman saying, "I think we shouldn't do that because it *insults* people," and we all look and say, "*What?*" You know,

even if we didn't *say* that, it might be in our *face* or on our *body*. And so
we got some women of color in a little *bunch*, and they all came on at the
same time.[35]

Germain's verbal emphases highlight the criticism Califia faced, while her
repetition of "little" focuses attention on how incremental change was
when women of color might feel isolated. The "we" and "them" hints at
the impediment that women of color could also see themselves as entering
a collective white women felt ownership over.

Visible racial parity in leadership was not reflected in the camp populations, but friendship networks, sexual orientation, and goals of coalition work brought more women of color. Anna María Soto and Carla Seco
(pseudonym) shared white friends in the Los Angeles Women's Community Chorus. One whom they trusted advised them to attend Califia. For
Soto (Califia Community collective member 1982–1987):

the thing that intrigued me about Califia was it was the only organization
doing antiracism work and work on class, which nobody was doing at the
time, and nobody is doing now. . . . I could always hang out with other Latinas, but I wanted to do coalition work. Because you know I could have
stayed in East L.A. and never bothered to step out, and I didn't want to do
that. And I believe the political, the personal is political. I wanted to reach
out to other women who were different and to see where I fit. And Califia
was really diverse. Anna María Soto[36]

As women who were already in an integrated performance group, Soto and
Seco branched out to gain training. Like other participants who experienced Califia over time, they agreed that it always included presentations
on class and race but that the degree of focus on racism evolved over time.[37]

By sheer numbers, the majority of women in the U.S. population and in
identified feminist groups were white. Nonetheless, limited women of color
participation in Califia's early years adversely affected women of color's
experience. Soto and another Chicana collective member initially felt es-
tranged from the Califia experiences while recognizing its importance:

Both of us were ready to do some political work, yet we knew nothing
about organizations or groups for women of color who happened to be
radical.

Califia did indeed have an impact. However, for us, as for many women
of color before us, the impact was not as profound or transforming as the

impact it had on white women. We went to all of the presentations, stayed up late, did all the readings, and still did not get the point. White women were crying and arguing, and we were left with a sense of observing it all rather than experiencing it. We knew that *something* was happening and we knew that we had to have it. We had to have it for ourselves as well as for other women of color who would never touch the Califia experience.[38]

Califia assembled something unique as a space without men or homophobia that addressed race and class. Radical political organizations for lesbians of color were just starting to form. Las Lesbianes Latinamericanas and Black Women of Color tentatively emerged from the NLFO conference of 1978 and coalesced into LOC. In the late 1970s and early 1980s the issues facing lesbians of color had been generally ignored in L.A., and most feminist political work was done in white-dominated groups.[39] Some women of color rejected association with white women, but these Chicana lesbians recognized Califia as a space they "had to have."[40]

Feminists of color collective members and white participants whose lovers were women of color were instrumental in making Califia more hospitable. West joined the entertainment committee and "had a mission from God, from the goddess, to recruit women [of color] to different camps . . . going out schmoozing with women, and having a legitimate . . . cause behind me—Califia. Like a pick-up line." Soto corroborated that as the collective shifted to having more women of color on it, women "started seeing more of us at parties and dances and things promoting, and there was a safety to come . . . to the camps."[41] In retrospect, Soto also credited white women's work to include women of color:

> [T]he white women were very very cool because most of the women of color back in those years were turned on to Califia by a white woman who they were either very, very close friends with or in a relationship *with*. And the white women who would bring her lover would bring them right up. . . . And we would make contact that way right away.

Stressing that there was no agreement to connect women of color with each other, Soto assumed that white women in cross-racial relationships initiated introductions to increase their lovers' sense of safety and comfort.[42]

Califia increased the racial diversity of the collective over a seven-year period through a combination of factors. Collective members expanded their numbers and replaced departing white leaders with women of color. If white leaders and participants had latent proprietary feelings about the space, women of color joined and spoke out anyway. Outspoken feminists of color helped make Califia more sensitive to them. Recruitment remained largely word-of-mouth through personal connections. Women approached lovers of current participants and those who seemed active in their communities.[43] Interracial work involved prioritizing multiple and potentially dissenting voices over efficiency and taking the time to consider the work of local groups occurring in tandem with Califia. It was a long process, but Califia stood as one of very few U.S. groups where people of color ever made up 50 percent of the leadership.

WHO SHOULD TEACH AND LEARN ABOUT RACISM?

An unintended consequence of recruitment was that women of color took over the antiracism training. Weiss, a white Jewish woman, had taken charge, but Díaz and two other women of color became spokeswomen and punched up the message. Women of color who did not attend the presentation and white women who went remember the new antiracism leadership as generally effective if tough, while these three were frustrated by responses to their labor. Escalating tensions over expectations for interracial work began in these middle years.

Collective member Weiss became the coordinator of the antiracism presentation after 1978, so that women of color would not be called on to do white women's work. She introduced foundational concepts: "that all white people are racist; that we have white privilege and the responsibility to use our privilege against racism; that the good intentions of white people often result in unintentional racism, and so on. She talk[ed] about the difference between racism and prejudice and present[ed] the statistics of the physical, economic, and social costs of racism for people of color."[44] Díaz chose to recruit a Peruvian and German American woman and an African American woman to coordinate the antiracism presentation with her. Retter Vargas recalled her introduction to Califia:

> María said at some point, "Califia is starting a woman of color workshop, and we need you and some other women, like doris davenport, to come and help organize it." The subtext there was "and kick butt." [laughs] So, I said, "OK" partly because it *is* conceivable that I knew Califia was there, but nobody had said, "Come and join us" or "Come and help," partly because they were afraid of me. So when María said, "Come and help," I said, "OK, I will."[45]

Retter Vargas's memory reflected the ways in which women of color could feel unwelcome at Califia before Díaz's outreach and indicated her perception of her role.

All three articulated racism with power and directness. The combination of their demeanors and white audience members' responses was emotionally charged. Díaz lamented in 1993 that white feminists only heard her message because she "was presenting it in ways that were softer."[46] In contrast to the "good cop" Díaz played, Retter saw herself as the "bad cop," someone women disliked or feared because of her direct style. She characterized davenport's message as affected by white women's perception of her as attractive: "a lot of women exoticized her because of *how* they perceived she looked. And so, *she* would *stand* there and, with a certain *dignity*, deliver the blows." Retter Vargas concluded, "In other words, people might listen to doris for the *wrong* reasons. They couldn't hear me because they were frightened. María, they *liked* her, but they weren't *hearing*."[47] White narrators across the board remembered Retter Vargas vividly but recalled davenport and Díaz to a much lesser extent. One of the white collective members was struck by the antiracism presentations but remembered details about Retter Vargas and davenport much better than she recalled Díaz:

> We had *fabulous* presentations, and we sat there, and we were *mesmerized*, and we *heard* them from different points of view. Doris davenport had a lot of things to say about *black* women, and she was a very educated person, and she was *tall* and *willowy*, and she had an *aloof air* about her. And she *walked* through the camps with skirts that *flowed* and *moved*, and she was *pretty* in that way. She *struck quite a figure*. And she had *poetry* and things like *that* that were *really* impactual. And that was *different* than Yolanda.[48]

Davenport in this memory signified black women and positive qualities of beauty, dignity, and intellect. Is this exoticizing, as Retter Vargas claimed or artistic as Germain amended? The fact that the presenters and most of the audience members were lesbians in a women's camp where a number of women have mentioned exploring sexual possibilities and that views on nudity differed by race and ethnicity attests to the potential for a sexually charged atmosphere. Heterosexual women sometimes objectify other women as role models with positive traits.[49] This possibility would be open to lesbian and bi women along with a more sexualized gaze. Davenport and Otero supported Retter Vargas's interpretation of sexualized othering, indicating the possibility of a broader fear of women of color participants' exoticization.[50]

Davenport commented on white feminists' perceptions of women of color as sensual and/or menial in her essay for *This Bridge Called My Back*.[51] The article supported Retter Vargas's memory of davenport delivering the blows and white Califians' recollections while it represented a shift in davenport's alliances. She related experiences of continuing racism in feminist circles on both coasts, and then asserted that black women found white women aesthetically, culturally, and sociopolitically disgusting because black women saw through the myth that white women were "the most envied, most desired (and beautiful), most powerful (controlling white boys) wimmin in existence." Within a scathing catalogue of white women's ugliness and failings, davenport mentioned, "Their hair, stringy and straight, is unattractive."[52] Two white narrators remembered a black woman degrading whites' hair as smelly. Merry vividly recounted the experience as painful, evoking tears and anger among white women. Myers, in contrast, laughed and said, "[I]t was very revealing to get into open and honest discussion."[53] For davenport, this myth of desirability was the root of white feminists' racism. They pulled rank against women of color because it was the only misplaced sense of power they had. Davenport attributed white women's racism to overcompensation for oppression as a colonized group in a misogynist culture. Recent scholarship continues to point out the importance of recognizing that different groups oppressed by a system will not necessarily unite but may turn on each other to ally with those in charge.[54]

By 1981, davenport was rejecting an early black civil rights model of working together as "the old, outdated philosophy of integration and assimilation." She seemed to believe that joining with whites would only expand a white model rather than alter that model to be inclusive or require adaptation on all sides. Like the Black Power leaders who prescribed separation in which whites taught whites while blacks focused on their own culture, she advocated self-segregation and self-determination through "a third world wimmin" movement.[55] Davenport's derogatory application of the term "boys" for men was consistent with separatism from men, which could have initially made Califia's retreat and other L.A. women-only setting appealing. As she became disenchanted with the realities of a racially integrated lesbian feminist community, however, she wrote to support racial minority women finding the commonality to work together apart from whites.

This was actually more complicated than she suggested because of cross-racial prejudices, separatist choices, and class differences. Califia sponsored West and other women of color to attend conferences, where they gained exposure to those doing political work against racism such as Angela Davis. West found "a lot of women of color were not cohesive," which she attributed to internalized racism.[56] Likewise, Soto remembered that at later Califia camps for women of color, Pacific Islanders refused to speak with Japanese Americans because of long-standing national conflicts over racial superiority and imperialism.[57] Soto and Seco had worked with Chicanos in their campus Movimiento Estudiantil Chicano de Aztlán (MEChA) but found it "too hard to work with the guys" and withdrew from members' pervasive homophobia.[58] Otero sharply distinguished the majority of LOC members, who were working class and dated among themselves, from davenport, Díaz, and Retter Vargas, who, Otero asserted, did not hang out with them at Catch One, the African American bar on Pico, and who did date whites.[59] Generally, axes of difference among feminists of color could hinder their work as was true in white-majority groups.

Retter Vargas's approach made more of an impact, in part, because she was more theatrically confrontational. She circulated in print and performance her views on racism, and her style was instructive for the pros and cons of marshalling humor, identification, anger, and pressure. Germain recalled:

> *One* time she was walking around Califia camp with a big white bandage over her eye. . . . And everyone was going up to her and saying, "*Yolanda*, oh my *God*! What *happened* to your eye? How come you've got that *bandage* on your eye?" And she says, "I'm *wearing* this bandage so that I only have to see half of the bullshit that's going on around here!" [laugh] Well it was *those* kind of things, you see, that were *creative* and that had some kind of *humor* to them I really loved.[60]

By eliciting feelings of sympathy, Retter Vargas's display held out the hope of linking a concern for physical well-being to an antiracist interest that was more theoretical to many white women. Using humor was a more acceptable way of raising consciousness about oppression than verbal attacks were because it released tensions while maintaining challenge on a symbolic level.[61] White women's contact with women of color and gradual identification with their concerns at least through comparison (e.g., for Germain, her heightened awareness of homophobia as a lesbian) complemented pointed discussions of racism in ways that the white-only antiracism training had not achieved.

White Califia participants recalled specific components of the antiracism presentations, such as guided fantasies and Retter Vargas's handouts as both transforming and intensely uncomfortable. Guided fantasies sought to point out that white women already had information to relate to racial oppression and further exposed the extent to which they needed to overcome racism. Participants visualized what their homes, work, and clothes would look like if they were another race. They were then taken through situations such as the theft of a coworker's money and trying to exchange a defective item at a department store and asked how coworkers or the sales clerk responded to them. Germain remembered that during discussion afterward, almost everyone had chosen to be black and felt fear and disrespect.[62] In a similar exercise, white women were asked to imagine themselves as white minorities in a land of women of color.[63] Through these kinds of self-teaching, participants could raise their awareness and empathy without necessarily being accused of racism. The fact that most women still thought in terms of black as the symbol for people of color despite the relatively large presence of Latinas at Califia and the number of Asian Americans and American Indians in L.A. indicates the extent to which it was difficult to move white Americans from a binary picture of race relations media emphasized. Empathy alone did not shift values, but it generated recognition of oppression. Since Califia women already had a desire to oppose dominant values, the exercise held potential for initiating individual antiracism actions.

Retter Vargas's presentation handouts took a more confrontational approach to push women beyond the plateaus they had hit and into action. She developed an assessment of where participants were coming from called "First Things First"[64] and a list of common excuses for not doing antiracist work called "The Excuse Closet."[65] Both contained elements of the "Rooting Out Racism" concentration on discomfort with race. "First Things First" was a survey that delved into racial stereotypes, asked about non–Euro-American geographic knowledge, and assessed white women's opinions about the roles that whites and people of color should play in antiracist work. Like the guided fantasy, one of the questions was "If I were not white, my next choice would be _____." Asked about reactions to this question and whether they gave reasons for their choices, Retter Vargas believed that white women drew on their fantasy and then might get slammed or that they hedged their answers depending on whether white women or women of color conducted the survey.[66] Years later, Retter Vargas continued to exhibit deep concern over eroticized race. Among possible interpretations, the choice of an alternate racial identity could have been based on exoticizing fantasy, a desire to experience more or less discrimination that one assumed different groups suffered, an attempt to match one's values to generalizations about other groups' values, or the racism one saw in one's associates.

"The Excuse Closet" sought to short-circuit platitudes that would undermine serious antiracist work. For example, when tensions rose, some would plead, "Why can't we all get along? Aren't we all people under the skin?" Retter Vargas would respond:

> Yes, we are on Thursday. But today is Tuesday. And we have two long days of work, and if you don't do the work between now and then, we're not going to get there. I agree with you, we are. But most of you use "We're all people under the skin" as an escape clause to not work on all the shit that's between Tuesday and Thursday.[67]

The splitting of "we" into an "I" and "you" with a burden of responsibility on the white "you" before returning to a reunited "we" highlights the tenuous nature of interracial antiracist work while reasserting that whites must take responsibility rather than retreat behind utopian visions of sameness that do not reflect real conditions. Retter Vargas explained that the process of ferreting out ingrained racism was very painful and took courage that would not be possible until white women cared as much about racism as they did about feminism or lesbianism.[68] The antiracism presentations followed those on sexism and classism in targeting members of dominant groups as culpable. Participants sometimes experienced presentations as denigrating their identities while expecting them to be supportive of those whose identities society oppressed.

There were a number of impediments to unlearning racism quickly. Frequently white lesbians new to the presentation did not understand why they were being separated from the women of color when everyone was together for the sexism and classism presentations.[69] Once a presenter told them that white people were raised to be racist and confronted them with their unconsciously racist behavior, there was a lot of unresponsiveness, denial, or redirection of emphasis to the anger of the women of color presenters. Rose Green recounted:

> *I'm* sitting on a couch *listening* to that and I thought, "Well, *I* sure as heck am not going to open up my mouth." And then why would I *do* that? To be confronted and attacked like that? So I knew enough, in a sense, to *protect* myself and shut *down* 'cause it didn't *feel* safe.[70]

Some participants recounted incomprehension and defensiveness in the moment but enduring benefits. Raven and Leon were especially cogent on this point. Raven was a militant separatist lesbian eighteen years before he transitioned to be a man. When he attended Califia camp around 1980, he felt attacked in the antiracism presentation and "shut down." In retrospect, he regretted that white attendees focused on Retter Vargas rather than on the feelings that came up and needed to be worked through. Raven attributed defensiveness to denial that lesbianism did not produce instant sisterhood but concluded that even when whites encounter homophobic discrimination, "I'm *still* and will *always have* more privilege than a woman of color." For years, Raven considered questions he learned there about racialized space and friendships: "When you *go* back to your community . . . who do you hang out with regularly? How many women of color do you have as friends? How many white events do you go to?" These questions and further unlearning-racism training led him to be critical of all-white spaces, but at the time as a "baby dyke," he thought, "Why are they *yelling* at us? [laugh] We're all having a good *time* here. Why are you *yelling* at us? Why are you getting so *pissed*?"[71] Narrators were brought up short by the concept that they inhabited a privileged position and contributed to other lesbians' oppression. Leon emphasizes the emotional stakes of working through denial:

> *Whoa! As the oppressor*, we didn't *know*. . . . [T]he *oppressed* people knew how the *oppressor* thought *and* knew how *they* thought, but the *oppressor* group *only* knew how *we* thought. And *all* of a sudden it was kind of *scary* to *realize* that—that there was an *unknown area*. And we were *challenged* to take it on to find *out*, to *become* more *interested*, to participate *more* in maybe a *less* comfortable situation. *But* we weren't made more *comfortable* in order to participate. And so, in *some* ways, I think that *backfired*. . . . The *separation* was being made really, really *extreme*, and, it was almost like a *longer bridge* to *cross*.[72]

The earliest racism presentations split women between oppressor and oppressed in theory, but Leon entered Califia when women of color were sharpening a message that has since further permeated feminist circles. Narrators were startled to perceive "how *much* the women of color *hated* the white women."[73] The combination of naïve assumptions of unity, resistance to being part of an oppressor category, and dismay at the level of hostility exhibited at the presentations slowed change. Nonetheless, narrators remembered what they were called upon to do: initiate an internal system for catching their own racist impulses, learn about and value other cultures, and take the lead in confronting other white people's racist jokes and discrimination.[74]

Retter Vargas's work extended beyond the presentation time to personal altercations and had unintended positive consequences. Germain remembered:

> We don't call her "Yolanda the Terrible" for *nothing*. And she would kick a lot of ass up there. *Boy*, I remember a *time* when she was talking with Betty Brooks. Betty Brooks is the *quintessential* middle-class *woman*. You were always saying, "Jeez Betty! Christ, will you *stop!*" . . . And *I heard Yolanda SCREAMING* and *yelling* and *cursing out* Betty up one side and down the other outdoors. And I was *way* far away. And I said, "Oh my God! What is this horrible *thing* that I'm hearing?" And I was very *curious* about it, which is kind of funny. Why would I be so curious about that? But *I was*, and *I* needed to *know* what was happening, and who was talking. And I came out, and I kept going closer and closer, and I saw *who* it was and *what* was going on. And I don't remember exactly what all the *words* were, but Betty was really getting her butt kicked. . . . And everything she said was being turned *around* you see.
>
> And I said to myself, "*You know*, I finally found a woman that's angrier than *I* am. And still she's not a maniac, and still she's not killing anybody. So *maybe my* anger is not what I thought was *endless*. It does come to a kind of a [laugh] a boundary, and it's just a little bit shy of *this woman's* boundary." And I said, "*Terrific! Great!*" To tell you the *truth*, I felt a whole lot *better*.

By Germain's account, a grave concern to hide how angry she was all the time underlay her need to know what was happening. She tried to hold herself back for fear her rage would explode into violence. Retter Vargas's ability to articulate anger and pain verbally reassured Germain that anger could be directed constructively without devolving into physical violence. Retter Vargas's productive closing became something to emulate:

> And *after all* of *this* the most *remarkable* thing happened in *my* estimation, which was after Yolanda had stopped telling Betty everything that was on her mind, she said, "You *know*, Betty," she says, "I'm *telling* you this because it *hurts* me. I'm *hurt* by this. I want to tell you about my *hurt*." And I thought, "Wow!" Now this is something! And this is *real*, and this is *smart* and *clever* because it isn't "Betty, I want to tell you that I've been scream-

ing at you because I *love* you." That would be such terrible *bullshit*, I would have *puked* right there. But what's *real*, and what's *clear* and what's *good* is that she said, "What's *behind* all this, Betty, is that you're *hurting* me. And you're *hurting* other people, and this is how you're *doing* it." And I was going, man, *wow*, that's some pretty *terrific, powerful stuff*! And I *loved* it. You see why I *love* Califia because there was no namby-pamby kind of bullshit.[75]

The presence of women of color at Califia heightened accusations of racism, including some directed at a founder of the group. Women of color's per-spectives helped to advance antiracist work in eye-opening ways for white participants. The three spokeswomen, however, felt that they were living the racism that was the impetus for their antiracist interventions.

Retter Vargas was representative of Díaz and davenport in believing that "the racism workshop didn't do any good, didn't do *enough* good. . . . the emotional price was too high." Women of color who did not attend the antiracism presentations, in contrast, thought the time was constructive.[76] Four feminists of color who gave a group interview agreed that women of color were expressly given the option not to attend, so they did not have to become examples for the white women. Women of color set up a separate meeting during the antiracism presentation to provide time together away from racist stereotypes and ignorance that arose during the presentations. Soto and others who had attended the presentation before would tell new-comers, "You know what, I would recommend that you don't go. But if you want to, go check it out."[77] Meeting away from white women left them feeling "connected" and "flying high." When white women and women of color came back together after the presentation, the dynamics of the camp changed. Not only did women of color feel bonded, but Donna Gó-mez (pseudonym) and West credited white women for trying to implement what they had learned by showing extra courtesy. Soto agreed that "sitting next to a white woman you'd never talked to before," there would be break-throughs after the presentations.[78] In retrospect, Soto, Gomez, and West recognized that Retter Vargas, Díaz, and davenport were angry and burnt-out from their antiracism work. They did what other women of color would not do and were equipped through their class background and formal edu-cation to identify with more privileged white attendees. Meanwhile, women like West, Gomez, and Soto benefited, looked forward to the workshop, and welcomed the dialogue that ensued. Eventually women of color collec-tive members compiled years of mailing lists and formed a Women of Color Network from which to create more women of color–only space.[79]

ETHNIC AWARENESS

After four years of presentations that bifurcated women into a monolithic white category and women of color (epitomized by African Americans), Jewish and biracial Califia women complicated assumptions of identical white experience. In doing so, they pushed feminists to looks at nuances of ethnic discrimination, but women of color mostly did not embrace arguments that could obscure the privileges that being labeled white conferred.

Jewish organizing reflected ways in which work on racism in lesbian communities nationwide sparked discussion about anti-Semitism.[80] In 1981, a Jewish women's SEA started to present workshops at Califia.[81] They planned to debunk myths about Jewish control over money and power and to dissect anti-Semitic remarks like "Gee, you don't look Jewish."[82] They associated what it means to "look" Jewish with voluntary and involuntary "race-passing." Jews of Eastern European descent vary in the degree to which they display a cluster of phenotypic traits associated with Ashkenazi Jews. This variation in combination with the degree to which others in a given community are aware of stereotypical markers makes it more or less difficult to stand out as "Jewish looking."[83] Members concluded, "In trying to define 'anti-Semitism' and 'Jew,' we began to question the validity of the 'concept of race.'" They rejected the other extreme that Jewish identity is religious adherence to Judaism and stressed that Jewish identity is ethnicity because members of the group all identified as Jewish despite adhering to a spectrum of beliefs from atheism to paganism, Christian Science, or Zen Buddhism. Opposition to identifying as a race is consistent with post-Holocaust thought while Jewish ethnicity follows the propensity of many white Califians to play up their ethnic identity alongside or instead of their whiteness.

Beyond the period of Califia, antiracism training distinguished between whiteness as unearned privilege and ethnicity as cultural roots. United States history includes discrimination against ethnic immigrants who, by the late twentieth century were all considered white: people of Irish, French, Germanic, Italian, and Slavic descent for example. Descendants of these groups may feel cultural pride in language, food, and customs specific to their ethnicity. Once recognized as "white," however, they gained legal standing and social privileges not afforded to those who were labeled nonwhite. In the 1980s, white ethnics still struggled to explain the dual position of white-skinned privilege and anti-ethnic biases such as anti-Semitism or anti–French Canadian sentiment in New England.

Jewish participants' memories of women of color denying that Jewish ethnicity counted in the racism equation are fraught with resentment. Looking at ethnicity could productively complicate conversations about discrimination but could also derail antiracism training by refocusing on white people's hardships. Jewish SEA members related assimilation to internalized anti-Semitism and lauded their "unwillingness to convert to Christianity or to assimilate totally into any given culture," which spoke to ethnicity rather than whiteness. They touched on the history and psychological dynamics of black-Jewish relations in the United States, citing common oppressions, positive aspects such as Jewish participation in passing civil rights legislation, and their assertion that "Jewish and black women are alike in that we are strong and matriarchal." Since minutes of their meeting reflect a brainstorming stage, it is not possible to know which ideas the Jewish group presented, but Retter Vargas had already dismissed resting on past accomplishments as an excuse for not doing continued antiracist work.[84] Women of color resisted comparisons between Jewish identity and racial minority status that decontextualized experiences and deflected attention from white-skinned privilege.[85]

Califia reflects the ways in which the stakes could be higher for Jewish lesbians. The history of the civil rights movement involved close work between Jewish Americans and African Americans. Ambivalence and distrust, however, arose from other aspects of black-Jewish relations—anti-Semitic comments by black Christian and Muslim leaders, the use of racism by Jewish Americans to assert their white privilege, and research published at that time implicating Jewish-Americans in the slave trade. Simultaneously, writers like Cherríe Moraga felt positively linked to Jews while comparing Jewish and black genocide. Barbara Smith agreed and characterized black-Jewish relations as expecting more from each other than either group expected from non-Jewish whites or gentiles generally.[86] Jewish Califia attendees were part of a nationwide feminist push to expose anti-Semitism and complicate racial identity with ethnicity.

White Jewish women's arguments of analogous oppression rang hollow to women of color in the context of presentations about white-skin privilege. Those who could not pass as white were also frequently uninterested in the predicament of light-skinned Latinas who were frustrated at being read as white. Barbara Forrest, a blonde-haired, blue-eyed Mexican American, strove to heighten awareness of mixed heritage and the "colorist" privileging of dark complexions among women of color. Because the women of color networking time was mostly social, Barbara lamented that "we [women of color] didn't deal with a lot of the internal -isms, you know, colorism, racism, whatever, among *ourselves*."[87] Retter Vargas and Díaz supported Forrest about biculturalism, but other women of color continued to interpret her insistence on inclusion as a diversion when racial lines were drawn based on whether people saw one as white.[88] The differing experience of Pam Chavez Hutson corroborated Forrest's. Although Hutson also was Hispanic through both parents, a white woman with a Hispanic husband adopted her and raised her with "a very conservative white middle-class background" that never discussed race.[89] Hutson came to Califia as part of her coming out process after a marriage and children and stressed eight times that "color was not an issue for me at that point in my life."[90] Soto's rejoinder after the third time was:

> And Pam was great. She kept saying, "You know, color's not, has never been an issue for me." At every workshop, "You know color's not an issue for me." And we'd look at her, the rest of the women of color, and we'd say, "Poor baby." [laughter] Come sit with us. [laughter]

Other women of color both welcomed Hutson and wanted her to raise her consciousness about race by attending the antiracism presentation. Hutson said she was not accepted as a woman of color because she did not identify as one until the end of Califia. At that point, when others said she should not be in women of color–only space, she started pushing the issue, "Wait a minute. Why are you telling me I'm not a woman of color? My father's name was Chavez, and my skin is brown, and I don't know where you think this came from, but. . . ."[91] Nonetheless, Hutson got a very different reception from Forrest in self-segregated spaces because she did not push hard for inclusion.

Bicultural ties also helped to explain tensions between women of color antiracism presenters at Califia and their racialized communities. Segregation and discrimination was significant in L.A. at large and among lesbians during the 1970s and 1980s.[92] Aside from very limited connections between Califia and LOC, most white-majority groups and women of color groups lacked coalition or sustained communication, and many radical women of color agreed that educating white women on racism distracted from their energies. The same strategies propounded by antiracism training guides led radical women of color who valued separatism not to appreciate the labor that women like Díaz, Retter Vargas, davenport, and the women of color collective members expended for Califia. The presenters had personal interests in forming a racially inclusive feminist community. Retter Vargas's biracial identity, the middle-class status of the presenters, gender separatist politics, cross-racial relationships, and the standing they gained as spokeswomen may have facilitated their interest in trying to forge a cross-cultural women's movement by attacking racism. These factors differentiated them and some of the leading women of color at Califia from their racially segregationist sisters, leading to criticism that they were not representative of women of color who focused on empowering other lesbians of color.[93]

FROM CR TO WWAR

Committed white Califia women rose to the challenge to address racism in the Los Angeles and San Francisco areas. They turned a SEA group into White Women Against Racism (WWAR) in the fall of 1979 and then reestablished that L.A. branch along with a northern one at Califia's first Bay Area camp in August 1980.[94] Their CR support meetings and initial antiracism workshop in the fall of 1979 occurred alongside others' antiracism workshops (e.g., the Lesbian Task Force of NOW in 1980) and individually led CR groups. Díaz and Retter Vargas credited LOC for persuasively pressuring white women to organize. Califia's climate and Retter Vargas's challenges to "wishy-washy white women" directly led to WWAR's formation.[95] L.A.–area WWAR members gained recruits through advertising and the weekly column they wrote in *The Lesbian News*.[96] They divided their time between providing a space for their members to get support about racism and doing presentations at schools, community colleges, and feminist sites, making them one of few active grassroots forces educating the public about racism.

Some white women derided WWAR as ineffectual or mired in internal politics.[97] Otero remembered the crowd at the L.A. gay and lesbian parade mocking a small WWAR contingent around 1984. She thought:

> [T]hese women were *truly* undervalued in the gay and lesbian community and just seemed like *outcasts* because they were trying to raise an issue that nobody wanted to listen to. . . . They weren't just concentrating on the gay community; they were doing it in the straight community, and I think *that* was really important work.[98]

While Otero, who had no interest in educating white women, approved of their work, criticism of WWAR came from those who did not want to read WWAR's moralizing tone and those with a stake in antiracist education at a time when not much work was being done. A positive portrayal of WWAR spread beyond California in antiracism circles. After moving from

L.A. in 1986, Bencangey attended an antiracism workshop in Atlanta that mainly drew East Coast and southeastern participants. An Atlanta man not only knew of WWAR, he caught her up on her organization's activities.[99] WWAR had been joined by a much wider circle of writings and presentations trying to interrupt racism in order to create a more harmonious society.[100]

COMPROMISING ON BREAD-AND-BUTTER ISSUES

Given how large a focus race relations were in Califia's middle years, it is not surprising that continuing differences over food became framed as a racial issue, and women of color similarly contested white assumptions behind entertainment choices. As new women sat down at the table with other Califia participants, the vegetarian fare continued to generate dissent. The presentation defending vegetarianism as feminist remained unintelligible despite the possibilities for posing vegetarianism as a way to redress world malnutrition, global environmental problems, imperialism in the service of corporate greed, American health concerns, and a speeded up culture. The solution that Califia meal planners found is a telling example of what was and was not too essential to compromise.

Nationally, the vegetarian counterculture linked to racial politics, but at Califia, women of color contested the menu as all "white people's food" while omnivores across race rejected vegetarianism. The debates over food at the camps illustrate the breadth of behavioral changes feminism would need to be holistic. Counterculture vegetarians captured the allure of good racial politics in the phrase "Don't eat white; eat right; and fight." Warren J. Belasco explained:

> Whiteness meant Wonder Bread, White Tower [hamburgers], Cool Whip, Minute Rice, instant mashed potatoes, peeled apples, . . . white collar, whitewash, White House, white racism. Brown meant whole wheat bread, unhulled rice, turbinado sugar, wildflower honey, unsulfured molasses, soy sauce, peasant yams, "black is beautiful."

Contemporary cookbooks like the famous vegetarian *Moosewood Cookbook* from 1977 eclectically mixed dishes from Asia (China, Japan, Vietnam, India), the Middle East, the Mediterranean, Eastern Europe, Mexico, and Brazil. African American "soul food" was vastly underrepresented, perhaps because southern cooking in general often included animal products.[101] Despite multiculturalism in the vegetarian movement nationally, Califia collective members around 1980 seem not to have known these recipes. "The bland food of white folks," complained davenport, "is legendary."[102] When collective members suggested adding "some tortillas . . . salsa and a little of this and a little of that," representatives advocating for different menus balked at the tokenism, demanding serious changes.[103] This led to an impasse; white cooks did not have recipes, and the women of color were divided as to whether taking on further kitchen duties would empower them or demote them to kitchen servants. Dominant food standards governed vegetarians' and women of color's competing calls for reform. The meat industry and assimilation campaigns against Mexican and Asian immigrants since the turn of the century had called on Americans to substitute white bread and meat for more nutritious traditional foods.

Resistance eventually beat back ideals. Disgruntled carnivores across racial backgrounds snuck in meat and lobbied for meat on their evaluation forms. West, Hutson, Raven, and Bernstein laughingly recounted women making car runs down from camp by the fourth or fifth day in search of hamburgers.[104] Leon related:

> I *do* remember the *cook* coming out with a McDonald's wrapper in her hand *FURIOUS*, just *furious*, and throwing the wrapper down on the ground and being *SO highly* insulted that anybody would go *out* of the camp and bring *meat in* [laugh]. And that, *that* was kind of a . . . *fun* one for me 'cause . . . my *father's* been vegetarian all his life, and the whole vegetarian *issue* is such a *scene.* . . . And somehow that was *obvious* at that time that that was the *feminist* thing to do. . . . It was *obvious*, but it wasn't obvious [pause] to *some* people. So I think, *maybe* there were some meat dishes served. . . . [T]he cook with the McDonald's wrapper did *not* want to make any. . . . She was *strongly* vegetarian, and it was part of the way she was changing the *world*. And there was no *way* they were going to get *her* to make a meatloaf for *meat*-eaters.[105]

Leon may have understood the philosophy behind vegetarianism and its connection to progressive political movements, but Raven remembered the same incident without ever connecting eating meat to supporting patriarchy.

As each week progressed, tensions heightened among women immersed in discussions of racism, classism, and sexism, and emotions began to explode. Collective members one year planned a chicken dinner at midweek with ice cream for dessert and a big dance. That dramatically reduced conflicts. Weiss laughingly swore that the combination of comfort food, including meat, and letting loose to music soothed people and paved the way for healing rifts that had formed so that women could go on to work together.[106] Jetter agreed there were continuous complaints until meat was presented as a side dish.[107] Brooks concurred:

> [A]nd so I'm telling you the people who were not *vegetarian* were having *fits* until we got that chicken in. . . . But people even wanted to make it have a little more *meat* there rather than just complete vegetarian, [laugh] and . . . at the *meetings* at night [laugh], these things were always brought *up*. And, of course, our answer . . . is so funny. I mean, you know, it's like you can say to the kids, "OK, you can't make it, so we'll let you cheat on it. You just bring your own *stuff* and keep it in your *cabin*," you know. I mean [laugh], it's just *horrible*. And that's . . . the *gift* of Califia. We *tried* to take on *all* these wonderful ideas about how to change the world.[108]

A combination of majority pressure and lack of resolve that vegetarianism held political importance continued to override purist vegetarians' objections. Raising "*all* these wonderful ideas" generated a climate of optimistic empowerment and a snowball effect of adding more ideas for change, but women hit a breaking point for understanding and integrating change into their lives within greater society.

High-energy dances dissipated hostilities,[109] but tensions over the kind of music played for dances at Califia extended racial generalizations. According to davenport, white women could not dance, and white music was unpleasantly undanceable and fostered lackluster parties that rival wakes.[110] Bernstein related that African American women and Chicanas criticized a camp in the 1980s for excluding music from their cultures. Because of her interest in Spanish-language music, Bernstein had brought tapes with Latino music, but she was the only white woman who had multicultural music. Unlike the food issue, where a paid cook and women on kitchen duty made the meals, an Asian American woman had volunteered to bring her sound equipment and records to the camp. In the midst of the uproar over representation, she packed up and left. Bernstein was fascinated that this D.J. had not been exposed to nor thought to bring any other kind of music, with its implications for how the music industry and a lot of women's music replicated whiteness.[111] This sole mention in interviews[112] of an Asian American woman during the first seven years of Califia and her hasty disappearance from a scene of contestation among black, Chicana, and white women is also a telling reminder of ways in which racial composition retained a majoritizing element.

In the 1970s and 1980s, when American society continued to struggle with desegregation in practice, Califia was part of a vanguard of feminists who taught women to unlearn racism to promote integrated work. After multiracial civil rights work in the 1960s, most groups had resegregated by either choice or inability to recruit women of color. When Califia founders created white-led antiracism presentations, they placed the burden of antiracism education on whites and produced a tame presentation that raised consciousness without producing vigorous work to integrate Califia. Women of color and white supporters who had a personal stake, such as close relationships to women of color, volunteered to do much of the recruiting that integrated the group. This work provided the candidates to make the collective 50 percent women of color as those women had demanded. For Califia, being part of the feminist movement's reincorporation of racial inclusion included a much tougher antiracism presentation run by women of color. Tensions at that presentation and presenters' expectations for white women to purge racist behavior from themselves quickly and fully led to burnout among the presenters and a combination of long-term upset and enduringly transformed perspectives for audience members. The presentations unintentionally raised the issue of the diversity in experience of white-skin privilege for Jewish and bicultural minorities. In contrast to the presenters, women of color who were not part of the antiracism training saw improvements in white women's attitudes and appreciated the time to network and discuss internalized racism among themselves. For all that the middle period of Califia was fraught with conflict, women were still willing to struggle with complexities in order to attain their ideal of an integrated feminist community. The community would be challenged further by external attacks from nationally recognized New Right leaders and policies as well as from internal disagreements over which alliances were most ideologically consistent and needed.

CHAPTER 6

THE RIGHT ATTACKS AND INTERNAL DIVISIONS

A NUMBER OF CALIFIA WOMEN have said that conservative attacks, combined with emphases on assimilation and individual gain among gay and lesbian Americans, portended the end of Califia. This chapter argues that Califia conferences waned because of a combination of key founders' departures, societal shifts that imperiled increasing numbers of Americans economically, and differences of opinion among feminists. New Right members attacked one founder while others turned to different projects. Neoliberal attempts to defund social services and public education hampered grassroots progressive organizing generally, and feminist educating outside universities specifically, by the mid-1980s. Established leaders in Califia collided with some multicultural feminists of color at and beyond Califia. Meanwhile, many lesbians in a broader Los Angeles scene shied away from separatist feminist politics in favor of work with gay men and/ or pursuit of recreation. Although the intractability of racism in the United States was a factor in Califia's faltering, Califia became a local model for organizing conference retreats and lesbians of color groups.

After Ronald Reagan's election to the presidency, federal politicians supported neoliberal goals of shifting resources from individual Americans to big business. Congress undercut the Johnson-era "war on poverty" by reducing the tax base for social services, cutting welfare programs during a recession, and opposing workers' collective bargaining. Tax restructuring gave the wealthiest elites a 5 percent increase in disposable income while the poorest Americans lost 15 percent. Congress privatized state-owned enterprises, deregulated businesses, financed the military through deficit spending, and ignored AIDS.[1] Before 1986 there was almost no federal investment in managing the AIDS epidemic. Reagan's budget gutted funding for the Centers for Disease Control, which prevented the CDC from combating AIDS with millions of dollars similar to what the federal government had poured into addressing a 1976 outbreak of Legionnaires disease that killed 29 American Legion veterans.[2] Gay activist groups raised funds to find medical ways to manage HIV's assault on the immune system. Gay and lesbian Americans started hospice services, political action groups, and direct action protests. The necessity for private citizens to address the pandemic inadvertently siphoned resources from some feminist activity.[3]

BETTY BROOKS BESIEGED

New Right gains imperiled social movements as well as public health and economic well-being. A controversy that ended Brooks's participation in Califia illustrates the ruinous effects the New Right had on countercultural individuals' lives and the movements in which they worked nationwide.[4] By 1982, only three original collective members continued to organize Califia. Betty Brooks, Marilyn Murphy, and Janet Stambolian had seven years of continuous experience. Irene Weiss had four years on the collective while the other eleven members were in their first or second years.

In 1982, Brooks was again fighting for her career. Conservative Christians extended their purview from the 1978 John Briggs Proposition 6 focus on lower education to the university system in 1982. Brooks was among those in their sights. New Right supporters attempted to destroy Women's Studies programs and campus women's centers as spaces that discussed feminism and lesbianism. These Christian Right members justified their actions with appeals to "traditional family values," claims of accountability to taxpayers or academic rigor, and denial that sexism needed to be addressed in society. The attacks highlighted the need to support feminism within the university system, the usefulness of feminist alternative educational sites outside mainstream society's financial and hierarchical constraints, and the dual position many feminists held within the academy and the community.

During the spring term in 1982 at California State University at Long Beach (CSULB), a small group of born-again Christian women pushed to reverse feminist influences on higher education. Differing with Brooks over the roles of religion and feminism, they targeted her and her introductory-level course "Women and Their Bodies." Brooks had witnessed Grace Brethren Church's student group members labeling pro-choice advocates "sinners" and gays and lesbians "sick" at their meetings. With her history of commitment to Christianity as emancipatory and to fighting male bias, she spoke out. Her subsequent public arguments with the group's campus preacher further riled Grace Brethren parishioners.[5] Part-time student Jessica Reynolds Shaver, her friend JoEllen Allen, and others claimed that Brooks's courses had a "lesbian emphasis," Women's Studies courses wrongly failed to espouse "traditional American values," and a women's center director named Denise Wheeler was at fault for declining to display their literature against ratifying a constitutional amendment to guarantee gender equality during the last year of the ERA campaign. Shaver and Allen first complained to the dean for educational policy and to Women's Studies Director Dr. Sondra Hale. Shaver proposed that Hale hire Allen as a "traditionalist" instructor and that the program include courses on marriage and the family. Women's Studies already offered home economics and a course called "Mothers and Daughters," but the curriculum reflected founding principles of Women's Studies programs as the "academic arm of the feminist movement."[6] In an interview with the student newspaper, Shaver argued in favor of traditional courses:

> I'd just like to see a lot of enthusiasm for the traditional family. . . .
>
> It didn't come naturally for me to be a homemaker. But instead of becoming a feminist, I became a Christian.
>
> The extreme feminist viewpoint which I see reflected in the textbooks used in Women's Studies is against male leadership in society and in the home and that male leadership was given by God.

Shaver claimed to want "balanced" discussion of all sides but would "like to see [the Women's Studies Program] eliminated if it's going to continue as it is."[7] Initially, fundamentalist activism used university channels to try to infuse their particular interpretations of Christianity into the state university.

Tapping into the swelling New Right movement provided the power to influence administrators. The initial protesting group wrote to conservative organizations and legislators, and by spring break, their ranks included the state chair of Eagle Forum, a national group founded by a leading antifeminist named Phyllis Schlafly. Aides to Republican Senators Ollie Speraw and Bill Richardson and Assemblyman Dennis Brown promised help. Attorney Thomas Burton represented the Eagle Forum and added this case to his record of attacking sex education in the public schools and the California Commission on the Status of Women.[8] According to the American Civil Liberties Union (ACLU) Women's Rights Project, this coalition pressured university administrators with threats of budgetary cuts.[9] University President Steven Horn, Academic Affairs Vice President Glendon Drake, Associate Vice President John Haller, and Social and Behavioral Sciences Dean Simeon Crowther met with them and agreed to a curriculum review for "Women and Their Bodies." The review was favorable, but

Shaver pursued matters with the support of Senator Speraw's office. Over the next months, despite the positive curriculum review, CSULB canceled Brooks's well-enrolled summer classes and notified her that her fall courses were being withdrawn. The dean of continuing education, Donna George, removed Brooks's name from catalogue listings for four courses she had regularly taught during her seven years there. Citing "substantial pressure at every level above [himself]," Crowther suspended Hale and revoked the Women's Studies Advisory Committee's established authority to hire teachers and determine qualifications.[10]

Accusations capitalized on traditional definitions of professionalism that excluded academic discussions of sexuality or social movement ties. An anonymous female student claimed that Brooks had shown the class "six close-up slides of male and female genitalia, one of which she (Brooks) said was of herself" and "[s]he showed films of people masturbating. There were films of couples having sex, including one of group sex, one of male homosexuals, and two of lesbian couples having sex."[11] Another charged that a guest lecturer "partially stripped in class to demonstrate a pelvic examination." Murphy wrote that the collective had scheduled Brooks "to show slides from her 'Women and Their Bodies' course" as part of Califia's 1980 sexism presentation with Germain, so slides similar to "cunt slides" may have been in the course. Brooks created them when professionally produced sex education materials were often not yet available.[12]

Associate Vice President Haller deployed the rhetoric of academic rigor as the binary opposite of courses with social movement influences. CSULB's one-unit weekend extension courses included basic self-defense based on Brooks's physical education field and another on women's sexuality from Brooks's Women's Studies specialization. Haller attacked both among programs he claimed "weakened [Women's Studies] by personal awareness classes that are throwbacks to the early 1970s." Claiming a need for academic rigor, this historian imagined a story of pure progress for social justice:

> For years these programs had this siege mentality . . . having to justify themselves to people and also trying to sensitize people to a need for such a program. I suppose that was all well and good because it served a function. But they need to go beyond that sensitizing and awareness approach to tough academic programs.[13]

Haller's interpretation made three assumptions: sensitizing people to societal problems could not be compatible with academic discourse, the courses lacked rigor, and all courses should conform to an unspecified "tough" standard regardless of department, number of credits, or target audience. A self-defense course that would be appropriate for Brooks's initial department (physical education) could not conform to Haller's field or perspective. Sexuality studies generally were too cutting-edge for history departments in the early 1980s.

In contrast to Haller's narrative, core faculty member Sherna Gluck's statement maintained that antifeminism and male-centrism remained immediate problems:

> The attack on feminists and on women's studies comes as no surprise in the current political climate. We are witnessing the systematic dismantling of all efforts that have been developed over the past decade-and-a-half to remedy social, economic, and political injustice: the ERA has been defeated, desegregation of schools halted, and reproductive rights attacked. What is a surprise is that a small group of religious bigots have met so little resistance from the University Administration. They seem to have easily succeeded in undermining our right to teach Women's Studies; our right to challenge the basically misogynistic perspective of all disciplines.[14]

As though feminist pedagogies and services had outlived their usefulness, the vice president and associate vice president announced plans to "restructure" the Women's Studies Program and alter the women's center. They replaced the women's center with a center for the continuing education of women, merged that with an adult reentry program, and reduced basic services such as rape victim and sexual harassment counseling that had been central.[15]

Dismantling ways the women's center addressed violence against women threatened to roll back feminist services on campus. "Restructuring" Women's Studies raised the question of academic freedom. The ACLU filed a lawsuit on behalf of the Women's Studies Advisory Committee, core faculty, and students on August 4, 1982, charging the unsympathetic CSULB administrators violated First and Fourteenth Amendment rights respecting academic freedom, due process, equal protection, and sex discrimination. University officials capitulated by reappointing Hale and rehiring Brooks for the fall semester after she underwent "sensitivity" training. They permitted the vaginal exam to remain in the course. The dean, however, retained control of the program.[16] Shaver vowed to gather more complaints against Brooks. Senator Speraw appealed to a myth of "objectivity" conservatives applied to progressives rather than themselves. He argued, "I think that when she's an avowed homosexual she loses her objectivity about the subject matter and then in theory she's an unfit teacher."[17] The ACLU pursued the case and amended it to include Brooks as a plaintiff who alleged sex discrimination, which set a precedent that influenced responses to attacks on academic feminists also occurring at Stanford, Berkeley, and UC Santa Cruz.[18]

While ACLU attorney Susan McGrievy constructed a case for individuals' legally guaranteed freedoms, Phyllis Schlafly and other evangelicals portrayed Brooks's work and feminism as state-supported perversions that should be purged to better society.[19] Schlafly editorialized under the dual headlines "It's Time Taxpayers Find Out What Universities Are Doing" and "ACLU Leaps to the Defense of Lesbianism Course." First she addressed the problem of using "women" as a euphemism for "feminist":

> The women's studies program . . . was pawned off on an unsuspecting university as something to benefit all women.
> The female faculty, however, converted it to a program to promote radical feminist-lesbian women's goals and values to the exclusion of traditional women's goals and values.[20]

Feminists believed that they benefit all women, and founding faculty in 1973—rather than later members—took feminism as their interpretive lens while recognizing that there were internal debates over that word. From the late 1960s, racial power movements created ethnic studies programs that incorporated liberation politics for analysis instead of relying on perspectives that assumed whiteness. Likewise, feminists initiated the academic study of women with feminist analyses to redress the sexism of previous methods. A CSULB Women's Studies faculty member wrote the founding preamble to the National Women's Studies Association Constitution of 1977, tightly linking her academic field with feminism:

> Women's Studies owes its existence to the movement for the liberation of women; the feminist movement exists because women are oppressed. . . .
> The uniqueness of Women's Studies has been and remains its refusal to accept sterile divisions between academy and community, between the growth of the mind and the health of the body, between intellect and passion, between the individual and society. . . . Women's Studies . . . is equipping women not only to enter society as whole, as productive human beings, but to transform the world to one that will be free of all oppression.[21]

Feminists tried to connect numerous issues, issues often seen as separate, and responded to hostile stereotypes against feminism by adopting the more neutral term Women's Studies.

In a move that continuously haunted the women's movement, Schlafly wedded feminism to pornography and to sexual acts she deemed to be perverse. She labeled feminist books about sexuality, relationships, and lesbianism pornographic, claiming that like a domino effect "they advise women how to become lesbians and to engage in every type of perverted sex, including group sex, orgies, bestiality, sadomasochism and bondage." Brooks's experience as a target of the Right led her to recognize that because anti-sex cultural conservatives generalized sexual representations as "pornography," "feminists cannot be on the side of the anti-pornographers. To be on that side is to put us with the Right."[22] This position pitted Brooks against MacKinnon and Dworkin's attempts to legislate against pornography and against groups like WAVAW, WAVPM, and WAP. Brooks headed FACT in southern California by 1985 to fight the L.A. antipornography ordinance, which had been drafted with MacKinnon's help by the County Commission on the Status of Women.[23] Schlafly concluded that taxpayers should inform themselves about how state funds were used, lest they support extremism and perversion.[24] Local evangelicals echoed her by trying to rally Californians with a petition against Women's Studies titled "Taxpayers for Academic Responsibility Petition."

The CSULB case was one example of conservative troops in an ongoing cultural war seeking an academic podium. National media attention, pressure from state legislators, and local church activism probably influenced CSULB's dean to prolong conflict by changing the hiring criteria to deny Brooks's rehiring in 1984.

Feminists like Brooks promoted experiential learning in the academy and in nonuniversity feminist groups like Califia and her self-defense courses. Feminist techniques filtered into universities as nonhierarchical, experiential, student-focused learning. Throughout Brooks's trials, Califia women wrote letters of support, listened regularly to KPFK Pacifica radio interviews with Brooks, and talked about the threat of the Right at camps.[25] They and other area feminists represented the dual strategy of providing feminist education within mainstream university structures and through alternative community channels. Part-time faculty frequently bridged the academy and the community. Within three years after the initial attack, "all part-time faculty associated with teaching women's sexuality, health issues, self-examination, or the course on the lesbian were pushed out . . .

by the dean." The ACLU emphasized the injustice that all of the fired Women's Studies teachers were lesbian, framing the suit as "a classic case of the Right's confrontation with radical lesbian feminism."[26] Brooks successfully won back pay and reinstatement but continued to receive harassment and threats to her job until she retired. Conservative politicians bent on defunding public education, administrators, students, and parents continued to threaten feminist academic programs nationwide for their unconventional pedagogy and discussions of sexuality and autonomy through the 1990s and into the 2000s.[27]

PERSONAL AND POLITICAL FALLOUT OVER CUSTODY

Meanwhile, a custody battle that diverted Murphy and Weiss's attention polarized feminists across the country. Murphy's youngest sister, Sharon, fled the Bay Area with her son after alleging in court that her ex-husband repeatedly beat her before and after their divorce and verbally, emotionally, and legally harassed her while they shared custody. Murphy's sister struggled for custody against the son of a high-profile feminist of color. The conflict played out in the mainstream and feminist press as well as through legal channels and private information gathering. The ex-husband and his mother characterized the Murphy sister as a racist, man-hating lesbian who, therefore, was unfit to raise a biracial male child.[28] The accusations brought to the fore fissures within feminism around race, sexual orientation, family loyalties, and disbelief when women identify as battered. The case also revealed the negative attitudes that courts and law enforcement held toward low-income lesbian mothers and radical feminism.

The conflict extended into Califia camp and participants' lives. Murphy wrote that an undercover private detective attended the July 1982 Califia Community to discover her sister's whereabouts. Murphy's research found that the detective agency used San Diego FBI connections and legal council to obtain welfare, food stamp, and school district records and local, state, and police intelligence files. Although a Freedom of Information Act request yielded no FBI records on Califia Community, the use of FBI information fit a pattern of FBI surveillance of progressive organizations. In 1983, detectives subpoenaed telephone records of Murphy, Germain, and a number of friends. They delivered letters to Murphy relatives, Califia women, and other friends in three states, which accused them of the federal offense of withholding information.[29] Germain remembered the ex-husband's mother calling her directly with the same threat.[30] An ex-lover of Murphy's sister informed on her in 1985. During the ensuing case, the court rejected photographic records of medical treatment for physical abuse and expert testimony and affidavits supporting the Murphy sister's depiction of herself as a battered woman.[31] She lost custody, and only saw her son under supervision.

Like Brooks, Marilyn Murphy and Weiss worked on the collective through the 1983 camps and then left Califia amid tumult in their lives. They continued feminist work through other venues. Murphy and Weiss advertised a feminist education program from their home in 1983 and then Murphy continued to write her "Lesbianic Logic" column when they did extended retirement travel.[32] They only attended subsequent Califia camps as paying registrants, which left the group in the hands of long-time attendees and new recruits.

WOMEN OF COLOR SPACES

Despite turmoil for established collective members, energetic younger members helped to expand Califia in 1982 to host its first Women of Color Califia Community. The seven women of color in the fourteen-member collective organized a four-day May event at a JCA camp by Malibu for a retreat "for feminist women to nurture, heal and educate each other."[33] The brochure retained the emphasis on sexism, racism and class and "the power of women to positively change their own lives and the world. . . ." Collective members advertised "an enormous potential in using a setting like Califia (feminist, woman-centered and spiritual), to create a unique experience of sisterhood and bonding among women of color." They knew that some radical feminists of color scorned Califia as hopelessly white despite years of integration work. The brochure conceded that the camp for women of color "was conceived by women who had attended past Califia camps and found them lacking in presentations and issues that were critical to their life experiences. Out of that concern, a statewide network was established and the Women of Color Califia Camp is now a reality. Join us!"[34]

In 1981, a feminist of color support, education, and action (SEA) group had formed the Women of Color Network. Califia occasionally held a session in the Bay Area, so the network became statewide and assembled a mailing list to encourage women of color to return. They got money from the regular Califia for the 1982 camp.[35] Their biggest challenges were coordinating with the collective and encouraging women of color resistant to Califia to come to one exclusively for women of color. The twenty members of the network who worked over the next year represented Latina, black, Chinese, and Japanese women. They recruited in other groups they attended such as LOC (which held its own retreats 1978–1983) and Gay and Lesbian Latinos Unidos (GLLU, formed in 1981). Attempts to contact American Indian women only became successful when they received a Native American women's mailing list and had northern California participants raising consciousness about native rights.[36] Network women faced resistance from women in their racial communities who saw Califia as white, insufficiently radical, and ineffective at addressing racism.[37] Some had attended a past Califia camp and vowed never to return. "Was the Network a front? Were the collective members sellouts? There were deep wounds in the women's movement—wounds that had opened and not been allowed to heal."[38] While trying to encourage women of color to participate in a Califia without whites but including bicultural women, network members also dealt with the Califia collective. Women of color collective members had to negotiate among "obstructionist" white collective members who wanted a collective member present at network meetings as they were at Jewish SEA group meetings, Califia women of color who split over whether to accept Califia money, and non-Califia women hostile to Califia sponsorship.[39] Despite these problems, network members used Califia funds for a camp that tried to better meet the needs of feminists of color.

The more than eighty women and their children at the Women of Color Califia camp followed a basic Califia event schedule but allowed flexibility in participation, which met with both appreciation and criticism.[40] There were presentations on feminism and class, as well as a political workshop led by Díaz and Retter Vargas "to identify, discuss and work in-depth on issues that separate us from one another."[41] West remembered a lot of talk about internalized racism while Soto remembered racial prejudice as problematic.[42] Other workshops tackled sterilization abuse and mothering, and films identified some issues and contributions of women of color to American society.[43] Soto and Gomez reminisced that "when the women of color met, you know, we'd meet, and it was wonderful for us *too*. We had the best time. It was wonderful for us. Our food was *better*. [laughter] Our music was *better*. Our dancing was *better*."[44] Adapting the Califia format to a setting exclusively for women of color increased their enjoyment by feeding and entertaining women in ways that were already culturally comfortable.

Written evaluations included praise for the opportunity to network and socialize with a large group of women of color. As usual, there were complaints about the quality of the food and lack of meat, and some women suggested that not hiring kitchen staff would increase the quality and a sense of community, as had occurred at most Califia camps. Women of Color Califia also received the recurring criticism that the space was not accessible to people with disabilities and not secure from men, who in this case were introduced into the setting as kitchen staff. While some evaluators supported the organization of the camp, others felt that there was a lack of responsibility among participants and a lack of leadership from the collective. Collective members of color were in a tenuous position because they could not count on the support that returning participants to the original Califia camps gave and, instead, had a higher percentage of attendees without respect for the way Califia camps operated.

This first camp generated hopes for networking and criticism of assimilation. Some felt secure and anticipated improved conditions because of the way collective members planned time and promoted change and responsibility. One evaluator, however, decried this style as Anglo. As part of a protracted denunciation, she claimed:

> Everyone has the white man's mentality. There is agression [*sic*] I sense flowing in the air. There is an imbalance of operating in the state of being & state of doing. I sense everyone is in the state of doing which calls for change & action. This is anglo style of behavior. The western notion of solving a problem is action & change. This is not so in every case, in every issue—it will only lead to more chaos etc. This is the message I keep hearing—CHANGE. I feel so sad, very sad, because all of you—Latinas, Blacks, Asians—your original culture you belong to where I belong. Our culture is far finer & superior—we share same thinking style but you have lost it. I want to do something . . . how? It was a privilege to be able to spend this weekend here. I made some friendship connections.[45]

This evaluator separated out certain ways of doing things as "white" or "Anglo" despite the actors being women of color. The underlying excitement at the opportunities that the Califia Women of Color camp presented should not be missed in her closing acknowledgment that she had made connections at the camp. Despite both harsh critique and constructive criticism, camps continued yearly with advertising that highlighted politics, networking, and cultural feminist "woman to woman space" for two hundred "sisters of color."[46]

Lesbian of color groups proliferated in L.A. in the 1980s, and despite strained relations with Califia due to perceptions of its whiteness, Califia provided a model for retreats that combined education, political organization, and community formation. The Califia model reached women who resisted coming to the original Califia camps. Otero went to one original Califia camp in 1980 or 1981 after she was recruited at an LOC meeting.[47] She attended a National LOC retreat conference in 1983 at the same campsite. She considered the LOC conference to be structured after the Califia model, but she felt much more at home there than at the white-majority Califia camp.[48] Lhyv Oakwomon, an African American radical lesbian feminist, was recruited to a Califia Women of Color camp through LOC because she "refused to have anything to do with Califia before then. And the reason why I had refused was because *I* felt at that time that they were waffling around the issue of racism." She says, "[S]exist self-betrayal . . . got to me so deeply I couldn't think about race." In retrospect, Oakwomon applauded Califia women for having the courage to discuss forms of privilege. She measured a woman's consciousness about racism, classism, and economic status to determine "the *degree* to which her feminism has affected her life" because "those investments that you have in the male-dominated society or the *privileges* that you have" are "your wake-up call." What she took from Califia was that its educational style was ideal for creating a model that addressed principles.[49]

The National LOC conference tested that model with its "sisters bonding" theme in 1983, and leadership included women who had attended Califia camps. Oakwomon and Forrest corresponded with potential participants, announced the conference, solicited input for topics and presenters, and tried to smooth over conflict about whether straight women should be presenters.[50] Despite the bonding theme, debate seems to have raged over lesbian separatism and the inclusion of lesbians of color who could pass as white like Forrest. Oakwomon defended separatism and woman-space as "political and social tools" with which women could "let off steam about our experiences of external oppression, confront our internalised oppressions, liberate and heal ourselves of the dehumanising effects of divide and conquer politics." She condemned the exclusion of women of color who appeared white as "vigorous exercises in futility" attributable to "internalised racism."[51] In a closing address, Kwambe Omdahda (Califia collective member 1979) met "uproaring cheers of unified approval" when she pronounced:

> We as womyn have come to realize that when we *choose* to identify as lesbi-
> ans of color we are making a choice that is synonymous with power. In or-
> der to generate that power into more effective force we must stop and take
> a long look at the ways in which we communicate . . . to confront some
> of the learned ways in which we hurt each other that are handed down to
> us through the society. . . . We take responsibility to create or join groups
> dedicated to issues unique to us as people of color, as womyn and as lesbi-

ans. It is important to acknowledge who we are, our culture, our roots, our community, our uniquie [*sic*] selves.[52]

This address dipped from a common feminist pool. Themes included conceiving of a group identity based on shared culture and community, forming resistive and nonoppressive ways of communicating, and rejecting oppressive learned behavior. Mirroring the struggle of antiracist white feminists to honor diversity, Omdahda devoted a sentence each to distinctive cultural contributions of Latin, native, Asian, and black sisters. Ironically, this crescendo was soon followed by the dissolution of the LOC, generally attributed to burnout.[53]

From the LOC Conference, Otero, other Chicanas, and a Peruvian lesbian formed Lesbianas Unidas. Otero found Lesbianas Unidas cohesive in contrast to the LOC because the Lesbianas Unidas members shared goals and did not contest the organization's finances. Their retreats echoed the LOC conference in being isolated from mainstream society and lasting for only a weekend rather than for a week. Otero remembered that participants confided "that they lived the whole *year* just to go to this *one* weekend *in* the mountains, so they could . . . *be* themselves and embrace *every* part of themselves at these retreats."[54] The importance of the Califia model was that "it made a statement . . . 'We're a collective, and we're going to talk about deeper issues than just get together and just party.'"[55] Like Califia, they too had talent shows where children and women performed songs and danced. Spanish served as a cultural bond. They generated money through dances and other fundraisers. Amid U.S. government–sponsored military campaigns in Central America in the news, Lesbianas Unidas sent proceeds from their fundraisers to hospitals in Central America in addition to funding a lesbian conference in Mexico City. As more Latinas moved to the Los Angeles area from Central America in the late 1980s, Lesbianas Unidas shifted from being Chicana-focused to more broadly Latina.[56]

The Califia model collided with ethnic nationalism when biracialism included European ancestry. Latinas came in all colors, and Otero recalls that Forrest and her sister wanted acknowledgment within LOC and Lesbianas Unidas. At the time, area Chicanas did tend to consider colorism a salient issue. They wanted to address "large agendas" and did not want to take time to deal with someone who at "every opportunity . . . became like La Llorona [the Mexican mythical crying woman] at these different groups where she would want the attention." Otero coded the Forrest sisters' behavior as "white" and disrupting of the group's focus on collective issues by "demanding attention on [their] specific individual issue."[57] The definitions of individual and collective seem based on the Forrest sisters being willing to keep trying to engage with a group that predominantly could not pass as white. Oakwomon, who was partially raised in Mexico, witnessed her friend Forrest's distress in LOC. She has continued to condemn colorism and accusations that Forrest "acts white":

> I had been raised in a country where . . . blancas with blonde hair, blue eyes, and white skin were mestizas in Mexico City. They were people of color. What my objection to . . . those women is, "You must not know what women of color look like." And you haven't been *around* enough if you think that she is particularly unique. . . . So I look at the Forrest women and I see Copper Canyon. They look at the Forrest women and they see blonde hair, blue eyes, white skin and project all the rest of the problems associated with—it's almost like one word, whiteskinblueeyesblondehair—you know, just one word. There are other ways, behavioral ways, to very clearly identify Barbara Forrest as Hispanic in origin. She is culturally Hispanic.[58]

Rather than see Forrest as an isolated case causing distraction, Oakwomon characterized "*endless* arguing over whether Barbara Forrest was a woman of color" as irrelevant and preventing better things from getting done.[59]

In addition to providing a model, Califia represented the continuation of a form of grassroots feminism and produced a network of women who supported feminist events. The beginning of a new women's center called Connexxus Women's Center/Centro de Mujeres demonstrated the struggle between grassroots and more bureaucratized feminist endeavors, the increasing voice of feminists of color, and the continued effects of Califia's contacts.

Connexxus signified a shift from the shoestring idealism of L.A. feminists who started a series of lesbian or women's centers in the early 1970s. Lauren Jardine gained experience as the director of Lesbian Central at the Gay Community Service Center between 1980 and 1984. Her departure from GCSC coincided with yet another rift between lesbians and the male-dominated GCSC.[60] Jardine and Adel Martínez cofounded Connexxus as "a woman-oriented space, a different way of providing services . . . to be done by women." Rather than simply strike out with the enthusiasm of grassroots activists, they first met with businesswomen in May 1984 to ensure that both energy and finances were available for another attempt at an autonomous women's service and cultural center.[61] This exploratory meeting occurred in the wake of bureaucratizing within NOW to ratify the

ERA and the establishment of lobbying groups like the National Gay Task Force to fight legal attacks on gays and lesbians. By the mid-1980s, the national climate privileged business and financial gain over a counterculture, and increasingly social justice workers waged their battles in courtrooms and legislatures more than in the streets.

The drawback of a focus on fiscal stability was that there was no guarantee that diverse women would have a say in planning and running the agency. To members of Lesbianas Unidas, the Lesbian Task Force of GLLU, Multi-Ethnic Gay and Lesbian Exchange (MEGLE), and LOC, Jardine and Martínez's attempt to break with grassroots beginnings in exchange for solvency replicated the exclusion of women of color and grassroots groups elsewhere. The initial meeting occurred without inviting input from any lesbian of color groups. Retter Vargas conferred with Lesbianas Unidas members after seeing a paucity of women of color at the organizational meeting. Lesbianas Unidas drafted a protest letter.[62] GLLU, MEGLE, and LOC also protested that input "from these underrepresented, underserved and underestimated constituencies ought to be an important part of any agency which purports, by virtue of its name, to represent an entire community. There is no excuse for these continued 'oversights.'" Although a relatively large number of attending businesswomen were women of color, the protesters asserted that "these women do not necessarily share the needs and concerns of groups of women which have not been included."[63] Martínez and Jardine drafted a conciliatory response requesting a meeting at a time convenient to their memberships "to ensure the total participation and representation you rightfully desire."[64]

By 1984, autonomous lesbians of color groups and caucuses of larger groups supplemented individual liaison work and balked at being added to white-founded or white-majority groups. During the first years of Connexxus, women of color associated with it pressed for increased visibility, rectification of racist incidents, and expanded access through clear statements that no one would be turned away for lack of funds and by setting up satellite sites such as Connexxus East.[65] Organizing and fundraising were crucial to Connexxus's continued existence, and Califia women supported Connexxus from the beginning.[66] Not only were some Califia women part of organizing the center, more attended fundraising as well as nonfundraiser dances, mixers, bingo, and talent shows.[67] Otero believed that Connexxus was able to tap into Califia's already established avenues for reaching and organizing women.

Califia was significant to other lesbian groups because it served as a model for providing education, political organizing, community formation, and creating separate space for women. The principles of basing group identity on shared culture, forming resistive language, and rejecting oppressive learned behavior were ones that other area lesbian groups utilized, and all were goals indicative of feminism. Finally, Califia's long existence had created a network of supporters of which successive groups made use.

BEYOND THE ORIGINAL CALIFIA

Lesbians of color demanded ground-level entrance into the planning of Connexxus to prevent continued marginalization of people of color. Likewise, a group of women of color pushed to run Califia Community in order to move it away from its white-marked roots to a more inclusive feminism. The proliferation of lesbian of color groups in Los Angeles, continued work from the Women of Color Network, and the exodus of initial collective members from Califia combined to shape the final stage of Califia Community's existence. Memories of the transfer of Califia leadership are marked by rancor. All agreed that Califia feminists of color asked to assume leadership of Califia and use its feminist education particularly for women of color, but disagreement arose over what led to the demise of Califia Community.

The tenth anniversary camp in 1985, which Kathy Wolfe videotaped, was the final regular Califia session and the fourth year of women of color camps. Attendees knew the main collective would not organize another camp. They discussed what should happen to the nonprofit status and remaining funds.[68] On February 1, 1986, a group of Califia women of color wrote a statement to the Califia Community "to ask that the leadership of CALIFIA Community be turned over to the women of color. Our white sisters have an opportunity to bond with us in recognition that feminist women of color leadership is a valid and necessary political stand for all women now."[69] The "Statement from Women of Color to the Califia Community" was indicative of the rise of multicultural feminism, which feminists of color expressed in *This Bridge Called My Back* and successive works and for which lesbians of color in Los Angeles campaigned by seeking inclusion in Connexxus.[70] The statement framed acceptance of their plan as solidarity with Califia and praised Califia as having "created a powerful model for feminist education and provided us with woman-space." These feminists of color objected:

> The women's movement can no longer be dominated by white women's analysis of oppression and theories of liberation. Because of institutional racism white women oppress women of color. Even when anti-racist fem-

inists work with women of color racist incidents occur and consciousness raising is done at the expense of women of color, for example racism is denied, ignored or justified.

Our women of color experience demands the comprehension of and resistance to all forms of oppression and exploitation. White women have been unwilling to translate their experience of oppression in ways that validate or include women of color. The articulation of our struggle is the leading edge of radical feminism. CALIFIA as a feminist institution is an ideal vehicle for that expression.

In our community women of color perspectives are not represented. CALIFIA is an established women's cultural institution and expresses women's culture signifigantly [sic]. Multicultural feminism defines and validates the conditions of all women's lives and struggles, creating the possibility of sisterhood and bonding.

We offer our model of leadership, feminist process and education to the community. Now is the time for CALIFIA Community to evolve towards it's [sic] ideals.[71]

These Califia women echoed close to two decades of work by feminists of color by objecting to dominant white feminists' analysis. Califia women were part of a broader attempt to develop fully a vocabulary of dissent, which drew connections among oppressions. Over the organization's decade of existence, it especially struggled with race relations. Like the lesbian feminist denunciation of an inherently straight feminism, Califia women of color were part of a trend. They rejected white-majority feminism as insufficient and proposed to lead feminists past racism to a fully integrated analysis of oppressions.

Women of color involved in the transfer of leadership and white participants connected transfer of responsibility for Califia to women of color with the departure of founding collective members after 1983 and burnout. Representing the spectrum of ages, equal percentages of white narrators (55 percent) and narrators of color (55.6 percent) believe that the energy to keep organizing Califia ran out.[72] Seven specified that Murphy and Weiss were linchpins and that others could not devote the time to organizing that their retirement and political commitment gave them.[73] Jewell added Brooks as an example of needed strong leadership, and Leon asserted that the CSULB firing of Betty was an attack on Califia:

> She had a *really* lot to offer and was *offering* it, like, *every hour.* And so when *she* was [under] personal *attack* like that, then the *Collective* was under personal attack because she was such a *big* contributor. And *I* think *that*

had a lot to *do* with the older women being *tired* is that they *weren't* just tired of producing *Califia*. I suspect if *that* hadn't happened, the Women's Studies program at Long Beach, that Califia may have weathered out several more years until the young people were *ready* to take it over.[74]

Linking Califia's end to leaders' departures, demoralization of established leaders, and burnout assigned the least blame while including an undertone that those who took on leadership were not ready. Murphy and Brooks's labor bore especially heavy representational burden. They embodied feminism to many participants for whom Califia was their major site of feminist CR and activity; conceptually, Califia could not survive without their efforts. Although the original Califia continued for two years past the 1983 season and Califia Women of Color carried on for two more years, the memories linking Califia to Murphy, Brooks, or Weiss represented a predisposition to personalize a movement through designated leaders who rose as public figures.

The burnout thesis connected with assertions that the times changed and became unfavorable to Califia's work. Four narrators noted that women had to prioritize career building because it had become difficult to survive economically under a conservative regime.[75] Like other Americans, Califia women struggled through the Reagan-era recession, which saw unemployment rates rise from 5.8 percent in 1979 to 7.1 percent in 1980, a high of 9.7 percent in 1982, and 7.2 percent in 1985.[76] Additionally, six narrators thought the political edge of Califia's feminism outlived its historical moment.[77] While its long-term participants had moved beyond introductory material, most lesbians in Los Angeles were turning to less-political venues, flocking to social and professional groups. This was a particular stress for women of color collective members who organized women of color camps, wanted to get a lot out of them, and wanted them to excel.[78]

Despite some recognition of larger economic and political changes, the Califia emphasis on personal experience colored narrators' interpretations. Continuous struggles over race relations throughout Califia's existence and participants' deep emotional attachments to its original methods influenced some narrators to attribute the dissolution of the group within two years of the transfer in leadership to women of color's decisions or to racism. Seven either stressed the arrogance of women of color in advancing their model of leadership as superior or framed the transfer as a result of white women's discomfort with the women of color. Women had that analysis despite the fact that the Califia collective decided to stop holding camps before the women of color contingent volunteered to continue and to transform Califia. Three long-term white participants who maintained close ties with each other asserted that Califia women of color prioritized spirituality at the expense of CR, ripping Califia from its political roots.[79]

A striking component of this interpretation is that only the narrators who themselves brought up why Califia ended eagerly blamed women of color. Terms of thick condemnation peppered these interviews— "polarizing," lack of "ethical behavior," "irresponsible," "divisive," "didn't follow through on their commitments," had not "taken care of Califia." Feelings of disappointment and distress bubbled to the surface almost two decades after Califia ended.

In contrast, near the end of their interviews, Catoggio and Manov, who were not participating in Califia by then but remained friends, constructed defenses of women of color. Catoggio claimed, from talking to those who were still active, that rather than dealing with the women of color by working together, "it was easier to just say, 'OK, you *take* it.'" Manov drew a parallel between Califia's end and that of the NLFO to add the possibility that white women tacitly gave women of color "permission to sort of *try* but without a lot of *support* for their efforts so they could try and *fail*."[80] A nonprofit status without resources would not be enough for the group to continue.

Feminists of color who were at the end emphasized their struggle with complex structural issues that differed from the original Califia. Califia feminists of color faced animosity from other women of color who considered them sell-outs for participating in Califia. As organizers of the camp, Califia feminists of color did not have the established authority among these women to demand the same type of mandatory participation that the original camps had. Spiritual practices became a method to start connections for basic networking.[81] While some white lesbian feminists had rejected spirituality along with organized religion and were able to live that philosophy among their associates, many American communities of people of color historically have found religious structure and spirituality to be useful tools to fight racism, especially where American Christians practiced their religion in racially segregated churches. A few organizers, like Oakwomon and Forrest's partner of the time, championed the non-European aspects of women's spirituality, such as sweat lodges and meditation. Cultural differences and racial tensions meant that the Califia Women of Color camps were like starting over. Women of color did not necessarily arrive at the camps with the effects of CR that Califia had developed for a decade and were not necessarily comfortable identifying themselves as feminists if they saw the latter as a white word.[82] Leaders, however, were impatient to move to a higher level of analysis to maintain their own interest and to demonstrate the success of multicultural feminism.[83] On top of that, women of color narrators cited financial and leadership problems. Their smaller scale weekend camps were always in the hole. They were in the difficult position of having attendees who owed them money. It became increasingly hard to sustain energy for planning the camps when they were from lower economic backgrounds and struggling to get ahead by finishing college and starting careers.[84]

This is not what white narrators heard. The CR framework, including racism presenters' use of personal experience to change white participants' behavior, inclined Califia women to explanations that placed blame and evoked intense guilt. Personalizing racism included expectations that white women would teach themselves to understand, accommodate, ask the right questions, and transform themselves into antiracist activists. Some expressed defeat and resentment that nothing they did would ever have been enough. Resentment intensified with the assumption that they would commit energy to the Califia Women of Color conferences when the camps were changing in a way with which they did not identify. After putting so much of their hopes and effort into Califia and gaining such benefits from participation, they felt simultaneously shut out and put upon to support its transformation into something else.

Califia's existence and demise illustrate important practices concerning feminisms in relation to the rise of the Right. As conservative backlash assailed progressives, feminists continued to mirror societal binary thinking in an attempt to purge women of dominant-group ways of thinking. The homogenizing results were insufficient. Their teachings could make complex connections such as the ways Jetter analyzed language, hegemonic thinking, and the selective use of the term terrorism, yet conclusions often posited one correct answer. Dualistic binaries and forms of feminism that prioritized gender and sexual orientation ultimately were not flexible enough to recognize how people are interconnected and map out common ground from which to work for positive change. Ultimately, Califia provided a format model to other groups, supported valuing identity-based community, and networked supporters for successive causes. Its demise, however, illustrates not only the complex relations between personal and structural factors but also the severe divisions that progressives inherited from the dominant society.

As Califia women left camp for the last time, many rejoined society revitalized and transformed with skills to assess power dynamics and try to make positive reforms. Their range of careers represented feminists elsewhere: business, helping professions such as nursing, counseling, teaching, and staffing feminist-inspired centers, media, or making inroads into the male-dominated trades. High-profile leaders like Brooks, Murphy, and Retter Vargas continued to champion lesbian and feminist causes. Brooks did so within her university and community courses while Murphy and Retter Vargas's community news and community center outlets made them lightning rods as the political climate changed.

LESBIAN FEMINISTS ATTACKED AS AIDING THE RIGHT

The demise of Califia was part of the decline of lesbian feminist activity in Los Angeles and reflected its struggle nationally. Through the 1980s, Califia women like Retter Vargas and Murphy continued to endorse lesbian feminist separatism while others shifted their views in line with developments in gay and lesbian movement work and multicultural feminism. In internal lesbian and gay disputes, lesbian feminists and gay men or lesbians working for reforms accused each other of being in league with conservative forces. These polarizing characterizations contested how to live free and responsible lives, how to fight reactionary forces, where to find compatriots, and—especially for lesbian feminists—the very definition of woman.

In 1988, Retter Vargas gained national attention, which embroiled her in controversy over the place of lesbian feminist separatism in a gay and lesbian movement. The way that the parties worded their positions illustrates persistent miscommunication. The mainstream mischaracterized separatists while liberal gays painted lesbian feminists as a flank of the Right to underscore problems with separatist ideology. A reporter for the national gay periodical, *The Advocate*, interviewed Retter Vargas after she and two other lesbian separatists were sensationally introduced as "women who hate men" on the Oprah Winfrey television show. Retter Vargas amended:

> I repeatedly say to people, it's not the boys that I hate—it is the expression of bad male behavior. Some of us as women model that behavior too, sometimes, that negative, yang behavior. . . . This is what separatists do: They hold the line for women's energy on the planet.[85]

She distinguished actions from identity but claimed the ability to attribute positive behavior to "women's energy" and negative actions to "male energy" regardless of the gender of the person exhibiting the activities.

Further into the article, Retter Vargas's views on prioritizing women transgressed a taboo within gay and lesbian AIDS work. She avowed that there were multiple ways to live a separatist life, from no contact with any male human or animal to her work heading Lesbian Central within the Los Angeles Gay and Lesbian Community Service Center.[86] Asked about working with gay men, she argued that gay men who considered themselves feminists should work to educate other men instead of barging in on lesbian spaces. Her sense that most gay men had more in common with straight men than with lesbians extended to her views on the AIDS epidemic and lesbians' participation in fighting the disease:

> And AIDS, once again, is asking women to take care of boys because they weren't able to control themselves. The boys are still asking for Mommy to come help them, and when lesbians want to play Mommy, I really despair. . . . One thing that made me very angry was when someone told me that 48,000 women per year die of breast cancer—that's more per year than have died of AIDS. And who's mobilizing for them? Nobody. I wanted to cry.[87]

In holding the line for women, Retter Vargas was criticizing the fact that the center devoted over 40 percent of its budget to AIDS services but only had sporadic lesbian health programs. Lesbians had been unsuccessful in negotiating terms of coalition that directly benefited them when AIDS was a growing epidemic that had only started gaining government funding. The characterization of gay male sexuality as uncontrolled, however, aligned with sex-negative moralizing from the Religious Right that failed to recognize a 1970s context in which sex without latex barriers was common for those who did not fear unwanted pregnancy because most sexually transmitted diseases were curable or manageable.

Director of Education Jeff Campbell demanded Retter Vargas resign in an irate memo copied to Deputy Director Torie Osborn. He compared Retter Vargas to anti–gay rights U.S. Representative William Dannemeyer of California (R., served 1979–1992),[88] dismissing her views as "sexist, prejudiced, and based upon hatred and misinformation." Campbell was most offended, understandably, by Retter Vargas's unwavering view that "gay men brought AIDS upon themselves" through their behavior. Claiming that her presence on the payroll was "ofensive [sic] to the vast majority of staff, volunteers and clients . . . [and] a source of contempt and ridicule of the entire Center by the community at large," he urged her "to take [her] abhorrent views elsewhere and resign immediately."[89] Directors successfully ousted Retter Vargas. Lesbian Central ceased to exist in 1989; with it went any lesbian health programming at the center. Discontinuation of lesbian health services underscored Retter Vargas's central critique that gay and lesbian coalitions tended to prioritize fighting a disease that was then most affecting males while ignoring an overwhelmingly female disease.[90] At a time when gay men were under attack from the Right, however, there was no space for critiques of funding priorities that implicated gay men in their plight.

Campbell's defense of gay men was shared by many who had lost loved ones to AIDS while New Right politicians and pastors since the 1980s had claimed that AIDS represented God's wrath against homosexuals. What was erased amid sensationalist sound bites was the possibility for internal dissent while gays and lesbians fought the Right, a space where critique did not necessarily come from neoliberalism. Retter Vargas reflected a wider concern among lesbian feminists that fundraising to combat AIDS inadvertently devastated lesbian work. For example, in 1986, Ivy Bottini (whom NY NOW purged from its presidency in 1971 for defending lesbians) joined Eric Rofes as cochairs of the No on La Rouche campaign. They and others rallied California gays and lesbians to oppose Proposition 64, which would have empowered state officials to mandate AIDS testing for individuals and segregate HIV-positive people from schools and travel routes, possibly isolating them in camps. The campaign raised $2.3 million, and the measure was defeated 72 percent to 28 percent.[91] Jinx Beers, owner of *The Lesbian News*, pointed out that during the campaign "donations to lesbian projects and other groups 'virtually dried up for several months,'" which had long-term consequences. Connexxus was devastated and finally closed in 1990. The Woman's Building shut its doors in 1991.[92] After Beers sold *The Lesbian News* in 1989, its new owners toned down political content over the next few years in favor of glossy, consumer, fashion, and socializing-oriented content, which garnered more paid advertisements. Bernstein lamented that of the region's original feminist periodicals, *The Lesbian News* was the only one that survived in name but it now targeted women with money for charity events and leisure activities like the Dinah Shore Golf Tournament while "some very good writers have gone by the wayside."[93] By the early 1990s, scant educational or activist spaces in Los Angeles or across the nation supported both lesbianism and feminism.

Until 1991, however, Murphy carved a niche for a Califia mindset within the pages of *The Lesbian News* through her "Lesbianic Logic" columns. Her column included injunctions against racism and anti-Semitism,[94] education about disability and age,[95] glorification of lesbian separatism,[96] and warnings about heteropatriarchy. Murphy received no negative responses to her CR on race, Judaism, disability, and age. Readers contested her lesbian separatist positions, however, as lesbians and gay men fought for equal protections under the law.

Since the mid-1980s, Murphy strongly censured heterosexual marriage in print along with lesbian behaviors that she believed imitated heterosexuality. In "Mother of the Groom," she explained why she did not attend her eldest child's wedding. For three years, she was proud of her son. He lived with his girlfriend without marital benefits like shared health insurance, tax returns, and credit records because they disapproved of how marriage institutionalized the inequality of women, extended state power, and gave a federal imprimatur to religious intolerance toward same-sex couples.[97] Tired of the financial and familial hassles and confident they could escape sexism, they decided to wed. Murphy argued to her readers that she could not attend a "ceremony which is the cornerstone of her past oppression as a married woman and her present oppression as a Lesbian." By analogy, she asserted:

> Men who abhor sexism do not join organization[s] which deny membership to women. White people who abhor racism do not join organizations which deny membership to people of color. Christians, believers and nonbelievers, who abhor anti-semitism [sic] do not join organizations which deny membership to Jews. Able bodied people do not join organizations which deny membership to disabled people. The refusal to join an organization which publicly and blatantly denies membership, and the benefits accruing to members, to persons different from themselves, is the very least that can be expected of those who profess belief in equality and civil rights for all.

Pointedly condemning heterosexual relatives who married and lesbians and gay men who supported those relatives, Murphy refused to collude with her own oppression and called on readers "to begin disturbing the consciences of our families and friends."[98] In 1985, the response was mixed. One letter to the editor thanked Murphy for helping the writer to clarify her own ambivalence and anger about attending heterosexual weddings. In another, a mother related her extreme grief at losing her son to his homophobia after she came out and divorced his father and concluded that being his mother was more important to her than working against relatives' homophobia. The third dismissed Murphy's column as "extremist," "self-righteous," and containing "ongoing hate-filled, self-pitying invective" "that appears to border on Neo-Nazi attidues [sic]." The letters represent a range of positions within the lesbian community, from the application of

radical feminist critiques of heterosexual marriage to a willingness to retreat from political ideology and overlook homophobia in favor of what is
"more familiar" to a lesbian predecessor of conservative talk show hosts like
Rush Limbaugh or Glenn Beck who casually label people Nazi or attack
feminists as "feminazis."[99]

Murphy also drew fire for her complicated take on lesbians choosing motherhood through artificial insemination. She believed that every
woman should have the right to choose pregnancy and approved of separating reproduction from sexual activity both to dismantle compulsory heterosexuality and to prevent men from claiming paternal rights. She did not discuss the legal implications for child support that her rejection of paternal
rights could entail. As long as male violence persisted, and as long as society taught everyone that women were born to serve men and children, she
saw no need for a male role model for children. Despite approving women's
right to decide whether to reproduce, Murphy opposed lesbians having babies as delusional. Murphy typically asserted her experiential authority:

> My credentials as an expert on motherhood include thirty-five years of
> mothering my four children. . . . I've also been intimately involved with
> my four sisters as they raised my twelve nieces and nephews, and with nu-
> merous friends, both Lesbian and non-Lesbians, who are mothers. And of
> course, I am a daughter, the eldest child of a mother whose behavior I have
> been scrutinizing for fifty-four years.

In Murphy's experience, dominant society perpetuated stereotypes about
mothering and children for heteropatriarchal purposes. Parents could not
ultimately control their children's beliefs and behaviors, so lesbians could
not know whether they would "produce the next generation's liberated
children." The desire to create someone who would always love one was
also self-deception. Therapists made livings from complaints about mothers, and nursing homes warehoused elders. Finally, Murphy criticized
would-be mothers whose love of children in the abstract signaled stereotypes about children, which could smother children's individuality.[100] In
part two, Murphy further tried to disabuse would-be mothers of idealized visions of motherhood.[101] A Latina Califia woman contested Murphy's
claim to experience: Murphy "never was, and is not now, a Lesbian choosing Motherhood. She establishes [later in her article] that her own Child-
bearing/rearing years were served wholly for the patriarchy."[102]

Both Retter Vargas and Murphy had years of experience as lesbian feminist separatists. They could not, however, successfully parlay their knowl-

edge into recognized expertise for audiences who maintained ties to men and did cogendered work to share in privileges that straight people had. The climate of the 1980s renewed debate over what constituted oppositional politics. Lesbian feminists could not gain a positive reception of positions that promoted abstaining from pleasure and enfranchisement for a potential political good.

COMMUNITY EDUCATION DISRUPTED

The 1980s were a challenging time for feminist groups. New Right members fervently attacked university personnel they considered radical as well as women's services. Those attacks harmed local community organizing and education. Brooks and other Women's Studies faculty who had to defend their careers no longer had time, energy, or money for nonprofit experiments like Califia. Neoliberal policies dismantled social welfare systems, expanded the income and wealth gaps between the wealthy and poor, and shrank the middle class. This left activists in a precarious position. Public and private funding for small group activism became scarcer and activists perceived more need to secure their individual economic futures. As founding Califia women aged, they needed or wanted to turn their attention to new endeavors. Women activists were especially vulnerable as they aged because they were more likely than men to care for ill or infirm loved ones and had fewer economic resources. The AIDS epidemic required enormous resources to develop care systems for the ill and dying and drug therapies that could manage the virus. The outbreak required activists' energies and money, since adequate government funding was not forthcoming.

Despite all that, Califia Community developed between 1982 and its conclusion in significant ways. Women kept joining the collective as others burned out; collective members of color started women of color camps; and ultimately they ran Califia Community themselves. Women of Color Califia was important, albeit short-lived, because it modified a concept to change with the times. It started when lesbian of color groups were proliferating in L.A. and women of color were pressing hard against continued racism in the broader community. Even though Califia ended, its legacies continued with its model for organizing and messages that shaped women's perspectives on justice.

ENDURING LEGACIES FOR "THE WEEK"

THE DEVELOPMENT OF CALIFIA COMMUNITY illustrates strengths and weaknesses of forms of feminism as well as how feminist work related to society. Feminists since the mid-1960s have sought to revolutionize the world; their sense of urgency and heightened expectations have built on previous New Left momentum. Califia participants reflected American feminists who tested alternative models of governance and revised assumptions, simultaneously supported and challenged each other, and encouraged political activism.

Assumptions endure that the "second wave generation" was essentialist, separatist, and antisex and exclusively promoted androgyny in ways that rejected femininity and could not understand gender fluidity. Overgeneralizations about feminism in the 1970s–1980s characterize all activists as having had a narrow set of beliefs and practices, including having "ignored racism, classism, and homophobia."[1] Laying out Califia's assets and struggles fosters reflection about the viability of that political generation's tactics while correcting dismissive stereotypes against 1970s–1980s feminists. Southern California feminists vigorously debated essentialism, the parameters for separatism, and what expressions of sexuality and gender were antisexist. Califia represented only some ways in which those debates played out. In the context of national feminist discussions about racial integration and institutional reform of work and welfare conditions, Califia's emphases on homophobia within sexism, on classism, and on racism belie claims that the "second wave generation" ignored these important facets of women's identification and societal prejudices.

This monograph is the first in-depth study of how feminists educated each other and their communities outside of Women's Studies courses. Within its first few years, Califia participants created an educational space with a flow of ideas that mirrored the competing views of the time. Their experiment was economically accessible, nonhierarchical, interactive, and woman focused. Hundreds of women came to Califia through L.A.'s network of feminist institutions and experienced powerful moments of insight and growth during the decade of campsite conferences. Collective members practiced consensus while participants experienced the collective's responsiveness when they voiced concerns at nightly community meetings or at the collective meetings held year round. Women encouraged each other to devote themselves intellectually, emotionally, materially, sexually, and politically to other women. They challenged cultural assumptions such as the romanticization of childhood. Women who entered temporary separatist spaces found freedom and safety from male violence and dominant society's control. Although there was debate in the wider feminist community over who could be feminist, Califia was emblematic of how stereotyping dominance and violence as male made many feminists hostile toward women who were labeled male at birth, male allies, and consensual SM while many initially could not conceive of lesbian battering and other woman-on-woman violence. Feminists have built and continue to build on the idea that gender and sexuality are socially constructed. Rather than shut down gender diversity, today's feminists often support those who transgress gender and sexual identity norms.[2]

Califia represented feminist struggles for bodily autonomy against violence and for integrated feminism. Like other community education that began with CR, the space criticized norms, exalted statuses dominant society considered inferior, and spurred action. Califia's appeal to corporeal, lived experience led women to join already established radical feminist groups like Fat Underground and Women Against Violence Against Women. Shortly thereafter, Califia women formed the San Fernando Valley Rape Crisis Service and White Women Against Racism. Califia became a model for education, community formation, separate space, and political organizing at lesbian of color groups' retreats and provided a funding network for Connexxus Women's Center/Centro de Mujeres. The experiential learning model ensured that Califia women emphasized everyday personalized cultural behaviors as ways of opposing patriarchal norms. It was typical of the 1970s–1980s feminist generation to transform culture as well as to engage in direct action and lobbying for institutional change.

In addition to supporting women when society dismissed them, Califia exposed privileges that were due to women's structural position or chosen actions in the world. Working-class participants made connections among class background, behavioral norms, and skills. The class presentation avoided anticommunist sentiment by considering ways middle-class standards disadvantaged working-class and impoverished people on a daily basis. Americans rarely consider or acknowledge those insights today. Califia's reliance on class backgrounds and interpersonal dynamics, however, constrained their ability to explain the effects of class mobility and to implement reforms in society.

Although women of color later deemed Califia's first years of teaching against racism insufficient, founders helped white women unlearn racism from Califia's beginning. Califia women ultimately grappled with the relationships among white-skin privilege, ethnicity, and biculturalism and produced White Women Against Racism as regional leaders in making race education more inclusive than a black-white model allowed. In addition to making change in the L.A. area, the Women of Color Network and committed white Califia participants attained parity in the collective between white women and women of color that progressive groups rarely achieved. At the same time that Califia emphasized antiracism work, women of color presenters felt burdened and white participants frequently felt attacked. It was challenging to select a tone that was effective and to manage self-care while working to change those who resisted owning their privilege.[3] American racism was too intractable for feminist work to destroy in two decades, but feminists built on civil rights activists' goals of raising consciousness to unlearn racism and protest its structural manifestations.

Califia's race and class work provide crucial lessons for twenty-first century class hierarchy and forms of de facto racial segregation. Jo Reger's work strongly indicates that racial integration or actions that address class persist as problems for contemporary feminism. Feminist groups continue to discuss racial diversity, and feminists of color continue to assert that white members deny white privilege. Dialogue about diversity does not necessarily translate into concrete plans for integrating organizations or practice, and Reger finds young feminists hardly discussing class at all.[4]

Throughout the 1970s and 1980s, expectations for personal transformation to mobilize women against oppressive conditions produced deeply emotional disappointments. Feminists felt besieged by numerous coercive aspects of society, including direct attacks like the attempts to fire Brooks and Retter Vargas. People did not agree on the most important changes to make, and they called each other out for not fully eliminating behaviors they realized were harmful or supported domination. Disappointment at those who seemed to exhibit complacency or advocated conduct that conflicted with feminist tenets led to infighting over whether men, heterosexual women, middle-class and white feminists, trans women, kinky dykes, and a host of others could work together for change. When women united through a feeling of commonality, unexpected realizations that some held an array of conflicting views, in addition to contestation over what was outside the bounds of "feminism," could feel like devastating betrayals. Furthermore, countercultural glorification of oppressed experience led to jockeying for the authority that came with most oppressed status.

A desire for safety through imagined similarities based on identity stood alongside the acknowledged need for alliances. Coalition building was crucial to making change against proponents of stasis. As Bernice Johnson Reagon argued in 1981 at the West Coast Women's Music Festival, "Coalition work is not done in your home. Coalition work has to be done in the streets. And it is some of the most dangerous work you can do. And you shouldn't look for comfort."[5] Strategic separatism granted women space to articulate their position and goals. Although Califia conferences, the West Coast Women's Music Festival, and other feminist spaces felt like "coming home" to many, those spaces were never just about safety and comfort. Califia advertised itself as "full of laughter, anger, conflict, joy, struggle, release, empowerment and personal growth."[6] Founders designed it to be uncomfortable in order to train women from different backgrounds with differing priorities to work together. Adding different constituents' grievances and analyses to a fluid agenda widened feminists' perspectives. Feminists have a long history of making gains based on fragile, imperfect, but sustained attempts to work through issues and find solutions collectively. Multicultural feminism furthered the necessity of looking at differences as interconnected and simultaneously operating in distinct ways for different people. For more than ten years, Califia sustained what feminists achieved nationally, a powerful sense of exhilaration at being among those struggling to repair divisions among women, so that coalition work could remain viable.

When women asked why everyone could not just get along (rather than struggling through antiracism training), Retter Vargas made the analogy to unlearning racism over the course of a symbolic week:

> And they used to say things like, [in a higher pitched voice] "Why can't we all get along. Aren't we all people under the skin?" I said, "Yes, we are on Thursday, but today's Tuesday. And we have two long days of work. And if you don't do the work between now and then, we're not going to *get* there. I agree with you. We *are*. But most of you use 'We're all people under the skin' as an escape clause to not work on all this shit that's between Tuesday and Thursday."[7]

In another literal and metaphoric use of the concept of week to address women at a multi-day gathering, Reagon argued that for movements to succeed at transforming the world, people had to set aside personal preferences in favor of wide alliances:

> Some folks we don't care too much about. . . . Everybody who is in this space at this time belongs here. And it's a good thing if you came. I don't care what you went through or what somebody did to you. Go for yourself. *You* give this weekend everything you can. Because no matter how much of a coalition space this is, it ain't nothing like the coalescing you've got to do tomorrow, and Tuesday and Wednesday, when you really get out there, back into the world: that is ours too.[8]

This book gave post–World War II inequalities, radical education, and New Left movements as context to assess Califia Community as an expression of 1970s and 1980s feminism. If a week represented the whole post-war period, many New Left movements sought that liberating weekend of equality—civil rights for racial equality, homophile rights and gay liberation, student rights, the antiwar movement, racial nationalism, the poor people's movement, and feminisms. Social movement history provides clues for how, as Brooks said, to "take our power" and get to the end of the week by adapting strategies to our present.

PATHS TO THE WEEKEND

It is beyond the scope of this history to finalize a program for getting to the metaphorical libratory weekend, but historical and contemporary guidance abounds. Califia and other concurrent feminist projects adapted previous radical visions for changes that would create a just society. Activists and scholars have roundly decried the limitations of identity politics since founding multicultural feminist discussions of intersecting oppressions steered activists away from prioritizing a single, unified identity.[9]

Social movement activists face uncertainty about whether they can succeed; they require creative thinking to adapt to changing power relations. One of Yolanda Retter Vargas's conditions for being interviewed was that I not subject her words to "pomohomo analysis." She did not want me to employ post-modernist queer theories that she felt obscure understanding. Although theorists about authorities reconfiguring their power to maintain the status quo add further insights, the history of social movements gives

concrete examples that plainly show activists and citizens need persever-
ance and creativity continually to press for participatory democracy, equality, and their meanings of freedom.

Califia was a bold educational retreat experiment at a time that was both
exhilarating and uncertain. Those who started and continued the experiment risked their time and reputations, faced criticisms, and innovated
to refine their project. Attendees used spaces such as the nightly community meeting and open collective meetings to provide ideas for improve-
ment, which allowed the collective to adapt Califia in ways that honed the
presentations and integrated more diversity. The permeability of the collective—with members leaving or joining every year—increased a sense of
cocreation rather than limiting ownership of the experiment solely to its
founders. Nonetheless, long-time participants who joined the collective did
feel ownership and resented the demise of the group.

Recent studies into creativity tightly link inventiveness to a "tolerance
for ambiguity."[10] In some areas, Califia participants demonstrated a willingness to tolerate the dissonance between what society told them and
women's own experience of disparaged traits like fatness, disability, and
low socioeconomic class. Everyone was equally subject to being called out
and asked to rethink her position. As often occurs when facing uncertainty,
however, the fear and anxiety uncertainty generate made it highly uncomfortable for Califia women to continue looking at some topics, especially issues that appeared to overlap with violence against women or issues about
which their minds were firmly decided. Facing harsh judgment from others
about positions on topics like race led many women to shut down and stop
sharing the ideas that might have had potential to further innovation.[11]

Califia provided a schedule and rituals that helped shore up participation and ingenuity. Research from psychology, religion, and even business argue that reliable routines ground people and offer a sense of connection, whether to like-minded people or also to people's concept of the
divine. Routines and rituals can therefore be effective to mitigate the fear,
anxiety, and resistance uncertainty provokes.[12] Grounding practices need
not be feminist Wicca rituals people like Jetter opposed and the Women
of Color Califia employed to unite participants. They could be routines
such as knowing that days, meals, and community meetings start at set
times or that there will be a talent show and closing circle at the end of the
conference.

Whatever grounds activists to deal with the emotions that attend uncertainty of success, the sense of community-building rituals foster holds
promise. Common cause and mutual regard are inherent to the civil rights

movement's "beloved community" or feminist "sisterhood." In practice, both civil rights workers and feminists coerced and pressured their members, but, nonetheless, something about connection holds promise for improved behavior. Martin Luther King, Jr. rooted his program for nonviolent resistance in a belief in human goodness and people's ability to develop compassion. Taking human capacity for goodness as a basic premise is important to social justice because suspicion of our own and other people's humanity tends to heighten distrust of diversity.[13] Beliefs in goodness and compassion tend to help people maintain a sense of openness, welcoming and wonder that translate into flexible thinking useful for heightening awareness of how people are interconnected.[14]

Work on multiculturalism argues that the abilities to welcome other people's experiences and to be open to wondering how the meaning of their experiences changes the way one understands the world further our capacity to manage meanings that overlap and partly contradict each other.[15] Comfort with ambiguity can help people resolve conflicts, find mutually beneficial compromises, and risk vulnerability.[16] When people can manage not to take critiques or other people's expressions of frustration personally, it is easier to learn from and integrate messages about how one benefits from unearned privileges or still behaves in oppressive ways that American culture teaches people to use. The ability to integrate constructive criticism is crucial to creativity and the ability to adapt.

AnaLouise Keating's program for teaching multiculturalism argues that when people simultaneously strive to develop empathy, compassion, openness, and trust and try to eliminate domination and manipulation, people can freely associate and share their differences in ways that respect differences and find common ground.[17] The process of sharing creatively transforms the group and makes them better able to understand in inclusive ways. In turn, they become better prepared to create a just and inclusive society that encompasses political change and the rest of human existence.

Supporting diversity and opposing prejudice encourages individuals' well-being and potential, which then serves the collective good. A social justice–oriented civic ethic is grounded in supporting people's well-being by fostering individuals' emotional welfare, range of knowledge (including distinguishing what is true from false through reason and experience), aesthetic understanding, sense of fulfillment, community with others, mutual control instead of authoritarianism, and appreciative understanding that others are unique and precious.[18]

Radical social movements have demonstrated that assisting individuals and the common good require a turn from today's glorification of individualism and privatized notions of freedom. Like Murphy's condemnation of sexist consumer capitalist individualism, other proponents of progressive social justice movements recognize ways in which enduringly discriminatory practices have been instituted in society, and how people are economically, socially, and emotionally interconnected and interdependent. As such, they reject the myth of "rugged individualism" where people think of themselves as independent and succeeding based solely on their own merit and individual work, a myth that shores up an adversarial concept that individuals should seek personal power or profit or do whatever they want at the expense of others.[19] The type of freedom that counters discrimination and makes room to champion diversity requires decreasing private, competing, and transitory interests. Even less radical mid-twentieth-century proponents of liberalism recognized that the pursuit of an interconnected form of freedom rather than fleeting, personal gains best cultivated people's potential and well-being but required a civic ethic.[20]

Championing diversity and liberation requires reassessing dominant assumptions beyond hyper-individualism. The tools for fashioning a vision and meanings that are multicultural and undermine stories that support a monocultural status quo already exist among us.[21] To return to identity issues, identity labels can be sources of comfort and strength, so it is worth listening to how people name themselves and what meaning they invest in those identifications. Identities can also create arbitrary divisions that provoke oppositions, reinforce hierarchies, and prevent us from recognizing our interconnectedness.[22] Keating argues that "status quo stories" use common sense explanations of reality to normalize unjust conditions and deny that change is possible.[23] Status quo ways of making sense of the world often rely on oppositional binaries (good-bad, black-white, male-female, and so on) instead of allowing for differences to complement each other. Dualism is detrimental because it encourages inflexibility and conflict between groups based on dismissive attitudes and unwillingness to consider alternatives. Likewise, claims that different social identities are permanent, unchanging categories or that some identities must take priority over others between or within people are problematic in a multicultural world.

Critical multiculturalism can start from the position that cultural identities are socially created rather than permanent, inherent truths.[24] We can relate to each other using what Keating calls "an unmapped common ground." Rather than utilizing predefined assumptions about common identities based on what we look like, where we come from, or the ideologies we wear on our sleeves, we can start from other connections, such as a desire to belong in the world and be understood.[25]

Jacqueline Lewis suggests people develop groups that continuously welcome in new people, invite sharing personal experience, support people to listen to others' experience and wonder how that changes the meanings we give to our own backgrounds. When group dynamics demonstrate an ethic of love and that becomes part of the group's collective identity, that compassionate identification binds members together as interrelated, interdependent people to help shape a group vision. This overarching narrative can help people reinterpret the memories of individuals' upbringing and identity to be more useful for quality of life and help one feel part of a greater good and geared toward listening to others and working together across boundaries.[26]

Listening to others' experiences, reinterpreting our own sense of meaning, and cocreating understanding that is more inclusive are acts that creatively transform how people see the world and their place in it because they reassess beliefs, values, assumptions, and what is true—all to expand well-being and potential. Such work takes energy and the ability to hold together meanings that seem to be in tension. Many people may find comfort in homogeneity, common sets of unambiguous beliefs, and assumed sameness based on superficial similarities. Cultural pluralism can be disquieting, but seeking to understand and incorporate differences without subsuming them to a dominant way helps us adapt to changing conditions and is at the heart of the coalition politics Reagon championed.

PREFACE

1. Charlotte Bunch and Sandra Pollack, *Learning Our Way: Essays in Feminist Education* (Trumansburg, NY: Crossing Press, 1983).
2. Nancy Whittier, *Feminist Generations: The Persistence of the Radical Women's Movement* (Philadelphia: Temple University Press, 1995), 5.
3. Sherna Berger Gluck and Daphne Patai, eds., *Women's Words: The Feminist Practice of Oral History* (New York: Routledge, 1991).

INTRODUCTION

1. Rosalyn Baxandall and Linda Gordon, eds., *Dear Sisters: Dispatches from the Women's Liberation Movement* (New York: Basic Books, 2000), 1.
2. There are books about projects that included an educational focus, e.g., Terry Wolverton, *Insurgent Muse: Life and Art at the Woman's Building* (San Francisco: City Lights, 2002).
3. Brooks interview, 1. All emphases are in the original transcripts based on speaker intonation.
4. Nancy Hewitt, ed., *No Permanent Waves: Recasting Histories of U.S. Feminism* (New Brunswick, NJ: Rutgers University Press, 2010).
5. Women's Graphic Collective, "Many Waves, One Ocean" [poster title], Chicago Women's Liberation Union (1972), http://cwluherstory.org/Online-Store.html, under "Large Poster Reprints."
6. Van Gosse, *The Movements of the New Left, 1950–1975: A Brief History with Documents* (Boston: Bedford/St. Martin's, 2005), vii; Anne Enke, *Finding the Movement: Sexuality, Contested Space, and Feminist Activism* (Durham: Duke University Press, 2007).
7. Jo Reger, *Everywhere and Nowhere: Contemporary Feminism in the United States* (New York: Oxford University Press, 2012), 6, 8.
8. Sara M. Evans, *Personal Politics: The Roots of Women's Liberation in the Civil Rights Movement and the New Left* (New York: Vintage, 1980 [1979]).
9. Judith Hole and Ellen Levine were among the first of many scholars to link the PCSW, EEOC, and founding of NOW. Hole and Levine, *Rebirth of Feminism* (New York: Quadrangle Books, 1971), 18–26, 42–43.
10. Clark A. Pomerleau, "Empowering Members, Not Overpowering Them: The National Organization for Women, Calls for Lesbian Inclusion, and California Influence, 1960s–1980s," *Journal of Homosexuality* 57.7 (2010): 842–861; Lillian Faderman and Stuart Timmons, *Gay L.A.: A History of Sexual Outlaws, Power Politics, and Lipstick Lesbians* (New York: Basic Books, 2006), 183.
11. Pomerleau, 842–861.
12. Benita Roth, *Separate Roads to Feminism: Black, Chicana, and White Feminist Movements in America's Second Wave* (Cambridge: Cambridge University Press, 2004); Wini Breines, *The Trouble Between Us: An Uneasy History of White and Black Women in*

the Feminist Movement (Oxford: Oxford University, 2006); Kimberly Springer, *Living for the Revolution: Black Feminist Organizations, 1968–1980* (Durham: Duke University Press, 2005); Anne Valk, *Radical Sisters: Second-Wave Feminism and Black Liberation in Washington, D.C.* (Urbana: University of Illinois, 2008); Maylei Blackwell, *¡Chicana Power!: Contested Histories of Feminism in the Chicano Movement* (Austin: University of Texas Press, 2011).

13. Valk, 186.

14. There is ample scholarly debate about coalition work across race, including Marlene Dixon, "The Restless Eagles: Women's Liberation 1969," in *The New Woman: A Motive Anthology of Women's Liberation*, ed. J. Cooke, Charlotte Bunch-Weeks, and Robin Morgan (Indianapolis: Bobbs-Merrill, 1970); Jo Freeman, *The Politics of Women's Liberation: A Case Study of an Emerging Movement and Its Relation to the Policy Process* (Authors Guild Backinprint.com, 2000 [1973]), 52–62; Cynthia Fuchs Epstein, "Ten Years Later: Perspectives on the Women's Movement," *Dissent* (Spring 1975): 169–176; Joan Cassell, *A Group Called Women: Sisterhood and Symbolism in the Feminist Movement* (New York: David McKay, 1977); Alice Echols, *Daring To Be Bad: Radical Feminism in America 1967–1975* (Minneapolis: University of Minnesota Press, 1989); Roth; Springer; Breines; Elizabeth Lapovsky Kennedy, "Socialist Feminism: What Difference Did It Make to the History of Women's Studies?" *Feminist Studies* 34.3 (Fall 2008): 497–525.

15. Women of Color (WOC) interview, 2, 15, 41.

16. Most specialists on feminism in the 1960s through 1980s attribute CR's origins to New York Radical Women (Anne Forer, Kathie Sarachild, Carol Hanisch, Elizabeth Sutherland Martínez, and Rosalyn Baxandall). Sara M. Evans, *Tidal Wave: How Women Changed America at Century's End* (New York: Free Press, 2003), 30. Sarachild first printed her outline for going from CR to radical feminist theory and action for the 1968 First National Women's Liberation Conference and then in Redstockings, ed., *Feminist Revolution* (1975, 1978). See Sarachild's "A Program for Consciousness-Raising," in Barbara A. Crow, ed., *Radical Feminism: A Documentary Reader* (New York: New York University Press, 2000), 273–276.

17. Rita Mae Brown, for example, expressed frustration in 1969 that her NOW CR group members discussed relationships with men to the exclusion of lesbian coupling. See Flora Davis, *Moving the Mountain: The Women's Movement in America since 1960* (New York: Simon & Schuster, 1991), 262–263; Pomerleau, 845.

18. Barbara Ehrenreich, "What Is Socialist Feminism?" [1976], in *Material Feminism: A Reader in Class, Difference, and Women's Lives*, edited by Rosemary Hennessy and Chrys Ingraham (New York: Routledge, 1997), 68.

19. See Roth; Springer.

20. See Valk.

21. Sherna Berger Gluck with Maylei Blackwell, Sharon Cotrell, and Karen S. harper, "Whose Feminism, Whose History?: Reflections on Excavating the History of (the) U.S. Women's Movement," in *Community Activism and Feminist Politics*, edited by Nancy A. Naples (New York: Routledge, 1998), 35, 40, 48.

22. Ibid, 37, 42–43.

23. Pomerleau, 852.

24. Marilyn Frye, "Some Reflections on Separatism and Power," in *Feminist Social Thought: A Reader*, edited by Diana T. Meyers (New York: Routledge, 1997), 408, 409.

25. Radicalesbians, "The Woman-Identified Woman," in *Out of the Closets: Voices of Gay Liberation*, edited by Karla Jay and Allen Young (New York: Jove/HBJ, 1977), 175–177; Pomerleau, 846–847, 850–851.

26. Echols, *Daring to Be Bad*, 283; ibid., 5.

27. Verta Taylor and Leila J. Rupp, "Women's Culture and Lesbian Feminist Activism: A Reconsideration of Cultural Feminism," *SIGNS* (Autumn 1993): 32–61.

28. An excerpted reprint is in print: Mari Jo Buhle and Paul Buhle, eds., *The Concise History of Woman Suffrage: Selections from* History of Woman Suffrage, *Edited by Elizabeth Cady Stanton, Susan B. Anthony, Matilda Joslyn Gage, and the National American Woman Suffrage Association* (Urbana: University of Illinois Press, 2005), xvii. Mary Church Terrell, *A Colored Woman in a White World*, Classics in Black Studies (Amherst, NY: Prometheus Books, 2005).

CHAPTER 1

1. Joanne J. Meyerowitz, ed., *Not June Cleaver: Women and Gender in Postwar America, 1945–1960* (Philadelphia: Temple University Press, 1994); Alice Kessler-Harris, *In Pursuit of Equity: Women, Men, and the Quest for Economic Citizenship in 20th-Century America* (New York: Oxford University Press, 2001); Stephanie Coontz, *The Way We Never Were: American Families and the Nostalgia Trap* (New York: Basic Books, 2000).

2. Michael Harrington, *The Other America: Poverty in the United States* (New York: Macmillan 1962), 178–179.

3. See Ruth Rosen's bibliography for postwar context. Rosen, *The World Split Open: How the Modern Women's Movement Changed America* (New York: Penguin Books, 2000), 401–428.

4. Kessler-Harris, 21–22, 26, 56–59.

5. Harrington, 190.

6. Sara Evans, *Tidal Wave*, xi–xii, 19; Rosen, xi; Freeman, 21–43.

7. Germain interview, 1–2, emphasis in the original.

8. Florence Howe, ed., *The Politics of Women's Studies: Testimony from 30 Founding Mothers* (New York: The Feminist Press at the City University of New York, 2000), xviii.

9. "History Highlight: Women Veterans and the WWII GI Bill of Rights," History & Collections: Women in Military Service for America Memorial Foundation, Inc. website, accessed 29 Sept. 2010, http://www.womensmemorial.org/H&C/History/history hl.html.

10. Rosen, 41–42.

11. Göran Hugo Olsson, Annika Rogell, Joslyn Barnes, Danny Glover, Axel Arnö, Angela Y. Davis, and Stokely Carmichael, *Black Power Mixtape 1967–1975: A Documentary in 9 Chapters* (New York: IFC Films, 2011).

12. Rosen, 42.

13. Howe, xvii–xviii; Constance B. Schultz and Elizabeth Hayes Turner, *Clio's Southern Sisters: Interviews with Leaders of the Southern Association for Women Historians* (Columbia, MO: University of Missouri Press, 2004), 8n14.

14. Eileen Boris and Nupur Chaudhuri, eds., *Voices of Women Historians: The Personal, the Political, the Professional* (Bloomington: Indiana University Press, 1999), 48, 68, 166.

15. Schultz and Turner, 137.

16. Ibid., 33, 38, 76–77, 96, 97, 138, 173; Howe, 58, 120; Boris and Chaudhuri, 2–3, 20, 48, 52–53, 68.

17. Schultz and Turner, 78; Howe, 18.

18. Schultz and Turner, 54; Howe, 71, 82, 171–172.

19. Howe, 66, 84–85, 90, 124–125; Schultz and Turner, 25, 64.

20. Boris and Chaudhuri, 4–5, 109.

21. Philip Jenkins, *Decade of Nightmares: The End of the Sixties and the Making of Eighties America* (New York: Oxford University Press, 2006), 28.

22. Howe, 247.

23. Pauline Valvo, "Nikolaj Frederik Severin Grundtvig: 1783–1872," National-Louis University Resources for Adult Education website (1 May 2005), accessed 28 January 2012, http://nl.edu/academics/cas/ace/resources/nfsgrundtvig.cfm.

24. Valvo.

25. Valvo.

26. John Glen, *Highlander: No Ordinary School*, 2nd ed. (Knoxville: University of Tennessee Press, 1996), 5.

27. Paul C. Mishler, *Raising Reds: The Young Pioneers, Radical Summer Camps, and Communist Political Culture in the United States* (New York: Columbia University Press, 1999), 10, 76.

28. Ibid., 2.

29. Ibid., 20–26, 30, 41, 44, 68, 70, 71, 84, 88, 96, 110, 135.

30. Glen, 10.

31. Myles Horton, *The Myles Horton Reader: Education for Social Change*, ed. Dale Jacobs, (Knoxville: University of Tennessee Press, 2003), 4.

32. Glen, 105.

33. Ibid., 66. Horton, 189, 240.

34. Horton, 191–192. Glen, 66.

35. Glen, 105, 219.

36. Horton, 122–124.

37. Ibid., 4, 7, 253, 276.

38. Horton, 121, 184, 187, 262–264.

39. Glen, 155–158, 162–163, 175–180, 193.

40. Moira Rachel Kenney, *Mapping Gay L.A.: The Intersection of Place and Politics* (Philadelphia: Temple University Press, 2001), 125.

41. Faderman and Timmons, 173, 182.

42. Ibid., 170, 389n6.

43. Kenney, 125.

44. Yolanda Retter, "Los Angeles Lesbian Chronology, 1970–1980," from the online Lesbian History Project (1996), accessed 20 March 2003, http://www-lib.usc.edu/~retter/main.html.

45. Baxandall and Gordon, 117.

46. Ibid., 118–119.

47. Aldebaran et al., "Statement from the Radical Feminist Therapy Collective," *Sister: Los Angeles Women's Center* 5.6 (Sept. 1974): 8.

48. Sara Golda Bracha Fishman [a.k.a. Aldebaran, a.k.a. Vivian F. Mayer], "Life in

the Fat Underground," *Radiance: The Magazine for Large Women* (Winter 1998), email version from Ariana Manov; Retter, "On the Side of Angels," 103.

49. NAAFA was later called National Association to Advance Fat Acceptance. Among the position papers Fat Underground would develop from their base at the Westside Women's Center were Anonymous, "Psychiatry" (1974), Aldebaran, "Compulsive Eating—In Six Easy Steps" (1974), Aldebaran, "Health of Fat People," Lynn Mabel-Lois, "Stereotype Yourself!" (1974), Lucia S. Williams, "Furniture in the Public" (1974), Aldebaran, "Fat: Let the Doctors Speak for Themselves" (1975), and Aldebaran, "The No-Cure 'Cure'" (1976), all found in Judy Freespirit's box at the June L. Mazer Lesbian Collection, Los Angeles, CA; Fishman, "Life in the Fat Underground."

50. Berkeley's Radical Psychiatry Center taught that people were fat because they ate too much because they were oppressed. By disproving the middle factor, Fat Underground directly attacked underlying factors oppressing fat women. Fishman, "Life in the Fat Underground." "When food intakes of obese individuals were accurately assessed and compared with people of normal weights, the intakes were identical." A. M. Bryans, *Canadian Journal of Public Health* (November 1967): 487, cited in Aldebaran, "Fat: Let the Doctors Speak." Concerning the failure of diets, reports such as the U.S. Department of Health, Education and Welfare's in 1966 and *Obesity* in 1974 concluded that because the body reduces metabolic rate and the amount of energy intake to operate when given decreased calories, people on diets would have to further reduce caloric intake and accept hunger to maintain reduced weight. Aldebaran, "Fat." Alvan Feinstein, M.D., wrote, "The few studies [of weight loss] containing long term results usually show a very low success rate—no more than about 1 or 2%." Alvan Feinstein, "How Do We Measure Accomplishment in Weight Reduction?" in *Obesity: Causes, Consequences, and Treatment* (Medcom Press, 1974), 86, cited in Aldebaran, "The No-Cure 'Cure'" (1976). Fishman, "Life in the Fat Underground." The 1960s study of fat, blue-collar Italian Americans in Roseto, Pennsylvania, found them virtually free of the diseases supposedly correlated with fatness. Although these Rosetans ate high-cholesterol foods, their subculture valued fatness, and they were "healthier than the average, average-sized American of the same age, sex and occupation." A Mayo Clinic study in 1952 found that people who maintained a heavy weight became coronary patients at the same rate as slim people and dieters but survived better than thin and dieting people. Aldebaran cites a number of doctors who warned that dieting impaired the heart, nerves, protein tissue, and body chemistry. Aldebaran, "Health of Fat People: The Scare-Story Your Doctor Won't Tell You," seven-page Fat Underground pamphlet of 1974.

51. The "communiqué" was "Fat Underground Communique," in *Sister* 5.4 (July 1974): 4. Vivian Mayer, "Fat Liberation: A Radical Therapy Approach" (unpublished manuscript, n.d.), 2, in Judy Freespirit's box at Mazer.

52. They circulated a generic letter for one's doctor demanding adequate medical attention without the assumption that problems are based on weight, without lectures, and with allowances like large size (42 cm) blood pressure cuffs so that a falsely high reading did not result from an overly tight cuff. Letter in Judy Freespirit's box at Mazer. Mayer, "Fat Liberation" recounts incidents of doctors refusing to examine fat women with fractured spines and instead telling them to exercise, and of a doctor who would not believe a fat woman was pregnant (she almost died of toxemia), 5.

53. Fishman, "Life in the Fat Underground."

54. Ibid.; Aldebaran, "We Are Not Our Enemies," *Sister* 4.10 (December 1973): 4; ibid., "Fat Liberation Manifesto," *Sister* 5.4 (July 1974): 4; ibid., "More Women Are on Diets than in Jail," *Sister* 5.8 (November 1974): 4. *Sister* also documented FU's investigation of women's clinics for fatphobia: Aldebaran, "Fat Underground Investigates Women's Clinic," *Sister* 5.9 (January 1975): 3.

55. Fishman, "Life in the Fat Underground." Aldebaran, "The No-Cure 'Cure'."

56. Ariana Manov interview, 26.

57. Judy Freespirit and Aldebaran, "Fat Liberation Manifesto," "The Fat Illusion," and other FU pamphlets are reprinted in Lisa Schoenfielder and Barb Wieser, eds., *Shadow on a Tightrope: Writings by Women on Fat Oppression* (San Francisco: Aunt Lute Books, 1983 [originally November 1973]), 52–53 (italics in the original).

58. Shirl Buss, "Clinic Fires Doctor for Racist, Fatist Attitudes," *The Lesbian Tide* 6.6 (May/June 1977): 20. Buss was not fat herself but helped FU prepare a video about fat liberation. Ariana Manov interview, 27. Cheri Lesh, "Big Hipped, Beautiful, and Fierce," *The Lesbian Tide* 7.3 (November/December 1977): 8–9.

59. Vivian Mayer, "The Fat Illusion," *Hagborn* (n.p., n.d., between late 1980 and January 1981), 3–4, from Betty Jetter's personal files. Marilyn Wann's *FAT!SO?: Because You Don't Have to Apologize for Your Size!* (Berkeley: Ten Speed Press, 1998) continues fat liberation and shows how activist publication has expanded since Fat Underground.

60. Faderman and Timmons, 190.

61. Robin Morgan, "Lesbianism and Feminism: Synonyms or Contradictions?: Keynote Address at Lesbian-Feminist Conference, Los Angeles, April 14, 1973." *The Lesbian Tide* (May/June 1973): 32.

62. Barbara McLean, "Diary of a Mad Organizer," *The Lesbian Tide* (May/June 1973): 35–41, here 36, italics and capitalization in the original.

63. Janice G. Raymond, *The Transsexual Empire: The Making of the She-Male* (New York: Athene Series, Teachers College Press, 1994 [1979]).

64. Ibid., 27. Some feminists have seen trans men as defecting from womanhood and assumed that FTMs ceased to care about female oppression and feminism if they gained male privilege from being recognized as men. A large proportion of trans men have gone through a stage of identifying as lesbians or lesbian feminists, perhaps because lesbianism and feminism disrupted normative womanhood. Henry Rubin, *Self-Made Men: Identity and Embodiment among Transsexual Men* (Nashville: Vanderbilt University, 2003), 84–85. The notion that trans people are motivated by gender privilege ignores trans women's experience of themselves as constantly misrecognized or punished for knowing they are women. When trans people seek medical transition, they want to be recognized as the gender they know themselves to be.

Feminism has informed transgender theory and practice, and transgender politics continues to add to feminism. Like white privilege or middle-class privilege, a transformative politics calls on FTMs who reap male privilege through transition to use it to speak out against oppression. Increasing numbers of feminists embrace trans women who want to be a part of feminism and recognize that feminist trans women are working through the transgressive definitions of woman that feminists have sought to create. When lesbian feminists accepted doctors' assignments of infants' gender and assumed essential qualities, they could not listen to individuals' self-assessments of their gender and needs. Like non-trans people, trans people span a spectrum from reactionary to radical. Some simply seek recognition that they are the normative woman or man they always knew themselves to be. For others, choices about their bodies and the way they live in the world reflect lifelong resistance to patriarchal gender division and carry on 1960s feminist reevaluations of traditional gender roles.

65. Catoggio interview, 62.

66. Retter, "On the Side of Angels," 135–136; Lois Bencangey interview, 1.

67. Maida Tilchen, "Lesbians and Women's Music," in *Women-Identified Women*, ed. Trudy Darty and Sandee Potter (Palo Alto, CA: Mayfield, 1984), 287–303. Frances Reid and Judy Dlugacz, prod. and dir., *The Changer: A Record of the Times* (Oakland: Olivia Records, 1991). Dee Mosbacher et al., prod. and dir., *Radical Harmonies* (San Francisco: Woman Vision, 2002).

68. Margie Adams, "Best Friend (The Unicorn Song)" and "We Shall Go Forth," arranged by Kay Gardner and Sue Fink (1977); Meg Christian, "The Rock Will Wear Away," arranged by Mary Dawkins; Cris Williamson, "Song of the Soul"; Bernice Reagon, "Every Woman Who Ever Loved a Woman," transcribed and arranged by Sue Fink, from *Believe I'll Run on See What the End's Gonna Be* album; Bernice Reagon (words and music), "Joanne Little," arranged by Bernice Reagon, Lynn Wilson, and Ann Buffington. All cited songs are from Betty Jetter's personal files.

69. "La Darke," traditional Serbo-Croatian folk song transcribed by Carole Petracca; "Bright Morning Star," traditional Appalacian folk song; Francesca Caccini, "La Liberazione de Ruggiero"; "De Colores," traditional with additional lyrics by Jennifer Woodal, Ginny Berson, and Holly Near, arranged by Joan Baez, additional music by Lynn Wilson. Betty Jetter's personal files.

70. Suni Paz, "Hasta la Victoria Siempre," arranged by Lynn Wilson with help from Sue Fink, for L.A. Women's Chorus (September 1977); Violeta Para (words and music), "Gracias a la Vida," arranged by Lynn Wilson for L.A. Women's Chorus (November 8, 1977); "De Colores." Betty Jetter's personal files.

71. Malvina Reynolds, "The Judge Said," lyrics only. Betty Jetter's personal files.

72. Susann Shonbaum, "The Fury," music transcribed and adopted by Sue Fink (n.d.); Flo Kennedy, "Battle Hymn of Women," lyrics without date. Betty Jetter's personal files.

73. "Sister-Woman-Sister," lyrics without date. Betty Jetter's personal files.

74. Bonnie Lockhart, "Still Ain't Satisfied," lyrics without date. Betty Jetter's personal files.

75. Mary Glavin, "New Woman Rising," music by Lynn Wilson, arranged for L.A. Women's Chorus by Ann Buffington and Lynn Wilson (March 27, 1978); Elaine Miller (words and arrangement), "Woman Spirit" (1970s); Ethel Smyth (words and music), "March of the Women: Shoulder to Shoulder," arranged by Lynn Wilson (1977); Joelyn Grippo and Sue Fink (words and music), "A Woman's Song" (1976); "For Bein' a Woman," arranged by Elaine Miller for women's chorus (n.d.); Susanne Morgan, "Women Energy." Betty Jetter's personal files.

76. Peggy LaMer and Elaine Miller, "Sisters Passin' Through," (n.d.), based on the American folk song "Passin' Through." James Oppenheim, "Bread and Roses," music by Caroline Kohlsaat, arranged by Anna Rubin (n.d.); "Cotton Mill Girls," traditional; Anna Rubin, "Sappho" (n.d.); Debbie Lempke, "The Bloods!," arranged by Carole Petracca and Sue Fink (n.d.); Patti Nicklaus (words and music), Patti Nicklaus, "W.A.V.A.W. Song," arranged by Lynn Wilson for women's chorus. Betty Jetter's personal files.

77. Malvina Reynolds, "What Have They Done to the Rain" and "The Judge Said"; Bonnie Lockhart, "Still Ain't Satisfied"; Margie Adams, "Best Friend"; Flo Kennedy, "Battle Hymn of Women"; Susanne Morgan, "Women Energy"; Programs from Betty Jetter's personal files.

78. Elsa Sue Fisher interview, 2–3, 8; Elsa Sue Fisher follow-up, 1.

79. Otero interview, 6.

80. P. A., "Law in a Contrived Vacuum: Z's Conviction Affirmed," *The Lesbian Tide* 5.4, corrected to 5 (March/April 1976): 6.

81. "New Evidence in Witch Trial," *The Lesbian Tide* 7.1 (July/August 1977): 16; P. A., 5. Sharon McDonald, "Z Budapest, Witch in Progress," *The Lesbian Tide* 9.5 (March/April 1980): 6–7.

82. Cheri Lesh, "Wicca Is Rebellion, Not Mysticism," *The Lesbian Tide* 6.5 (March/April 1977): 19.

83. Helen Hancken, "Bearded Womon Honors Ancestors," *The Lesbian Tide* 5.3 corrected to 4 (January/February 1976): 28.

84. Z Budapest, "How the Grinch Stole Winter Solstice," *The Lesbian Tide* 5.4 (January/February 1976): 29.

85. Ibid., "The Movement Should Support Its Stars," and The Editorial and Political Collective, "Editorial: But Who Would Support the Movement?," *The Lesbian Tide* 6.5 (March/April 1977): 14–15.

CHAPTER 2

1. Betty Willis Brooks, "All the Teachers Are the Taught, and All the Taught Are the Teachers: Califia Community" (unpublished manuscript, n.d. [post-1982?]), 1–2, Lesbian Legacy Collection at ONE (LLC); Betty Brooks with Sylvia Russell interview, 2–3. The Ecumenical Institute was an interdenominational live-in community the World Council of Churches started in Chicago in the 1950s that combined equal task-sharing and teaching between men and women for societal change. Brooks was affiliated first with the Methodist Church and then with the progressive denomination United Church of Christ.

2. Cathy Olson gave a "Self-Defense for Women" course through Santa Monica City College and offered to help women form self-defense collectives through Westside Women's Center. Retter, "On the Side of Angels," 138. Maureen, "Self Defense," *Sister* 4.2 (February 1972): 9. Rural feminists built intentional communities and published self-defense articles with step-by-step photographed techniques in *Country Women*. Betty Braver, "Rape," *Country Women* 10 (April 1974): 44–48; ibid., "Self Defense: Between Mothers and Daughters," *Country Women* 11 (July 1974): 46–52; Dyani, "Self Defense," *Country Women* 12 (August 1974): 47; Sue Katz, "Kick Ass for Women," *Country Women* 14 (February 1975): 50–55; Dana Densmore, "Ja Shin Do," *Country Women* 16 (June 1975): 58–59; Barbara, "The Nature of Self-Defense," *Country Women* 24 (April 1977): 21; Marty Pate with Jill Wilson, "Tai Chi: A Learning Cycle," *Country Women* 28 (March 1978): 6–7; Betty Braver, "Karate: The Art of the Open Hand," *Country Women* 28 (March 1978): 24–26.

3. "Dirty Street Fighting," *Human Behavior* (October 1973): 17; and "Twelve Tips on Self-Defense" from CSULB in LLC subject files; "Self-Defense for Women," *Sister* (February/March 1977): 9.

4. Retter, "On the Side of Angels," 137.

5. Joan Robins, "Betty Brooks: One Woman Wave Maker," *Sister* 5.6 (September 1974): 1.

6. Retter, "On the Side of Angels," 138.

7. Brooks follow-up interview, 1.

8. "Purge of Feminists in ♀'s Phys Ed," *Sister* 5.5 (August 1974): 1. Joan Robins, "Betty Brooks: One Woman Wave Maker," *Sister* 5.6 (September 1974): 1.

9. Randi Firus, "Brooks—Profile in Unsubtle Persuasion," *Daily Forty-Niner* (October 17, 1979): 12, LLC subject files, Betty Willis Brooks.

10. Marilyn Murphy, Lesbianic Logic columns, "'Our Proud Present,'" *The Lesbian News* 9.5 (December 1983): 23; "Feminist Yesterdays," ibid. 9.10 (May 1984): 23–24; "Some Girls Never Learn," ibid. 12.3 (November 1986): 29; Jetter interview, 1–2.

11. Roth, 135–136.

12. Marilyn Murphy, "Califia Community," in Bunch and Pollack, 138.

13. Cheryl Gould, "New ♀ Institute Opens," *The Lesbian Tide* 4.5 (January 1975): 11, 29. *Sagaris* was a synonym for the double-edged ax of the Amazons also called a *labyris*.

14. Brooks interview, 3; Echols, *Daring to Be Bad*, 265–268; Rosen, 254–257, 258–259.

15. Gould, 11.

16. Jackie St. Joan, "The Ideas and the Realities: Sagaris, Session I," in Bunch and Pollack, 117–125.

17. Catoggio interview, 6.

18. Echols, *Daring to Be Bad*, 265–268.

19. Rosen, 256, based on her interview of Atkinson.

20. Catoggio interview, 7–8.

21. Gould, 29. St. Joan, 116.

22. Echols, *Daring to Be Bad*, 268.

23. Rosen, 256–257.

24. Ibid., 258.

25. Catoggio interview, 6–7, 8, 9.

26. Select Committee to Study Governmental Operations with Respect to Intelligence Activities (The Church Committee), *Final Report* (Washington, D.C.: GPO, 1976), 3, 2–27, reprinted in Robert Griffith and Paula Baker, eds., *Major Problems in American History Since 1945*, 3rd ed. (Boston: Houghton Mifflin, 2007), 252–255.

27. Roberta Salpiers gives a good example of the waste involved. Of the 646-page FBI file on her, the FBI eventually released 388 pages to her. Half of that consisted of duplicated material. A great deal of the nonduplicated material, such as movement publications and newspaper articles, was already public. Roberta Salpiers, "U.S. Government Surveillance and the Women's Liberation Movement, 1968–1973: A Case Study," *Feminist Studies* 34.3 (Fall 2008): 431–455.

28. Rosen, 239–260. Echols, *Daring to Be Bad*, 8, 248, 301–302n25; Davis, 138, 141–142. Roxanne Dunbar-Ortiz, *Outlaw Woman: A Memoir of the War Years, 1960–1975* (San Francisco: City Lights, 2001), 222, 225–265, esp. 245, 257–260.

29. Margaret Rose Gladney, "A Chain Reaction of Dreams: Lillian Smith and Laurel Falls Camp," *Journal of American Culture* 5.3, (Fall 1982): 50–55. Charles Payne, *I've Got the Light of Freedom: The Organizing Tradition and the Mississippi Freedom Struggle* (Berkeley: University of California Press, 1997); Horton.

30. Brooks, "All the Teachers Are the Taught," 2.

31. Brooks follow-up interview, 1. Nobody in the group was from Morro Bay, but a professor opened her home in La Jolla for their meeting.

32. Brooks, "All the Teachers Are the Taught," 3.

33. The public planning meeting on November 16, 1975, resulted in the following people joining as collective members: Margaret Barker, Mary Glavin, Donna Hill, Cecilia Lami, Janet Stambolian (a socialist feminist), and Sue Williams. Barker, Hill, Lami, and Marilyn Pearsol resigned before the Califia Camp and, according to Brooks, were replaced by "another Sagaris woman," Sue Dunne a.k.a. Cybele, Ahshe Greene, Gail Harris, Anne Perna, and Shirley Virgil. Brooks, "All the Teachers Are the Taught," 4.

34. Murphy, in Bunch and Pollack, 139. Brooks, "All the Teachers Are the Taught," 3. Founded in 1973, the Women's Building was a white-dominated center that housed art programs, dances, lectures, and businesses. Retter, "On the Side of Angels," 124–127.

35. Murphy, in Bunch and Pollack, 139. Brooks, "All the Teachers Are the Taught," 4.

36. Califia bridged European and American traditions as a reference from García Ordóñez de Montalvo's 1510 *Las Sergas de Esplandián* (Adventures of Esplandián). The story is set on an island called California replete with pearls, gold, and beautiful black Amazon women who are led by Queen Califia. Fortified by steep cliffs and rock shores, Califia and her Amazons allowed men on the island only once per year, as walking sperm donors, a concept that repeats Strabo's ancient Greek description of Amazons. Hernán Cortés led about 650 Spaniards in eleven ships from Cuba up the western coast of Mexico in 1519 and mentioned California as a "great island of fabulous wealth" after his men met American Indians who had pearls. Mark J. Denger, "Spanish and Mexican California: Explorations and Conquest of California," for the California State Military Department's "The California Military Museum: Preserving California's Military History" website, last accessed 22 March 2003, http://militarymuseum.org/ExConXA .html. Like feminists between 1970 and 1975, Califia collective members connected with the Amazon tradition that stemmed from ancient Greek mythology. They foreshadowed women of color cultural references, however, by choosing a name that combined Old and New World references.

37. Brooks follow-up interview, 4.

38. Brooks, "All the Teachers Are the Taught," 6.

39. Paulo Freire's writing influenced radical American educators at the time. His program for *conscientização*, or critical consciousness, guided oppressed people from a starting point of perceiving social, political, and economic contradictions that limited their freedom to realizing "the 'untested feasibility' which lies beyond the limit-situations" and taking "action against the oppressive elements of reality." Paulo Freire, *Pedagogy of the Oppressed*, 30th Anniversary Edition, trans. Myra Bergman Ramos, intro. Donaldo Macedo (New York: Continuum, 2000 [1970]), 35, chapter 3, esp. 113–119.

40. Freire, 72–73, 81.

41. Brooks, "All the Teachers Are the Taught," 5.

42. Catoggio interview, 4–5.

43. "Come to Califia Community" brochures from LLC and June L. Mazer Lesbian Collection (Mazer).

44. Camp de Benneville in the Angelus Forest held 150 women and 30 children for 1977–1978. Camp Cielo in 1979 held 250 people. Brochures 1977–1979, LLC.

45. Brochures 1977–1983 list successive sites. Califia conferences in 1979 were at a Camp Fire Girls Camp Cielo (seventeen miles northeast of Santa Barbara) and at the Women's Buildings in L.A. and in San Francisco. In 1980 Califia met at Cottontail Ranch a half-hour from L.A. in Malibu Canyon, a YMCA Camp Arbolado in Angelus Oaks (San Bernardino National Forest), and 4H Camp Las Posadas in Angwin, CA, an hour and a half from San Francisco. Califia 1981 met twice at Cottontail, at Echo Lake Camp by Berkeley, and at Camp Cielo again. Califia 1982 held two camps at the Jewish Camp JCA in Malibu and one at another Angelus Forest Camp Radford (Angelus Oaks area). Califia 1983 started at Hollywoodland Camp in L.A., returned to Camp Cielo, and had another Thanksgiving weekend.

46. Brochure 1977, LLC. Brooks interview, 36. Myers interview, 1. Bernstein interview, 4. With inflation, the 2012 values of these costs are approximately $2,950 for the 1975 $700 fee, $300 for the 1976 $75 fee, $200 for $50, $100 for $25, and $40 for the $10 deposit.

47. "Ahshe on Class," July 1976 tape deposited at Mazer. Catoggio interview, 54.

48. Brochure 1978, 2, from the personal files of Wanda Jewell and Diane F. Germain.

49. Murphy, in Bunch and Pollack, 140, 142.

50. Brooks, "All the Teachers Are the Taught," 5.

51. Weiss follow-up interview, 1. Women of Color group interview (WOC interview hereafter), 56.

52. Jetter interview, 2. Bernstein interview, 3. Jetter met Murphy at the NOW California State Conferences. Jetter was a long-term member of NOW–San Fernando Valley while Murphy was in NOW–Orange County.

53. Elsa Sue Fisher interview, 2. Catoggio interview, 5. Muriel Fisher interview, 1.

54. Bencangey interview, 1.

55. Wanda Jewell learned from a friend who had attended in 1976. Diane F. Germain entered in 1978 through her friend, Yvonne King, who was the lifeguard. Jewell interview, 1–2. Germain interview, 3.

56. Brochure 1977.

57. Brooks, "All the Teachers Are the Taught," 6. Murphy, in Bunch and Pollack, 145.

58. Brooks, "All the Teachers Are the Taught," 6.

59. Brochure 1979, LLC.

60. Manov interview, 2. Diane F. Germain, "Feminist Art and Education at Califia: My Personal Experience," in Bunch and Pollock, 154. Bencangey interview, 5.

61. Bencangey, Bernstein, Brooks, Catoggio, Díaz, Elsa Sue Fisher, Muriel Fisher, Germain, Jetter, Jewell, Kaufmann, Manov, Merry, Murphy, Sabry, and Weiss interviews; Marilyn Murphy, in Bunch and Pollack, 139.

62. Bencangey interview, 1. Catoggio interview, 5. Elsa Sue Fisher interview, 4. Kaufmann interview, 1–2. Jetter interview, 3. Merry interview, 17–18. Murphy interview, 1. Weiss interview, 1. Off-tape Bernstein and Sabry confirmed other accounts that each started a long-term relationship with a partner during Califia.

63. Murphy interview, 1. Weiss interview, 1.

64. Elsa Sue Fisher interview, 4.

65. Catoggio interview, 9.

66. Elsa Sue Fisher interview, 3.

67. Jetter interview, 3.

68. Bernstein interview, 3.

69. Germain interview, 4.

70. Bencangey interview, 5.

71. Bernstein interview, 5.

72. Germain follow-up interview, 5. The cunt slides were one of the most memorable sexuality presentations. Jetter interview, 33–34.

73. Jetter interview, 33–34. Otero interview, 30–31.

74. "Califia Sexuality Workshop," Jewell's notes from attending, from Wanda Jewell's personal files.

75. Jetter interview, 32.

76. Merry interview, 18–19.

77. Bernstein interview, 18.

78. Brooks interview, 7.

79. Merry interview, 18.

80. Bencangey interview, 5. Bernstein interview, 17. Manov interview, 25. Merry interview, 17.

81. Of those attending the 1976–1978 camps, Bernstein had found the Gay Community Service Center in 1976 in her process of coming out. Jetter and Marilyn Murphy were both married at first contact with Califia but divorced within a year. Jeanne Murphy also came out in midlife and has joked that she knew she would become a lesbian when her sister, Marilyn, came out to her. Bencangey had been out for two years. Myers came out in the late 1970s after a life without romantic interest in men. Elsa Fisher felt she chose to be lesbian rather than bisexual while her mother, Muriel, became strictly lesbian after divorcing her husband. Jewell entered the collective using her married name and completed her coming out after her first two years (brochure 1978). Bernstein interview, 2. Jetter interview, 2, 19. Murphy interview, 13. Bencangey interview, 8. Myers, follow-up interview, 1. Elsa Sue Fisher interview, 10, 19. Manov interview, 2.

82. Jetter interview, 17–18.

83. Brooks interview, 7.

84. There has been no discussion of whether heterosexual feminists found this offensive. Germain interview, 34. Retter interview, 1. Manov interview, 18.

85. Germain interview, 11–12.

86. Kaufmann interview, 1–2.

87. Bencangey interview, 5.

88. Manov interview, 25–26.

89. Bencangey interview, 5, 7. Bernstein interview, 5. Brooks interview, 18, 26–27, 55. Catoggio interview, 1–2. Elsa Sue Fisher interview, 4, 31. Germain interview, 3, 26, 36, 37. Jewell interview, 2, 9, 17. Kaufmann interview, 12. Merry interview, 2, 17–19, 27. Sabry interview, 17. Seco interview, 4, 26, 28. Weiss interview, 32.

90. Germain, follow-up interview, 5.

91. Merry interview, 2, 27. Weiss interview, 32. Seco interview, 4. Elsa Sue Fisher interview, 31. Manov interview, 25.

92. Otero interview, 7–8.

93. Weiss interview, 32.

94. Weiss interview, 32.

95. Echols, *Daring to Be Bad*, 5, 283. Taylor and Rupp.

96. Weiss interview, 14, 16.

97. Susan Krieger, *The Mirror Dance: Identity in a Women's Community* (Philadelphia: Temple University Press, 1983), xii–xv, 5, 12.

98. Kaufmann interview, 11–12. Sabry interview, 5–6.

99. Joy Fisher, "The Califia Experiment," *The Lesbian Tide* 6.2 (September/October 1976): 4.

100. Weiss interview, 24.

101. Murphy, in Bunch and Pollock, 142.

102. "Song of Unity (A Woman's Anthem)," with lyrics by Ann Denham with the assistance of Audry Sheats, Billie Hamilton, and Charlotte Clarke. Betty Jetter's personal files.

103. WOC interview, 38.

104. Joy Fisher, "The Califia Experiment," 4.

105. Taylor and Rupp.

106. Jewell interview, 9, 1.

107. Joy Fisher, "The Califia Experiment," 5.

108. Jetter interview, 4–5.

109. Jetter interview, 3.

110. Weiss interview, 24, 28.

111. Brooks interview, 18, 55.

112. Catoggio interview, 50.

113. Fisher, "The Califia Experiment," 5.

114. "Califia Land Project" *The Lesbian Tide* 6.3 (November/December 1976): 26.

115. "Califia Plans Urban Commune" *The Lesbian Tide* 6.4 (January/February 1977): 16.

116. Brooks, follow-up interview, 2.

117. Journals of the period that published about women-only land communities included *Country Women, Maize: A Lesbian Country Magazine, Off Our Backs*, and Southern Oregon's *Womanspirit* (1974–1984). A number of first-person accounts, participant-observer studies, and ethnographies document the network of women's lands called the Southern Oregon Women's Community: Sue, Nelly, Dian, Carol, and Billie, *Country Lesbians: The Story of the Womanshare Collective* (Grants Pass, OR: Womanshare Books, 1976); Joyce Cheney, ed., *Lesbian Land* (Minneapolis: Word Weavers, 1985); Katharine Matthaei Sprecher, "Lesbian Intentional Communities in Rural Southwestern Oregon: Discussion on Separatism, Environmentalism, and Community Conflict," MA thesis, California Institute of Integral Studies (1997); La Verne Gagehabib and Barbara Summerhawk, *Circles of Power: Shifting Dynamics in a Lesbian-Centered Community* (Norwich, VT: New Victoria Publishers, 2000); Hawk Madrone, *Weeding at Dawn: A Lesbian Country Life* (Binghamton, NY: Harrington Park Press, 2000); Catriona Sandilands, "Lesbian Separatist Communities and the Experience of Nature: Toward a Queer Ecology," *Organization & Environment* 15 (June 2002): 131–163; Catherine B. Kleiner, "Doin' It for Themselves: Lesbian Land Communities in Southern Oregon, 1970–1995," PhD diss., University of New Mexico (2003); Jennifer Marie Almquist, "Incredible Lives: An Ethnography of Southern Oregon Womyn's Lands," MA thesis, interdisciplinary studies, Oregon State University (2004).

118. Jewell, personal conversation on July 10, 2002.

119. Catoggio interview, 27–28, 29.

120. Bernstein interview, 6–7.

121. Japanese researchers continue to publish medicinal benefits of green tea as an antioxidant that blocks destructive effects of free radicals, lowers lipids and blood pressure, fights bacteria, viruses, toxins, and cancer, hinders tooth decay, and deodorizes the body. The benefits of green tea are also touted in women's health books regarding aging. Purifying and balancing qualities could have been metaphorically transferred to conceptions of mental illness as caused by impurity and imbalance. Yukihiko Hara, *Green Tea: Health Benefits and Applications,* Food Science and Technology series, ed. Owen R. Fennema et al. (New York: Marcel Dekker, 2001). Takehiko Yamamoto et al., eds., *Chemistry and Applications of Green Tea* (Boca Raton: CRC Press, 1997).

122. Jetter interview, 13–14.

123. Elsa Sue Fisher interview, 22. Brooks interview, 12.

124. "Ahshe Green on Class."

125. Manov interview, 19–20.

126. Gay and lesbian historians have produced growing evidence that people who expressed same-gender attraction have been susceptible to imprisonment in mental wards and debilitating torture through nonconsensual drug therapy, electroshock, and lobotomies. Gary Atkins, *Gay Seattle: Stories of Exile and Belonging* (Seattle: University of Washington Press, 2003), 34–52.

127. Phyllis Chesler, *Women and Madness* (New York: Avon, 1972). Esther Newton supported Chesler's critique with a mostly personal account that linked designations of mental illness to frustration over patriarchal suppression. She cited Ronald Laing and Aaron Esterson's 1971 *Sanity, Madness and the Family: Families of Schizophrenics* as evidence that "much of so-called schizophrenic behavior is a predictable and purposeful response to certain techniques of mental torture": denial, restriction of autonomy, fusion with mother, father's paranoia regarding sexual intentions of other men, mystification, contradiction, and tabooed areas. Esther Newton, "High School Crack-Up," in *Amazon Expedition: A Lesbianfeminist Anthology,* ed. Phyllis Birkby et al. (Albion, CA: Times Change Press, 1973), 43–54, here 44.

128. Elsa Sue Fisher interview, 21.

129. Merry interview, 15.

130. Jetter recalled that her partner at the time volunteered, pressured Jetter to sign up for a shift, but then left Jetter alone to supervise Sappha. Jetter spent the next two hours nearby as Sappha masturbated. Upset and miffed, Jetter became another voice saying Califia could not care for Sappha. Jetter interview, 14.

131. Brooks interview, 13.

132. Manov interview, 20.

133. Murphy, in Bunch and Pollack, 141.

134. Ibid.

135. Freeman, 119–124.

136. Manov interview, 28.

137. Jewell interview, 13–14.

138. Seco interview, 1–2.

139. Catoggio interview, 55–56.

140. WOC interview, 33–34.

141. Jetter interview, 38–39.

142. Weiss interview, 13. WOC interview, 33–34.

143. Seco interview, 2.

144. "Califia Community at de Benneville" (n.d.), 2, from Jewell's personal files.

145. Bernstein interview, 3.

146. Jetter interview, 51–52.

147. Frances Moore Lappé, *Diet for a Small Planet* (New York: Ballantine Books, 1971), 5–9, 18–24, italics in original. Warren J. Belasco, *Appetite for Change: How the Counterculture Took on the Food Industry 1966–1988* (New York: Pantheon Books, 1989), 19–20, 133, 172, 259n26.

148. Belasco, 16.

149. Ibid., 26.

150. Françoise d'Eaubonne, "The Time for Ecofeminism," trans. Ruth Hottell, in *Ecology: Key Concepts in Critical Theory*, edited by Carolyn Merchant and Roger S. Gottlieb (Atlantic Highlands, N.J.: Humanities Press International, 1994).

151. Eric Schlosser, *Fast Food Nation: The Dark Side of the All-American Meal* (New York: Perennial, 2002 [2001]), 5, 19–24.

152. Carol Adams, "The Oedible Complex: Feminism and Vegetarianism" in Gina Covina and Laurel Galana, eds., *The Lesbian Reader: An Amazon Quarterly Anthology* (Berkeley: Amazon Press, 1975), 147, 150.

153. Belasco, 54. Lappé, 28–29. The National Academy of Science concluded that Americans exceeded protein recommendations by 45 percent.

154. Myers interview, 4.

155. Jewell interview, 3, 4–5, 6, 7, 11, 12, 16, 17.

156. Ibid., 1, 2, 11.

CHAPTER 3

1. Assessments about how males oppressed females proliferated from the late 1960s, building on suffrage-era critiques, post–World War II authors like Simone de Beauvoir, Elinor Flexnor, Eve Merriam, Betty Friedan, and Aileen Kraditor, and women's personal experience. Kate Weigand, *Red Feminism: American Communism and the Making of Women's Liberation* (Baltimore: Johns Hopkins University Press, 2001), 140–148.

2. Murphy, in Bunch and Pollack, 146; and camp schedules (Mazer, LLC). For the long duration of the lesbian-straight split, see Pomerleau, 842–861.

3. Weigand, 147. Elinor Flexnor, *Century of Struggle* (1959), Kate Millett, *Sexual Politics* (1970), Anne Koedt et al., eds., *Radical Feminism* (1972), Del Martin and Phyllis Lyon, *Lesbian/Woman* (1972), Dolores Klaich, *Woman + Woman* (1974), Vivian Fornick and Barbara Moran, eds., *Woman in Sexist Society* (1971), Adrienne Rich, *Of Woman Born* (1976), Toni Cade [Bambara], ed., *Black Woman* (1970), Gerda Lerner, ed., *Black Woman in White America* (1972). Califia Community Letter, (June 1978), Germain's personal files. "Califia Community at de Benneville" (n.d. [1978]), Jewell's personal files.

4. "Recommended Reading List," n.d. (after 1979), Mazer archive. James Baldwin, *Notes of a Native Son* (1955) and *Fire Next Time* (1963), Betty Berzon and Robert Leighton, eds., *Positively Gay* (1979), Lorraine Bethel and Barbara Smith, eds., *Conditions: Five, the Black Women's Issue* (1979), Cade (1970), Phyllis Chesler, *With Child* (1979), Mary Daly, *Gyn/Ecology* (1978), Angela Davis, *If They Come in the Morning* (1971), Anthony and Rosalind Dworkin, *The Minority Report: An Introduction to Racial, Ethnic and Gender Relations* (1976), Zillah R. Eisenstein, ed., *Capitalist Patri-*

archy and the Case for Socialist Feminism (1978), Flexnor (1959), Sally Gearhardt, *The Wanderground* (1978), Gornick and Moran (1971), Susan Griffin, *Woman and Nature* (1978), Lorraine Hansberry, *To Be Young, Gifted and Black* (1971), Jeanne Wakatsuki Houston, *Farewell to Manzanar* (1973), Jordan Winthrop, *White Over Black* (1968), Maxine Hong Kingston, *Warrior Woman* (1975), Klaich (1974), Louis Knowles and Kenneth Pruitt, eds., *Institutional Racism in America* (1969), Koedt (1973), Joyce A. Ladner, ed., *The Death of White Sociology* (1973), Frances Moore Lappé, *Diet for a Small Planet* (1971), Martin and Lyon (1972), Millett (1970), Juliet Mitchell, *Woman's Estate* (1971), Ann Petry, ed., *In Darkness and Confusion* (1947), Marge Piercy, *Woman on the Edge of Time* (1976), Armando B. Rendon, *Chicano Manifesto* (1971), Rich (1976), Adrienne Rich, *On Lies, Secrets, and Silence* (1979), Sheila Rowbotham, *Women, Resistance & Revolution* (1972) and *Woman's Consciousness, Man's World* (1973), Barry N. Schwartz and Robert Disch, *White Racism* (1970), Stan Steiner, *The New Indians* (1968), Margaret Walker, *Jubilee* (1966), Michelle Wallace, *Black Macho and the Myth of the Superwoman* (1979), Monique Wittig and Sandy Zeig, *Lesbian Peoples: Materials for a Dictionary* (1975), and poetry of Nikki Giovanni, Janice Mirikitani, June Jordan, Audre Lorde, and Alice Walker.

5. Weiss interview, 14.

6. Brooks, "All the Teachers Are the Taught," 6, capitalization in the original. Ellen Messer-Davidow, "Acting Otherwise," in *Provoking Agents: Gender and Agency in Theory and Practice*, edited by Judith Kegan Gardiner (Urbana: University of Illinois Press, 1995), 37.

7. Myers interview, 7.

8. Murphy, in Bunch and Pollack, 145.

9. Jetter interview, 37.

10. Merry interview, 1, 6.

11. Murphy, in Bunch and Pollack, 146.

12. Marilyn Murphy, "Lesbianism as a Special Issue" (1976), 2 [with "First Califia" handwritten on the mimeograph], in Mazer.

13. *The Lesbian Tide* ran articles condemning NBC movies like "Flowers of Evil" and "Born Innocent" for perpetuating stereotypes that lesbians murdered vulnerable old people, engaged in sadomasochism, and raped girls. See Jeanne Cordova, Karla Jay, Gudrun Fonfa, and Janie Elven, "Community Mows Under 'Flowers of Evil,'" *The Lesbian Tide* 4.5 (January, 1975): 16–18. "Lesbian Feminists Protest 'Born Innocent,'" *The Lesbian Tide* 5.3 corrected to 5.4 (January/February 1976): 17.

14. Murphy, in Bunch and Pollack, 147.

15. Gay Revolution Party Women's Caucus, "Realesbians and Politicalesbians," in Karla Jay and Allen Young, *Out of the Closets: Voices of Gay Liberation* (New York: Jove/HBJ, 1977 [1972]), 177–181. Marilyn Murphy, "Thinking about Bisexuality," Lesbianic Logic column, *The Lesbian News* 9.7 (February 1984): 26–27, and reprinted in April 1989.

16. Elsa Sue Fisher interview, 19.

17. Merry interview, 23.

18. Alix Dobkin, "View from Gay Head," *Lavender Jane Loves Women* (Women Wax Works, 1973). Ibid., *Alix Dobkin's Adventures in Women's Music* (New York: Tomato Publications, 1979), 37, italics in original.

19. Murphy, in Bunch and Pollack, 146–147. Weiss interview, 15.

20. Amber L. Hollibaugh, *My Dangerous Desires: A Queer Girl Dreaming Her Way Home* (Durham: Duke, 2000), 122–123, 125.

21. Retter Vargas interview, 18. Irene Weiss personal conversation.

22. Marilyn Murphy, "Pretty in Pink," *The Lesbian News* 11.12 (July 1986): 46–47.

23. Marilynn Cruz Rodriguez, "Pretty in Pink. Y Que?" *The Lesbian News* 12.2 (September 1986): 35–36.

24. Jetter interview, 12.

25. Naomi Wolf coined the term "victim feminism," which antifeminist fathers' rights organizations have adopted. Naomi Wolf, *Fire with Fire: The New Female Power and How to Use It* (New York: Random House, 1994), 135.

26. Catoggio interview, 56.

27. Jetter interview, 39–41.

28. Muriel Fisher interview, 12.

29. Albright interview, 12.

30. Nancy A. Matthews, *Confronting Rape: The Feminist Anti-Rape Movement and the State* (New York: Routledge, 1994), xvii, 75–77. Ibid., "Surmounting a Legacy: The Expansion of Racial Diversity in a Local Anti-Rape Movement," in *Violence Against Women: The Bloody Footprints*, ed. Pauline Bart and Eileen Geil Moran (Newbury Park, CA: Sage, 1993), 177, 180.

31. Kalivoda interview, 14.

32. Matthews, "Surmounting a Legacy," 183–184, 190. Ibid., "Feminist Clashes with the State: Tactical Choices by State-Funded Rape Crisis Centers," in *Feminist Organizations: Harvest of the New Women's Movement*, ed. Myra Marx Ferree and Patricia Yancey Martin (Philadelphia: Temple University Press, 1995), 293–297.

33. Peggy Reeves Sanday, *A Woman Scorned: Acquaintance Rape on Trial* (New York: Doubleday, 1996), 174.

34. Rosen, 182. Lisa Duggan and Nan D. Hunter, *Sex Wars: Sexual Dissent and Political Culture* (New York: Routledge, 1995), 20.

35. Interview transcripts: Albright, Cattogio, Forrest, Germain, Jetter, Leon, Merry, Jeanne Murphy, Oakwomon, Otero, Raven, Retter Vargas, West in Women of Color interview. Marilyn Murphy, "Do We 'Only Hurt the Ones We Love'?," *Lesbian News* 8.12 (July 1983): 24; and "It Could Have Been Worse," *Lesbian News* 11.10 (May 1986): 53–54.

36. *The Lesbian Tide*, 5.4 corrected to 5.5 (March/April 1976): 10 and 5.6 (May/June 1976): 4–5.

37. "The Sexes: Really Socking It to Women," *Time* 109.6 (February 7, 1977), accessed January 3, 2011, http://www.time.com/time/magazine/article/0,9171,914772,00.html; Duggan and Hunter, 21–22; Susan Brownmiller, *In Our Time: Memoir of a Revolution* (New York: The Dial Press, 1999), 298.

38. Brownmiller, 298–300.

39. Manov interview, 23. Brooks interview, 22. Retter, "On the Side of Angels," 139–140.

40. Dani Adams, "PORNOGRAPHY = VIOLENCE" (n.d.), 1–5, "Women Against Violence Against Women LA" folder, LLC, ONE Archives.

41. Echols, *Daring to Be Bad*, 288. Robin Morgan, "Theory and Practice," in *Going Too Far: The Personal Chronicle of a Feminist* (New York: Vintage Books, [1974] 1978), 169.

42. Germain interview, 6.

43. Kaufmann interview, 4.

44. Brooke, "Feminist Conference: Porn Again," *Off Our Backs*, 9.10 (Washington: Nov 30, 1979), 24, accessed 4 January 2011, http://www.webcitation.org/query?url= http://www.geocities.com/wikispace/oob.1979.html&date=2009-10-26+00:12:27.

45. Pat Califia, *Public Sex: The Culture of Radical Sex* (Pittsburgh: Cleis Press, 1994), 121.

46. Duggan and Hunter, 34, 44–46; Brownmiller, 317–322.

47. Duggan and Hunter, 26.

48. Hollibaugh, 133.

49. Alice Echols, *Daring to Be Bad*, 289.

50. Robin Morgan, *Going Too Far*, 181.

51. Los Angeles Coalition against Assaults against Women and WAVAW organized resistance to SM in Los Angeles. Retter, interview, 293. Atkinson talked to an offshoot of the New York–based Masochists' Liberation Front about "Why I'm Against S/M Liberation." Atkinson agreed with the SM group's analysis that sadomasochism pervaded society while society discriminated against SM practitioners. She interpreted the simultaneous pervasiveness and rejection as proof that "the Establishment" did not want to identify with SM because embracing SM would help "women to understand in such overt and brutal terms the very nature of the power relationship." SM liberationists' interest in recognition from dominant society seemed to signal the antithesis of feminist goals but was akin to gay rights and other forms of sexual liberation. Robin Ruth Linden et al., eds., *Against Sadomasochism: A Radical Feminist Analysis* (East Palo Alto, CA: Frog in the Well, 1982), 91.

52. Postwar gay male culture included strains of SM and pornography. The first gay motorcycle club, the Satyrs, formed in southern California in 1954 and embraced intense masculine sexuality while creating space for sexual taboos like sadomasochism. Within a decade, gay leatherman motorcycle clubs had spread from Los Angeles and San Francisco across the country. Mark Thompson, ed., *Leatherfolk: Radical Sex, People, Politics, and Practice* (Los Angeles: Alyson Books, 2001 [1991]), xv, xviii–xix, 91–105. During the 1970s, in addition to pornographic movies hitting mainstream theaters, images of gay male SM increased with Tom of Finland's hypermasculine gay depictions of anonymous gay male sex, including pictures that circulated without fanfare until his first U.S. exhibits in Los Angeles and San Francisco in 1978. Mica Ramakers, *Dirty Pictures: Tom of Finland, Masculinity, and Homosexuality* (New York: St. Martin's Press, 2000), 106–107. In 1977, Robin Morgan's "The Politics of Sado-Masochistic Fantasies" connected SM to male practices and posited that the new debates among lesbian feminists over SM reflected "a possible by-product of the new 'bonding' within the 'gay community', a way of gaining male approval from many homosexual 'brothers.' . . ." Linden, *Against Sadomasochism*, 122, n. 8.

53. Jeanne Cordova, "Towards a Feminist Expression of Sado-Masochism," *The Lesbian Tide* 6.3 (November/December 1976): 14–17. The workshop took place at the Women's Health & Healing Conference in October 1976. Although the public debate in the Los Angeles lesbian feminist community seems to have begun with this article, Cordova mentioned that other forums had discussed SM (e.g., Oregon's WomanShare and San Francisco's Janus Society), 14.

54. Liz Brown, Holly Near, Judy Dlugacz, Frances Reid, Karlene Faith, Sally Savitz,

Amy Horowitz, and Liz Stevens, "Letter to the Editor," *The Lesbian Tide* 6.4 (January/February 1977): 18.

55. "Letter to the Editor," *The Lesbian Tide*, 6.4 (January/February 1977): 19.

56. Raven interview, 22.

57. Barbara Ruth, "Cathexis (on the nature of S&M)," *The Lesbian Tide* 6.6 (May/June 1977): 10–11.

58. Z Budapest, ". . . Responses on S&M," *The Lesbian Tide* 6.6 (May/June 1977): 26.

59. Cerridwen Fallingstar, ". . . Responses on S&M," *The Lesbian Tide* 6.6 (May/June 1977): 26.

60. Brooks interview, 38. Germain interview, 13.

61. Jetter interview, 34.

62. The recurring charge against SM that it shored up sexist role assignments of "natural masochism" to females and "natural sadism" to males reflects essentialist feminism and an incomplete understanding of kinky sex. Practitioners renamed SM "BDSM" in the 1980s for bondage/discipline, dominance/submission, and sadism/masochism (announcement for L.A.'s Leather and Lace in *The Lesbian News* 9.10 [May 1984]: 10). There has been a substantial phenomenon of women dominants with male submissives as well as dominant-submissive role-playing among gay men or lesbians where one man in the couple would be submissive and one woman of the pair would be dominant.

63. Germain interview, 12, 13; follow-up 2, 4, 6.

64. Weiss interview, 17–18.

65. Raven interview, 22–23.

66. "Califia Announces '83 Gatherings," *Gayzette* (April 21, 1983) n.p., in Mazer. Pam Hutson also recalled hours of discussion within Califia about the problem of feminists associating their group with Pat Califia. WOC interview, 28.

67. Seco interview, 22, 23. Leon interview, 37–38, 42.

68. Brooks interview, 38–40. In contrast, Murphy lumped together lesbian battering, parental corporal punishment of their children ("a swat on the bottom"), and lesbian BDSM as violence against females: Murphy, "Do We 'Only Hurt the Ones We Love'?," 24.

69. Forrest interview, 6.

70. Manov interview, 29–30.

71. Catoggio interview, 42–45. Jetter interview, 36.

72. Gayle Rubin, "Thinking Sex: Notes for a Radical Theory of the Politics of Sexuality," in *Pleasure and Danger: Exploring Female Sexuality*, ed. Carole S. Vance (Boston: Routledge & Kegan Paul, 1984), 267–319.

73. Ibid., 304–306.

74. Ibid., 309.

75. Ibid., 275–283.

76. "Pagoda Temple of Love: A Lesbian Spiritual and Cultural Community," in *Lesbian Culture: An Anthology: The Lives, Work, Ideas, Art and Visions of Lesbians Past and Present*, ed. Julia Penelope and Susan J. Wolfe (Freedom, CA: The Crossing Press, 1993), 418–419.

77. Hollibaugh, 44–45.

78. Ibid., 49.

79. Muriel Fisher interview, 6.

80. Hollibaugh, 54.

81. Ibid., 47–48.

82. Germain, in Bunch and Pollack, 157.

83. Germain interview, 35–36.

84. Germain, in Bunch and Pollack, 157.

85. Ibid., 157.

86. Kalivoda interview, 2.

87. Murphy, in Bunch and Pollack, 145.

88. Germain interview, 36.

89. Murphy, in Bunch and Pollack, 143–144.

90. Germain interview, 37.

91. Del Martin, *Battered Wives* (San Francisco: Glide Publications, 1979), 19.

92. Carol Zisowitz Stearns and Peter N. Stearns, *Anger: The Struggle for Emotional Control in American History* (Chicago: University of Chicago Press, 1986), 192, 201–2.

93. Adrienne Rich, "Compulsory Heterosexuality and Lesbian Existence," *Signs* 5.4 (1980), reprinted by Antelope Publications's feminist pamphlet series (Denver, CO: Antelope Publications, 1982).

94. Raven interview, 17.

95. Kerry Lobel, ed., *Naming the Violence: Speaking Out about Lesbian Battering* (Seattle: Seal Press, 1986), 2, 95–97, 152–153.

96. Jetter interview, 41–42.

97. Lobel, *Naming the Violence*, 2, 194, 219.

98. Carol Seajay, "Violence between Women," *Country Women* 26 (September 1977): 16–18.

99. Lobel, *Naming the Violence*, 152.

100. Kerry Lobel, "Domestic Violence Hits Close to Home," *The Lesbian News* 8.3 (October 1982): 1–2.

101. Lobel, *Naming the Violence*, 77–78, 104. Suzanne Pharr, *Homophobia: A Weapon Of Sexism* (Little Rock: Chardon Press, 1988), 34–36.

102. Lobel, *Naming the Violence*, 106.

103. Lobel, "Domestic Violence" 1.

104. Lobel, *Naming the Violence*, 173–174.

105. Jetter interview, 7–10.

106. Interviews: Bernstein, 24; Brooks, 10; Catoggio, 39, 56; Germain, 13–14; Kalivoda, 7; Kaufman (pseudonym), 1, 4, 14; Manov, 22; Seco, 5.

107. Germain interview, 14.

108. Kalivoda interview, 7–8.

109. Kathy Wolfe, producer, Califia Community master videotape 6, "Betty Jetter," November 1985, Wolfe Video Distribution Archives, San Jose, CA. Jetter utilized Casey Miller and Kate Swift's *Words and Women* (New York: Anchor Press/Doubleday, 1976) and Dale Spender's *Man Made Language* (London: Routledge & Kegan Paul, 1980).

110. Kathy Wolfe, Califia Community master videotape 7, "Betty Jetter."

CHAPTER 4

1. Mary Inman, *In Women's Defense* (Los Angeles: The Committee to Organize the Advancement of Women, 1940); Weigand, 28, 33, 35–38.

2. Selma James, "Introduction to *The Power of Women and the Subversion of the Community*," in *Materialist Feminism: A Reader in Class, Difference, and Women's Lives*, ed. Rosemary Hennessy and Chrys Ingraham (New York: Routledge, 1997 [1972]), 37.

3. Weigand, 6.

4. Greg Mitchell, *Tricky Dick and the Pink Lady: Richard Nixon vs. Helen Gahagan Douglas: Sexual Politics and the Red Scare, 1950* (New York: Random House, 1998), 170, 233.

5. Lisa McGirr, *Suburban Warriors: The Origins of the New American Right* (Princeton, NJ: Princeton UP, 2001), 25–26, 35.

6. Thomas W. Evans, *The Education of Ronald Reagan: The General Electric Years and the Untold Story of His Conversion to Conservatism* (New York: Columbia University Press, 2006).

7. Matthew Dallek, *The Right Moment: Ronald Reagan's First Victory and the Decisive Turning Point in American Politics* (New York: Free Press, 2000), 89.

8. Ibid., 180, 186, 190.

9. Deirdre English, Barbara Epstein, Barbara Haber, and Judy MacLean, "The Impasse of Socialist Feminism: A Conversation," in *Women, Class, and the Feminist Imagination*, ed. Karen V. Hansen and Ilene J. Philipson (Philadelphia: Temple University Press, 1990 [1986]), 304.

10. Karen V. Hansen, "Women's Unions and the Search for a Political Identity," in Hansen and Philipson, 215–222, 229–232.

11. English et al., 310.

12. Faderman and Timmons, 173.

13. A reprint of the Chicago Women's Liberation Union's "Socialist Feminism—A Strategy for the Women's Movement" warned that finding classed social, psychological, and economic patterns from personal experiences without a structural analysis of society would lead "toward a kind of formless isolation rather than to a condition in which we can fight for and win power over our own lives." Hyde Park Chapter, Chicago Women's Liberation Union, "Socialist Feminism—A Strategy for the Women's Movement," *Sisters* 4.2 (February 1972): n.p. *Sisters* reprinted the introduction to the Furies' collected essays about how class-based tensions among women harmed activism in "Class and Feminism," *Sisters* 5.12 (April 1975): 9; reprinted in Charlotte Bunch and Nancy Myron, eds., *Class and Feminism: A Collection of Essays from The Furies* (Baltimore: Diana Press, Inc., 1974). A review of Sheila Rowbotham's *Women, Resistance and Revolution* praised Rowbotham for reconstructing working-class women's historical activism from Puritan times to 1971 Algeria. Julia Stein, "Women, Resistance and Revolution: A Marxist-Feminist View," *Sisters* 5.12 (April 1975): 10. Sharon Bas Hannah, a Fat Underground member, echoed the Furies by discussing classed attitudes as someone from a mixed class background. Sharon Bas Hannah, "Seeing It from Both Sides and Too Brightly," *Sisters* 5.12 (April 1975): 10. Edith White argued that her Jewish immigrant union family did not scorn upward mobility the way some parts of the feminist movement did. Edith White, "Is Upward Mobility Wrong?," *Sisters* 5.12 (April 1975): 11.

14. Paul A. Jargowsky, *Poverty and Place: Ghettos, Barrios, and the American City* (New York: Russell Sage Foundation, 1997), viii, x, 3, 14.

15. "Ahshe Green on Class," cassette tape, Mazer. Betty Jetter helped to tape her presentation and distribute copies for the price of the cassette.

16. Manov interview, 8–9.

17. Jetter follow-up interview, 2.

18. Jetter interview, 1, 23.

19. Marilyn Murphy, "One of the Murphy Girls," in *Out of the Class Closet: Lesbians Speak*, ed. Julia Penelope (Freedom, CA: The Crossing Press, 1994), 300.

20. Hansen, 215, 222.

21. "Ahshe Green on Class."

22. Green divided her presentation into eleven topics for class comparison: luck/hard work, eccentricity/conformity, material bonding/romance and common interests, material/verbal support, spending against emergencies/successful saving, extended family/nuclear family, the myth of perpetual happiness, physical violence/verbal manipulation, upward/downward mobility, guilt as middle class, and a sliding scale as benefiting downwardly mobile middle-class women.

23. "Ahshe Green on Class."

24. Lee Evans, "Dykes of Poverty: Coming Home," *Lesbian Ethics* 4.2 (Spring 1991): 7–18, here 17.

25. "Ahshe Green on Class."

26. Bunch and Myron, 15, 19–20, 24.

27. Rita Mae Brown, "The Last Straw," *A Plain Brown Rapper* (Oakland: Diana Press, 1976), 97–106.

28. "Ahshe Green on Class."

29. Murphy, "One of the Murphy Girls," 310.

30. Germain, follow-up, 1; Weiss interview, 9.

31. "Ahshe Green on Class."

32. Mary Glavin, "The Passing Game," Germain's personal files.

33. Murphy, "Califia Community," 148–149.

34. Forrest interview, 19.

35. Merry interview, 3.

36. Ibid., 4.

37. "Ahshe Speaks," *Country Women* 23 (February 1977): 4–8.

38. Marilyn Murphy, "Did Your Mother Do Volunteer Work?" Betty Jetter's personal files.

39. It is unclear whether or when Green joined Bhagwan Shree Rajneesh. No narrator knew her whereabouts after 1978. Rajneesh, a guru from India, mixed eastern and western religions and philosophies along with forms of therapy and meditation. For the times, an attractive aspect of his thought was his advice to be totally free in sex. He gained American followers by the early 1970s and moved from India to the United States in 1981, when a disciple bought a 64,299-acre ranch in Eastern Oregon to set up Rajneeshpuram. The center closed in 1985 amid serious criminal charges—infecting salad bars in The Dalles with salmonella to decrease voter turnout at a contested county election, other poisonings, electronic eavesdropping conspiracy, immigration fraud, lying to federal officials, harboring fugitives, criminal conspiracy, burglary, racketeering, arson, assault, murder. Lewis F. Carter, *Charisma and Control in Rajneeshpuram: The Role of Shared Values in the Creation of a Community* (New York: Cambridge University Press, 1990), 224–225, 236–237.

40. Catoggio interview, 15, 10–17.

41. Murphy, "Volunteer," 4–5.

42. Kalivoda interview, 1.

43. Germain interview, 5.

44. Bencangey interview, 3.

45. Germain interview, 18.

46. "Califia Community Collective Presentation" (class handwritten in), Germain's personal files, n.d., 6.

47. "Califia Community at de Benneville" (n.d.), 2, from Jewell's personal papers.

48. Weiss interview, 1.

49. Forrest interview, 22.

50. Bunch and Myron, 10.

51. Manov interview, 6–7.

52. Oakwomon interview, 20. Retter Vargas interview, 14.

53. Forrest interview, 30. Otero interview, 24.

54. Brooks follow-up interview, 4.

55. Elsa Sue Fisher interview, 9–13.

56. Manov interview, 4–6.

57. WOC interview, 24.

58. Murphy, in Bunch and Pollack, 149.

59. Otero interview, 4–5, 20.

60. Díaz interview, 3.

61. WOC interview, 3.

62. "Ahshe on Class."

63. WOC interview, 4.

64. Diana Pearce, "The Feminization of Poverty: Women, Work, and Welfare," *Urban and Social Change Review* (February 1978): 28–36, here 28–31, 34.

65. Elliott Currie, Robert Dunn, and David Fogarty, "The Fading Dream: Economic Crisis and the New Inequality," in Hansen and Philipson, 319, 321–322, 330.

66. "Poverty Status of People by Family Relationship, Race, and Hispanic Origin: 1959–2000," Table 2, last accessed 18 January 2010, http://www.census.gov/hhes/www/poverty/histpov/perindex.html. Statistics for 1976–1987 do not include American Indian or Asian American people and underrepresent by maintaining the formula that providing for basic needs requires three times the cost of food.

67. Johnnie Tillmon, "Welfare Is a Women's Issue," *Ms.* (Spring 1972): 111–116.

68. Blackwell, 147–149.

69. "Welfare—Myths and Facts," in Betty Jetter's personal files.

70. Forrest interview, 22.

CHAPTER 5

1. Matthew D. Lassiter, *The Silent Majority: Suburban Politics in the Sunbelt South* (Princeton, NJ: Princeton University Press, 2006), 1–2, 9–12, 135.

2. Dallek, 45–60.

3. Lisa Duggan, *The Twilight of Equality?: Neoliberalism, Cultural Politics, and the Attack on Democracy* (Boston: Beacon Press, 2003), 37–39.

4. Brochure 1977: "will include history, sexuality, spirituality, class, ethics, race, political and economic systems, organizing skill and strategies—specifically as they relate to the social and political struggles throughout the world," from LLC.

5. Brochure 1978, LLC.

208 NOTES TO PAGES 123-128

6. One of the antiracism manuals recommended by Califia is indicative of support-ing the Black Power message for whites teaching whites: Judy H. Katz, *White Awareness: Handbook for Anti-Racism Training* (Norman: University of Oklahoma, 1978), 15–16. Carmichael in 1967 stressed, "If the white man wants to help he can go home and free his own people." Stokely Carmichael and Charles V. Hamilton, *Black Power: Politics of Liberation* (New York: Vintage, 1967). Eldridge Cleaver agreed in his 1968 essay collec-tion, *Soul on Ice* (New York: Dell, 1968). Malcolm X in 1970 concluded, "Whites who are sincere should organize themselves and figure out some strategies to break down the prejudice that exists in white communities. This is where they can function more in-telligently and more effectively, in the white community itself, and this has never been done." Malcolm X, *By Any Means Necessary: Speeches, Interviews, and a Letter by Mal-colm X*, ed. George Breitman (New York: Pathfinder, 1970), 164.

7. Katz, 17.

8. Germain interview, 17.

9. Sara Winter, "Rooting Out Racism" (unpublished manuscript, n.d.), 7 pages, here pages 1–2, from Mazer. The Winter piece was handed out to be read before the racism presentation and also came in a photocopied version that appeared to be published but contained no citation.

10. Winter, 3–7.

11. Bencangey interview, 5.

12. Women of color who attended Califia during its first four years tended to find out about it through white friends or recruiters. Díaz heard about Califia through a white-dominated group when a Califia woman distributed brochures and talked up the camp during a Southern California Women for Understanding meeting. Bencangey in-terview, 1. Bunch and Pollack, 161.

13. Bencangey interview, 6.

14. Díaz interview, 1–2.

15. Califia's brochures consistently stated these goals.

16. The Califia Outreach Task Force solicited women of color in 1979 with a let-ter that promised, "Califia, a women's community and collective, is attempting to deal meaningfully with racism in the women's community. *We need you!* Come and get the high that comes from doing something that makes a difference." They planned to make the collective at least one-third women of color and had committed one thousand dol-lars to pay fees for women of color to attend the camps. "Women of Color" flyer/let-ter (1979), LLC Califia Community file, bold in original; Murphy, in Bunch and Pol-lack, 150.

17. Retter Vargas interview, 2. The original woman of color delegate was Margaret Sloan, formerly of NBFO.

18. Janet R. Jakobsen, *Working Alliances and the Politics of Difference: Diversity and Feminist Ethics* (Bloomington: Indiana University Press, 1998), 5, 9, 62–65.

19. Hole and Levine, 112–113.

20. Murphy, in Bunch and Pollack, 150.

21. Brooks was resigned that lesbian feminists were Califia's community because "[w]hoever came was our community." Brooks follow-up interview, 3. Jetter (presenter from ca. 1978 on and collective member ca. 1984–1985) and Albright (collective 1980–1981) began attending Califia while married but then came out. Califia was part of the coming-out process of other narrators as well (Pam Hutson, Wanda Jewell, Vicki

Leon, Alice Myers, Joan McNeil, Karen Merry, Jeanne Murphy, Marilyn Murphy, Lillian West).

22. Germain interview, 9.

23. WOC interview, 2, 6.

24. Cherríe Moraga, *Loving in the War Years: lo que nunca pasó por sus labios* (Boston: South End Press, 1983), 128–129.

25. Retter Vargas interview, 4.

26. Jakobsen, 5, 9.

27. Germain interview, 26.

28. Bencangey's interview corroborated Díaz's actions and the sense that little care had been put into integrating women of color. Bencangey became part of White Women Against Racism. Bencangey interview, 6–7.

29. Of the 1978 collective, Liz Bernstein, Anne Perna, Kathy Proud, Wanda Jewell, and Shari Schulz did not return for the 1979 season. Betty Brooks, Marilyn Murphy, Alice Myers, Janet Stambolian, and Irene Weiss remained active members. Josy Catoggio took a leave of absence after a personal conflict with Murphy and did not return. Catoggio interview, 32. Brooks follow-up interview, 3. Personal conversation with Elsa Fisher. The 1979 collective added three black women—Kwambe Omdahda, Glenda J. Osborne, and Denise A. Woods—along with Carol R. Rabaut (white). Brochures for 1978 and 1979 from LLC in conjunction with interviews and a Women of Color Califia address list for Camp JCA, Malibu, CA. Brooks credited Murphy with a lot of the integration of the collective and pointed to Murphy's closer ties to women of color (her first female lover was a black woman) and work giving lectures from Gerda Lerner's *Black Women in White America: A Documentary History* (New York: Pantheon, 1972). Brooks follow-up interview, 4.

30. The 1980 collective retained Betty Brooks, Marilyn Murphy, Alice Myers, Glenda Osborne, Carol Rabaut, Janet Stambolian, and Irene Weiss. Karen Williams and Denise Woods took leaves of absence. The collective added Dani Adams (white), Rose Greene (white Jewish), Kari Hildebrand (white), Carol Albright (white), and Lois Nevius (white). 1980 brochure in LLC.

31. Bunch and Pollack, 160, lists terms for the 1981 collective's racial composition: Christina M. Alvarez (bicultural), Betty W. Brooks, Dawn Darington (bicultural), Barbara E. Forrest (bicultural white/Latina), Diane Germain (white), Kari Hildebrand, Jan Hines (white), Yvonne King (white), Marilyn Murphy, Alice Myers, Carol Albright, Lois Nevius, Glenda Osborne, Carla Seco (pseudonym, Chicana), Anna María Soto (Chicana), Janet Stambolian, and Irene Weiss.

32. The 1982 collective added Ann Cariño (black), Mary Louise Lorang (white), Marj Suárez (Chicana), and Lillian West (black), while no longer listing Dawn Darington, Kari Hildebrand, Alice Myers, Carol Albright, and Glenda Osborne. 1982 brochure in LLC. See Chapter 3 for NLFO.

33. In 1983 Cariño, Seco, Soto, Suárez, and West remained, but Alvarez and Forrest left. The collective added Suzanne Bedford, Paula Fisher, Betty Jetter, Rosalie Ortega, Kate Rosenblatt, and Sarah Stroud. Stroud is the only one in Women of Color Network records. "Califia Community Women of Color Network 1982" and "Women of Color Califia Camp JCA Malibu, CA."

34. In 1984 Brooks, Germain, Lorang, Murphy, Ortega, Rosenblatt, Stambolian, Suárez, and Weiss left. They were replaced by Tory Collett, Maria Christina Cortez,

Patty Drasin, Shelly Garside, Teri Hupfer, Karen Merry, and Sheri Persion. A Maria Cortez is in the Women of Color records.

35. Germain interview, 26–27.

36. WOC interview, 2.

37. Ibid., 4.

38. Bunch and Pollack, 161.

39. Untitled update (April 28, 1978) in Lesbians of Color file at LLC. Louis Jacinto, "Lydia Otero: GLLU's Eighth Year Begins," *Unidad* (February/March 1989): 1–2. Retter, "On the Side of Angels," 121, 185–186, 196–199.

40. Otero interview, 6.

41. WOC interview, 18, 24.

42. Ibid., 40.

43. Germain interview, 27.

44. Murphy, in Bunch and Pollack, 150–151.

45. Retter Vargas interview, 2.

46. Retter, "On the Side of Angels," 131–132.

47. Retter Vargas interview, 15–16.

48. Germain interview, 24. In a personal conversation Germain amended this recollection by characterizing her description of davenport's beauty as artistic rather than sexual. Ability to remember Retter better than or to the exclusion of Díaz and davenport was true of Brooks, Raven, and Jetter among others.

49. Sarah Banet-Weiser, *The Most Beautiful Girl in the World: Beauty Pageants and National Identity* (Berkeley: University of California Press, 1999).

50. "[T]he worst, the *terror* I would have is to take off *my* clothes and be around *white* women—that just sounded horrible—and be objectified in that way." Otero interview, 8.

51. Doris davenport, "The Pathology of Racism: A Conversation with Third World Wimmin," in *This Bridge Called My Back: Writings by Radical Women of Color*, edited by Cherríe Moraga and Gloria Anzaldúa (Watertown, MA: Persephone, 1981), 85–90, here 86.

52. Davenport, 87.

53. Merry interview, 9. Myers interview, 2.

54. Janet R. Jakobsen, "Different Differences: Theory and the Practice of Women's Studies," in Elizabeth Lapovsky Kennedy and Agatha Beins, eds., *Women's Studies for the Future: Foundations, Interrogations, Politics* (Piscataway, NJ: Rutgers University Press, 2005), 125–142.

55. Davenport, 88–90.

56. WOC interview, 21.

57. Ibid., 60.

58. Ibid., 13.

59. Otero interview, 10. Forrest interview, 8.

60. Germain interview, 24.

61. Katherine A. Jankowski, *Deaf Empowerment: Emergence, Struggle, and Rhetoric* (Washington, DC: Gallaudet University Press, 1997), 88, whose source was M. Douglas, "The Social Control of Cognition: Some Factors in Joke Perception," *Man* 3 (1968): 361–376.

62. Germain interview, 20.

63. Retter Vargas interview, 8.

64. Retter, "First Things First" (unpublished, 1979), from Mazer.

65. Retter, "Some Myths about Racism Or The Wonderbread Woman's Excuse Closet" in *Spinning Off* (May 1980), 5 [excerpted from *A Handbook for Racism Workshops* 1980], Mazer's personal file on Yolanda G. Retter and hereafter cited as "Excuse Closet."

66. Retter Vargas interview, 9.

67. Ibid., 16.

68. "Excuse Closet."

69. Albright interview, 17–18; Leon interview, 24.

70. Green interview, 20.

71. Raven interview, 3–6, 25.

72. Leon interview, 25.

73. Jeanne Murphy interview, 5, corroborated by Green, Merry, Myers, Raven.

74. Albright interview, 18; Bencangey interview, 7; Catoggio interview, 34; Germain interview, 17; Fisher interview, 17; Leon interview, 25; Merry interview, 4–5, 12; Jeanne Murphy interview, 5–6; Raven interview, 4, 6.

75. Germain interview, 20–21. Retter Vargas amended this story in a personal conversation, clarifying that she gave herself the name "Yolanda the Terrible."

76. Retter Vargas interview, 25.

77. WOC interview, 24–27.

78. Ibid., 40–41.

79. Ibid., 47–49, 56.

80. Elly Bulkin, "Hard Ground: Jewish Identity, Racism, and Anti-Semitism," in Elly Bulkin, Minnie Bruce Pratt, and Barbara Smith, *Yours in Struggle: Three Feminist Perspectives on Anti-Semitism and Racism* (Ithaca, NY: Firebrand Books, 1984), 94.

81. Both West and Soto remembered consistent organizing by Jewish women, while neither Bencangey nor Bernstein did. Bencangey and Bernstein both identified as Jewish but married into Judaism from Christian backgrounds. It is unclear how the Jewish women's group constituted itself, but there seems to have been some criterion that prioritized women who grew up Jewish and held strong Jewish identification despite converts' adoption of Jewish symbols like the Star of David and mezuzah. WOC interview, 37; Bencangey interview, 8; Bernstein interview, 9.

82. "Notes from Califia Jewish Women's Group Meeting on November 11, 1984," from Germain's personal files. Germain attended to represent the collective.

83. Joan E. Biren explained the complex pulls between wanting to assimilate and hating to pass for a Gentile in "That's Funny, You Don't Look Like a Jewish Lesbian," in Evelyn Torton Beck, *Nice Jewish Girls: A Lesbian Anthology* (Watertown, MA: Persephone, 1980), 122–123. As someone who "did not 'need' a nose job," had no New York accent, had an "Americanized" last name (Biren from Bironholtz), and had been raised to assimilate, it took Biren a decade after coming out as a lesbian to affirm her Jewish identity. The photographs she included of Jewish women purposefully wearing Jewish symbols such as the Star of David, a *chai*, or a yarmulke, or symbols that combine Jewish and lesbian identity, such as a labrys with a Star of David or buttons with puns like "Clitzpah," depicted tactics used by some Califia women. The homes of the lesbians who identified with Judaism were observed during interviews as being adorned with Jewish art. Weiss had an artistic plate that integrated the Star of David with the *chai* while Muriel

Fisher (who was born Jewish) and Bernstein and Bencangey (who had both married Jewish men) had menorahs. Additionally, Bencangey had a mezuah on her doorframe and wore a Star of David necklace.

84. I.e., "I have worked in the Civil Rights Movement and need that to be taken into account" from the "Excuse Closet."

85. "Notes from Califia Jewish Women's Group Meeting on November 11, 1984."

86. Barbara Smith, "Between a Rock and a Hard Place," in Bulkin et al., 71–73.

87. Forrest interview, 8.

88. In addition to Forrest and Hutson, the women of color group interviewed remembered other women of Latina descent whom they identified as having "lived white." WOC interview, 14.

89. Ibid., 31.

90. Ibid., 3 (twice), 7, 8 (twice), 10, 11, 53.

91. Ibid., 11.

92. In 1979 LOC members picketed West Hollywood's Palms lesbian bar because they claimed that employees asked them, unlike whites, for three pieces of identification and denied them nonalcoholic drinks. When a black woman accused Palms employees of hassling her two years later and kicking her out in a letter to the editor, *The Lesbian News* editors and readers (some identifying as white and others as women of color) rejected her account and defended the bar. One letter attacked her as an example of black obsession with being among whites and of "too many blacks coming in." The exchange reflects a combination of ingrained racism and dismissal of racially motivated bias. *The Lesbian News* 6.1 (June 1981): 15. *The Lesbian News* 6.12 (July 1981): 15–16. *The Lesbian News* 7.1 (August 1981): 23. Another event in 1981 kept racial division in the spotlight. Women of color criticized the West Coast Women's Comedy and Music Festival, organized by a Jewish comic, for excluding them and not having a sliding scale. While some white women opposed these accusations as divisive, the non-Califia group, Jewish Feminists, evenhandedly supported women of color's critiques against classism while noting that the organizer had been stereotyped as money-grubbing, power-hungry, and aggressive. Retter Vargas concluded that divisiveness was inevitable because no space was free from the accumulated mistrust, denial, and power differentials within the Los Angeles lesbian community. Retter, "On the Side of Angels," 268–271.

93. Personal conversation with Lydia Otero.

94. The camp was Camp Las Posadas, one half-hour north of San Francisco. Tracy Robb, "Interview with Carol [Schmidt]," part of a master's thesis in Human Development with specializations in Multicultural Studies, Women's Studies, and Administration at Pacific Oaks College, stored at Mazer. Schmidt joined WWAR in 1980 and "heard that a group of that name had sort of organized in the fall of 1979 but fell apart. Some of those people—Linda Barone, Lois Bencangey and Norma Esfeld—had put on a four-Saturday workshop at the Center for Feminist Therapy around November, 1979, which [she] attended . . ." (4). In contrast, Retter, "On the Side of Angels," dated the group to July 1980 (264), and Murphy, in Bunch and Pollack put the formation between 1980 and 1981 (152).

95. Díaz interview, 6. Retter, "On the Side of Angels," 264. Tracy Robb, "Interview of Carol [Schmidt]," 4.

96. Tracy Robb, "Interview with Shirl [Buss]," 3; and ibid., "Interview with Robin [Podolsky]," 4, at Mazer.

97. Joan (claiming to represent Committee Against Ineffectiveness), letter to the editor, *LN* 8.12 (July 1983): 35. Kathy Sabry (pseudonym) interview, 11. Schmidt and Otero provided examples of internal divisions. In Tracy Robb's interview with Schmidt, Schmidt remembered a disastrous workshop on leadership with women of color where "all whites ended up being put down in a set-up situation." After Schmidt wrote a furious letter to Díaz and Retter, Schmidt claimed Díaz stopped speaking to her and "began to tear down WWAR to Lois [Bencangey]." Otero remembered Retter "would make fun of them constantly too." Otero interview, 17.

98. Otero interview, 17.

99. Bencangey interview, 5.

100. Over the years, Kathy Wolfe collected some materials on racism that extended beyond Califia and were available in Los Angeles. A "Statement to a Racism Workshop" explored stereotypes and the extent to which white women had helped women of color. *Lesbian Connection* 5.5 (July 1982). Terry Wolverton, Margaret Hobart, and Tyaga prepared materials in January 1984 for their antiracism workshop, including Retter's "Excuse Closet," Ricky Sherover-Marcuse of Oakland's "Towards a Perspective on Unlearning Racism: 12 Working Assumptions" and "A Working Definition of Racism," and selections from *This Bridge Called My Back*. By 1985, The Ida B. Wells Task Force of Aradia Inc. in Grand Rapids, MI, circulated an *Antiracism Newsletter*. The Santa Cruz monthly, *Matrix Women's Newsmagazine*, dedicated its 12.4 June 1987 issue to racism. Califia file from Kathy Wolfe.

101. Belasco, 48, 61–62.

102. Davenport, 87.

103. Germain interview, 25–26. She remembered the collective's changing the food in response to davenport's complaints.

104. WOC interview, 30. Raven interview, 15. Bernstein interview, 3.

105. Leon interview, 34–35.

106. Weiss interview, 23–24.

107. Jetter interview, 52.

108. Brooks interview, 14–15.

109. Jeanne Murphy interview, 6.

110. Davenport, 87.

111. Bernstein interview, 6. If Otero's description of this Asian American woman as a "tenant landlord" who advertised as a DJ in the *Lesbian News* during the 1980s is accurate, assimilation to white class norms might be at work in her lack of musical exposure. Otero, personal communication.

112. Soto mentioned that it was not until women of color took control of Califia that Asian American women came. This presented a whole new set of conflicts as women did not want to interact because of historic military conflicts among the Asian countries from which they descended. WOC interview, 60.

CHAPTER 6

1. William C. Berman, *America's Right Turn: From Nixon to Bush* (Baltimore: Johns Hopkins University Press, 1994), 92–93, 95.

2. Randy Shilts, *And the Band Played On: Politics, People, and the AIDS Epidemic* (New York: St. Martin's Griffin, 1987), 80, 90, 143, 186.

3. The Reagan administration consistently vetoed Congressional funding for AIDS research and preventive education. Not until after news reports that actor Rock Hudson had needed to go to Paris for AIDS treatment did the administration approve funding increases under threat of Congressional subpoena. Reagan did not mention AIDS in a public policy speech until May 1987. By then 20,849 Americans had died prematurely of AIDS. Another 170,000 died by 1993. Shilts, 187, 578–579, 596. Executive quiescence catalyzed protest groups in New York City such as AIDS Coalition to Unleash Power (ACT-UP: March 1987), Queer Nation (March 1990), and Lesbian Avengers (June 1992), which spread to California and across the nation, reinterpreting demonstrations and street theater for the 1990s.

4. Alice Myers (collective member 1978–1982) resigned to care for her mother, and Glenda Osborne (collective 1979–1982) also left. Betty Brooks, Marilyn Murphy, Irene Weiss, and Janet Stambolian resigned from the collective after the 1983 season. Women who had attended camps since the 1970s constituted a minority of successive collective members—Betty Jetter began attending in 1976, Karen Merry in 1977, Yvonne King in 1977, Diane Germain 1978, Carla Seco 1978/79, and Anna María Soto 1978/79.

5. Betty Brooks had brought her "Community Organizing" class to meetings of Grace Brethren Church's student group, Zeta Chi. Betty W. Brooks, "A New Kind of Harrassment [*sic*]," 5, Betty Brooks file, LLC.

6. Doreen Carvajal, "Turmoil Seen for CSULB Women's Studies," *Press Telegram* (July 2, 1982): B1, B5, Betty Brooks file, LLC; Sandra Hale, "Our Attempt to Practice Feminism in the Women's Studies Program," *Frontiers* 8.3 (1986): 39–43, here 42.

7. William Orton and Vicky Hendley, "A Voice from the 'Right,'" *The Summer Union: The Student's Newspaper Cal State University Long Beach* 2.2 (July 6, 1982): 1, 7, 8, Betty Brooks file, LLC.

8. Hale, 40.

9. ACLU Women's Rights Project, "Cal State Long Beach Women's Studies Program vs. Cal State University Administration," Betty Brooks file, LLC.

10. Orton and Hendley, 1. Vicky Hendley, "Crowther Cuts Women's Studies," *The Summer Union: The Student's Newspaper Cal State University Long Beach* 2.2 (July 6, 1982): 1, 8, Betty Brooks file, LLC. Sherna Berger Gluck, "Reflections on Linking the Academy and the Community," *Frontiers: A Journal of Women's Studies* 8.3 (1986): 46–49, 48.

11. Hendley, 8.

12. Betty Brooks listed her course materials in "A New Kind of Harrassment" as *Our Bodies Our Selves*; *Women, Health, and Choice*; *Women and the Crisis in Sex Hormones*; *How to Stay Out of the Gynecologist's Office*; and audiovisuals "showing the sexual anatomy, home and hospital births, early abortions and some sexually explicit material," 6.

13. Carvajal, "Turmoil."

14. Hendley, 8.

15. "There Is Good News and Bad News," *The Lesbian News* 8.3 (October 1982): 3.

16. "Chronology of the Attack on CSULB Women's Studies Program," in Mazer. Brooks probably authored the chronology; many of its sentences and paragraphs appear in her "A New Kind of Harrassment." Brooks's partial reinstatement was contingent on "counseling by school administrators that her classes would be under surveillance for 'improper use of language,' 'questionable teaching style,' and lack of proper 'political perspective.'" ACLU Women's Rights Project. Ironically, rather than focusing the coun-

seling on academic rigor, Brooks told ACLU attorney Susan McGrievy that the campus dean lectured her on "sensitivity." Doreen Carvajal, "L.B. Women's Studies Instructor to Resume Teaching Duties in Fall," *Press Telegram* (August 21, 1982), 1, Betty Brooks file, LLC.

17. Carvajal, "L.B."

18. Those attacked were Professors Estelle Freeman at Stanford, Merle Woo at Berkeley, and Nancy Shaw at Santa Cruz. ACLU Women's Rights Project; "Long Beach Instructor Joins ACLU Suit," *L.A. Herald Examiner* (Sept. 14, 1982), n.p., Betty Brooks file, LLC.

19. Letter from Betty Willis Brooks, Ed.D., to Ramona Ripston, Executive Director of ACLU Foundation of Southern California, September 29, 1982, Betty Brooks file, LLC.

20. Phyllis Schlafly, "ACLU Leaps to the Defense of Lesbianism Course," *Oklahoma City Times* (October 15, 1982): 42.

21. Hale, 40. Gluck, 47. The preamble still marks Women's Studies' origins. See "National Women's Studies Association Constitution," last checked 12 December 2003, http://www.nwsa.org/constitution.htm.

22. George Mendenhall, "Classroom Spies Accuse Prof. of Teaching Porn," *Bay Area Reporter* (March 27, 1986): 10, 13, Betty Brooks file, LLC.

23. Mary Beth Crain, "Strange Bedfellows, Dangerous Precedents," *L.A. Weekly* (May 24–30, 1985): 39–40, which pictures Brooks and describes her as a "sex educator and First Amendment crusader." Betty Brooks file, LLC.

24. Schlafly, 42.

25. WOC interview, 29. Seco interview, 25. Myers interview, 7.

26. Sharon L. Sievers, "What Have We Won, What Have We Lost?," *Frontiers: A Journal of Women's Studies* 8.3 (1986): 44.

27. Duggan, *The Twilight of Inequality*, Chap. 2.

28. Cheryl McCall, "Maya Angelou: The Writer-Poet Continues to Find Art in Her Life as She Makes an Emotional Return to Her Native South," *People Weekly* 17.9 (March 8, 1982): 92, 95–96, 99, here 95–96. Fran Moira, "Maya Angelou on the 'Child Stealing' Case," *Off Our Backs* 26.3 (March 31, 1986): 20.

29. Marilyn Murphy, "A Small Injustice," *The Lesbian News* 11.7 (Feb. 1986): 52; ibid., "It Could Have Been Worse," 53–54.

30. Germain follow-up interview, 8.

31. Murphy, "It Could Have Been Worse," 53.

32. Murphy and Weiss advertised their Southern California Center for Women's Education by February 1983 in the *Lesbian News* 8.7 (Feb 1983): 19. From July 1983 through June 1984, their SCCWE advertisement and some of Murphy's columns indicated that they were traveling.

33. Christina Alvarez (1981–1982), Ann Cariño (1982–1984), Barbara Forrest (1981–1982), Carla Seco (pseudonym 1981–1984), Anna María Soto (1981–1984), Marj Suárez (1982–1983), Lillian West (1982–1984). "Califia Community Women of Color Network—1982," at Mazer. Califia brochures list of collective members.

34. "Women of Color Califia Community 1982" brochure.

35. WOC interview, 56–57.

36. Letter from Eagle Weyant to the Women of Color Network (n.d.), Yolanda Retter Vargas's personal files.

37. "Califia Community Women of Color Network—1982," Mazer; Bunch and Pollack, 162.

38. Bunch and Pollack, 166. Soto and West recalled that other women of color considered them suspect because they worked with white Califia collective women. WOC interview, 22, 49.

39. Bunch and Pollack, 162–163.

40. "Women of Color Califia, Camp JCA Malibu, CA," Mazer.

41. "Women of Color Califia Community brochure 1982," LLC.

42. WOC interview, 59–60.

43. Films were *La Chicana* by Silvia Morales, *Mitsuye & Nellie* by Mitsuye Yamada and Nellie Wong, *Huelga, The Emerging Woman, Jade Snow, Salt of the Earth, Mother Is on Strike,* and *The Life and Times of Rosie the Riveter.*

44. WOC interview, 57.

45. "Evaluations from the Women of Color Califia," Mazer.

46. "Women of Color 'Networking'" flyer, LLC.

47. Otero recalled that Lesbians of Color held many social events such as camping trips and parties. She remembered that drug dealing and use at the conference was in keeping with the party atmosphere of the times. Otero interview, 3, 4.

48. Otero interview, 1, 9. The National Lesbians of Color Conference was held 8–11 September 1983 in Malibu for 220 women.

49. Oakwomon interview, 6, 10, 14, 17.

50. Oakwomon and Forrest, letter (April 10, 1983), Mazer subject file Lesbians of Color Conference 1983, part 1. Otero identified Díaz and Retter Vargas as helping to organize the conference as well. Otero interview, 11.

51. Oakwomon letter (January 13, 1984), Mazer subject file Lesbians of Color Conference 1983, part 1. British spelling in the original.

52. Kwambe Om Dah Dah and Rha Medeen statement for final gathering of the Lesbians of Color Conference. Underlining in original. Retter Vargas personal files.

53. Forrest and Retter Vargas attributed the group's decline to burnout, whereas Otero believed secretiveness about finances generated divisions. Forrest interview, 7. Otero interview, 11–12. Retter, "On the Side of Angels," 276.

54. Otero interview, 2.

55. Ibid., 3.

56. Ibid., 11, 12, 22, 25.

57. Ibid., 22–23.

58. Oakwomon interview, 11.

59. Ibid., 33–34.

60. Seco interview, 37.

61. Wendy Averill, "Spotlight: Lauren Jardine, Co-Executive Director, Connexxus," *The Lesbian News* 10.10 (May 1985): 47.

62. Retter Vargas follow-up interview, 2. Otero interview, 29.

63. Letter from Gay and Lesbian Latinos Unidos—Lesbian Task Force, Multi-Ethnic Gay and Lesbian Exchange, and Lesbians of Color sent to Adel Martínez, Lauren Jardine, Roz Allen, and Jeane Cordova, June 11, 1984, LLC Lesbianas Unidas and Connexxus file.

64. Letter from Adel Martínez and Lauren Jardine sent to Gay and Lesbian Latinos Unidos (Lesbian Task Force), Multi-Ethnic Gay and Lesbian Exchange, and Lesbians of Color, June 17, 1984, Lesbianas Unidas and Connexxus file. LLC.

65. Women of Color Forum Minutes, March 15, 1987 in Connexxus Latina Services Advisory, Mazer, Task Force subject file, 1–2.

66. Interviews: Kalivoda, 2; Greene, 29; Seco, 37; Otero, 28.

67. Averill, 48.

68. Interviews: Seco, 33; Germain, 47; Elsa Sue Fisher, 5; Muriel Fisher, 2.

69. "Statement from Women of Color to the Califia Community," February 1, 1986. LLC.

70. The trend for services and inclusion would continue in 1989 with a Latino AIDS project, called Bien Estar, and GLLU members speaking at straight Latino places and at white gay places for inclusion. Otero interview, 14–15.

71. "Statement from Women of Color to the Califia Community."

72. Twenty-seven narrators gave opinions as to why Califia ended when it did. Of these, nineteen were white women and eight were women of color. Based on references to age in their interviews, in 1986, two white narrators were in their sixties, six were in their fifties, three were in their forties, four were in their thirties, and three were in their twenties. Although two women of color were in their forties, five were in their thirties, and two were in their twenties. On burnout or lack of central energy, see interviews: Albright, 36–37; Bencangey, 8; Bernstein, 23; Muriel Fisher, 2; Forrest, 31; Germain, 46; Greene, 29; Jewell, 17; Leon, 46–47; Merry, 31; Jeanne Murphy, 27; Myers, 13; Gómez, Soto, and West in WOC interview, 20, 50; Seco, 30.

73. Interviews that all paired Murphy and Weiss as guiding forces: Albright, 36–37; Bencangey, 8; Gómez in WOC interview, 40; Greene, 29; Seco, 30; Soto in WOC interview, 20. Jewell connected Murphy and Brooks as key leaders. Jewell interview, 17.

74. Leon interview, 47.

75. Brooks follow-up interview, 4. Forrest interview, 31. Germain interview, 46. Soto, WOC interview, 19.

76. U.S. Department of Labor Bureau of Labor Statistics: http://stats.bls.gov/cps /prev_yrs.htm; and the Labor Research Association U.S. union membership, 1948– 2002, last accessed 29 July 2004, http://www.laborresearch.org/charts.php?id=29 last.

77. Interviews: Greene, 29; Kalivoda, 3, 5; Merry, 29, 31; Jeanne Murphy, 27; Myers, 13; Retter Vargas, 21.

78. WOC interview, 50.

79. Interviews: Brooks, 53–54; Catoggio, 55; Díaz, 29–31; Elsa Sue Fisher, 4–6; Kalivoda, 3; Jetter, 5–6, 7, 47–49; Jeanne Murphy, 26–27; Oakwomon, 18–19; Weiss, 7–8; Germain follow-up interview, 8.

80. Catoggio interview, 55; Manov interview, 32.

81. Seco interview, 33, 35; Soto and West in WOC interview, 22, 49.

82. Hutson, Soto, and West in WOC interview, 50–51.

83. Oakwomon interview, 18–19; Seco interview, 29–30; Gómez and Soto in WOC interview, 50.

84. Soto in WOC interview, 58, 63; Seco interview, 32; Retter Vargas follow-up interview, 1.

85. Melissa Limmer, "A World Apart: Lesbian Separatists Hold the Line for Women's Energy," The Advocate (October 10, 1988): 26–27.

86. After years of dissent, men at the Gay Community Service Center finally added "and Lesbian" to its name in 1980. Retter, "On the Side of Angels," 213.

87. Limmer verified that the latest figures from the 1988 Statistical Abstract of the United States recorded that 40,400 women died of breast cancer in 1985 and between

12,450 and 13,830 people died of AIDS in 1987, according to the National Center for Health Statistics (27). By the end of Reagan's second term, nearly 30,000 people had died of AIDS. Fundraising for breast cancer research has since become public among women and their partners.

88. Dannemeyer called for mandatory AIDS testing in 1988 after the failed Proposition 64 of 1986. Michael Bronski, "Why Reagan Ignored AIDS," *The Advocate: Online Exclusives*, posted 9 June 2004, last accessed 27 August 2004, http://www.advocate.com/html/stories/917/917_reagan_bronski.asp.

89. Jeff Campbell, memo to Yolanda Retter (November 16, 1988). Mazer people file for Yolanda Retter.

90. Retter, "On the Side of Angels," 312.

91. Ibid., 225–226.

92. Ibid., 227, 312, 323.

93. Bernstein interview, 8.

94. Marilyn Murphy, "Thanksgiving Day," *The Lesbian News* 13.4 (November 1987): 29; ibid., "She's Jewish, You Know!" *The Lesbian News* 13.5 (December 1987): 10; ibid., "At a Celebration for Hitler's Birthday," *The Lesbian News* 15.11 (June 1990): 25.

95. Ibid., "The Summer of '73," *The Lesbian News* 10.12 (July 1985): 34–35; ibid., "Money, Homophobia & Death in the Closet," *The Lesbian News* 11.2 (September 1985): 44–45; ibid., "More About Wills," *The Lesbian News* 11.3 (October 1985): 48–49; ibid., "Aging in April," *The Lesbian News* 12.8 (April 1987): 27; ibid., "Old Is In: The West Coast Celebration by and for Old Lesbians," *The Lesbian News* 12.10 (June 1987): 30–31; ibid., "And the Walls Came Tumbling Down," *The Lesbian News* 12.12 (July 1987): 28.

96. Ibid., "Our Town," *The Lesbian News* 10.7 (February 1985): 34–35; ibid., "Color Me Lavender," *The Lesbian News* 10.9 (April 1985): 46, a reprint of her first article in August 1982; ibid., "Beachtree: My Kind of Place," *The Lesbian News* 11.4 (November 1985): 43–44; ibid., "RV Living: Lesbian Style," *The Lesbian News* 12.6 (February 1987): 26; ibid., "Letter from Florida," *The Lesbian News* 13.10 (May 1988): 34.

97. Ibid., "Mother of the Groom," *The Lesbian News* 10.6 (January 1985): 30.

98. Ibid., 31.

99. "Letters to the Editor," *The Lesbian News* 10.8 (March 1985): 34, and 10.9 (April 1985).

100. Marilyn Murphy, "And Baby Makes Two—Part I," *The Lesbian News* 12.2 (Sept. 1986): 34.

101. Ibid., "And Baby Makes Two—Part II," *The Lesbian News* 12.2 [should be number 3] (October 1986): 30–31.

102. Letter to the Editor, *The Lesbian News* 12.4 (December 1986): 26.

CONCLUSION

1. Reger, 87.

2. Ibid., 183.

3. Counseling professionals have since written guides to communicating emotional positions while decreasing conflict, as well as advice for self-care. Marshall B. Rosenberg, *Nonviolent Communication: A Language of Compassion*, 5th printing (Encinitas, CA:

PuddleDancer, 2001). Laura van Dernoot Lipsky with Connie Burke, *Trauma Stewardship: An Everyday Guide to Caring for Self While Caring for Others* (San Francisco: Berrett-Koehler, 2009).

4. Reger, 155–156.

5. Bernice Johnson Reagon, "Coalition Politics: Turning the Century," in *Home Girls: A Black Feminist Anthology*, ed. Barbara Smith (New York: Kitchen Table: Women of Color Press, 1983), 359.

6. "Come to Califia Community 1982" brochure.

7. Retter Vargas interview, 16.

8. Reagon, 368.

9. Gloria T. Hull, Patricia Bell Scott, and Barbara Smith, *All the Women Are White, All the Blacks Are Men, but Some of Us Are Brave: Black Women's Studies* (New York: Feminist Press, 1982); Cherríe Moraga and Gloria Anzaldúa, *This Bridge Called My Back: Writings by Radical Women of Color* (New York: Kitchen Table, 1983); Moraga, *Loving in the War Years*; Audre Lorde, *Sister Outsider* (Freedom, CA: The Crossing Press, 1984); Gloria Anzaldúa, *Borderlands/La Frontera: The New Mestiza* (San Francisco: Spinsters/Aunt Lute, 1987).

10. Jonathan Fields, *Uncertainty: Turning Fear and Doubt into Fuel for Brilliance* (New York: Portfolio/Penguin, 2011), 18–19.

11. Ibid., 32.

12. Ibid., 46, 57.

13. Amardo Rodríguez, *Diversity as Liberation (II): Introducing a New Understanding of Diversity* (Cresskill, NJ: Hampton Press, Inc., 2003), xv.

14. Pamela Wat supplied the vocabulary of "wonder" at Denton Unitarian Universalist Fellowship and in personal conversation, 20 March 2012. AnaLouise Keating, *Teaching Transformation: Transcultural Classroom Dialogues* (New York: Palgrave Mac-Millan, 2007), 36.

15. Jacqueline J. Lewis, *The Power of Stories: A Guide for Leading Multi-racial and Multi-cultural Congregations* (Nashville: Abingdon Press, 2008), 24–25, 31, 63.

16. Ibid., 3, 29, 50, 52.

17. Keating, 37; Rodríguez, xi.

18. Henry Nelson Wieman, *Creative Freedom: Vocation of Liberal Religion*, ed. Creighton Peden and Larry E. Axel (New York: The Pilgrim Press, 1982), 10, 53, 69.

19. Keating, 26, 28, 35.

20. Wieman, 3.

21. Lewis, 4.

22. Keating, 35.

23. Ibid., xii.

24. Ibid., 3, 6, 13.

25. Ibid., 37.

26. Lewis, 52–53, 95.

REFERENCES

ORAL HISTORY INTERVIEWS

The author conducted all of the following interviews and deposited the transcripts at the June L. Mazer Lesbian Collection, Los Angeles, CA.

Albright, Carol. Grenada Hills, CA. 13 July 2002.
Bencangey, Lois. Valley Village, CA. 8 August 2000.
Bernstein, Jane Deckert. Burbank, CA. 9 August 2000.
Brooks, Betty Willis. With Sylvia Russell. Downey, CA. 14 July 2002.
———. Follow-up interview. San Clemente, CA. 1–2 August 2003.
Catoggio, Josy. Altadena, CA. 12 July 2002.
Díaz, María Dolores. Tucson, AZ. 20 January 2002.
Fisher, Elsa Sue. Long Beach, CA. 11 July 2002.
———. Follow-up interview. Long Beach, CA. 28 July 2003.
Fisher, Muriel. San Diego, CA. 11 August 2000.
Forrest, Barbara. Albuquerque, NM. 24 May 2001.
Germain, Diane F. San Diego, CA. 11 August 2000.
———. Follow-ups with Diane F. Germain. San Diego, CA. 17 July 2002, 10 April, 2003, 13–15 April 2003, 31 July 2004.
Greene, Rose. Santa Monica, CA. 14 July 2002.
Jetter, Betty. Pasadena, CA. 12 July 2002.
———. Follow-up interview. Pasadena, CA. 28 July 2003.
Jewell, Wanda. Los Angeles, CA. 10 July 2002.
Kalivoda, Kal. Van Nuys, CA. 10 August 2000.
Kaufmann, Bonnie (pseud.). Los Angeles, CA. 12 July 2002.
Leon, Vicki. San Diego, CA. 17 July 2002.
Manov, Ariana. Highland Park, CA. 14 July 2002.
McNeill, Joan. Apache Junction, AZ. 16 March 2002.
Merry, Karen. San Diego, CA. 18 July 2002.
Murphy, Jeanne. Apache Junction, AZ. 29 March 2002.
Myers, Alice J. Los Angeles, CA. 9 August 2000.
———. Follow-up interview. Los Angeles, CA. 27 July 2003.
Oakwomon, Lhyv. Albuquerque, NM. 28 May 2001.
Otero, Lydia. Tucson, AZ. 12 March 2004.
Raven, Daniel. Tucson, AZ. 27 January 2002.
Retter Vargas, Yolanda. Los Angeles, CA. 10 August 2000.
———. Follow-up interview. Van Nuys, CA. 29 July 2003.
Sabry, Kathy (pseud.). Los Angeles, CA. 13 July 2002.
Seco, Carla (pseud.). Pasadena, CA. 14 July 2002.
Weiss, Irene. Apache Junction, AZ. 2 March 2002.
Women of Color Interview with Donna Gómez (pseud.), Pam Chavez Hutson, Anna María Soto, and Lillian West. Sylmar, CA. 13 July 2002.

COLLECTIONS

June L. Mazer Lesbian Collection, Los Angeles, CA.

Lesbian Legacy Collection of ONE National Gay & Lesbian Archives, Los Angeles, CA. (LLC).

Personal files of Betty Jetter, stored at the Bancroft Library at the University of California Berkeley, CA.

Personal papers of Diane F. Germain, in her possession.

Personal papers of Wanda Jewell, in her possession.

Personal papers of Lori Mennella, in her possession.

Personal papers of Yolanda G. Retter Vargas, in her possession.

Personal papers for Califia Community of Kathy Wolfe, in author's possession.

Videos for Califia Community of Kathy Wolfe, in Wolfe archive, 21640 Almaden Road, San Jose, CA 95120.

PUBLISHED SOURCES

A., P. "Law in a Contrived Vacuum: Z's Conviction Affirmed." *The Lesbian Tide.* 5.4 corrected to 5 (March/April 1976): 6.

Adams, Carol. "The Oedible Complex: Feminism and Vegetarianism." In *The Lesbian Reader: An Amazon Quarterly Anthology*, edited by Gina Covina and Laurel Galana. Berkeley: Amazon Press, 1975.

"Ahshe Speaks." *Country Women* 23 (February 1977): 4–8.

Aldebaran. "Fat Underground Investigates Women's Clinic." *Sister* 5.9 (January 1975): 3.

———. "More Women Are on Diets Than in Jail." *Sister* 5.8 (November 1974): 4.

———. "We Are Not Our Enemies." *Sister: Los Angeles Women's Center* 4.10 (December 1973): 4.

Aldebaran et al. "Statement from the Radical Feminist Therapy Collective." *Sister: Los Angeles Women's Center* 5.6 (September 1974): 8.

Almquist, Jennifer Marie. "Incredible Lives: An Ethnography of Southern Oregon Womyn's Lands." MA thesis. Oregon State University, 2004.

Anzaldúa, Gloria. *Borderlands/La Frontera: The New Mestiza.* San Francisco: Spinsters/Aunt Lute, 1987.

Atkins, Gary. *Gay Seattle: Stories of Exile and Belonging.* Seattle: University of Washington Press, 2003.

Averill, Wendy. "Spotlight: Lauren Jardine, Co-Executive Director, Connexxus." *The Lesbian News* 10.10 (May 1985): 47.

Banet-Weiser, Sarah. *The Most Beautiful Girl in the World: Beauty Pageants and National Identity.* Berkeley: University of California Press, 1999.

Barbara. "The Nature of Self-Defense." *Country Women* 24 (April 1977): 21.

Bas Hannah, Sharon. "Seeing It from Both Sides and Too Brightly," *Sisters* 5.12 (April 1975): 10.

Baxandall, Rosalyn, and Linda Gordon, eds. *Dear Sisters: Dispatches from the Women's Liberation Movement.* New York: Basic Books, 2000.

Beck, Evelyn Torton. *Nice Jewish Girls: A Lesbian Anthology.* Watertown, MA: Persephone, 1980.

Belasco, Warren J. *Appetite for Change: How the Counterculture Took on the Food Industry, 1966–1988.* New York: Pantheon Books, 1989.

Berman, William C. *America's Right Turn: From Nixon to Bush.* Baltimore: Johns Hopkins University Press, 1994.

Biren, Joan E. "That's Funny, You Don't Look Like a Jewish Lesbian." In Evelyn Torton Beck, *Nice Jewish Girls: A Lesbian Anthology.* Watertown, MA: Persephone, 1980.

Blackwell, Maylei. ¡*Chicana Power!: Contested Histories of Feminism in the Chicano Movement.* Austin: University of Texas Press, 2011.

Boris, Eileen, and Nupur Chaudhuri, eds. *Voices of Women Historians: The Personal, the Political, the Professional.* Bloomington: Indiana University Press, 1999.

Braver, Betty. "Karate: The Art of the Open Hand." *Country Women* 28 (March 1978): 24–26.

———. "Rape." *Country Women* 10 (April 1974): 44–48.

———. "Self Defense: Between Mothers and Daughters." *Country Women* 11 (July 1974): 46–52.

Breines, Wini. *The Trouble Between Us: An Uneasy History of White and Black Women in the Feminist Movement.* Oxford: Oxford University, 2006.

Brown, Liz, et al. "Letter to the Editor." *The Lesbian Tide* 6.4 (January/February 1977): 18.

Brown, Rita Mae. *Plain Brown Rapper.* Oakland: Diana Press, 1976.

Brownmiller, Susan. *In Our Time: Memoir of a Revolution.* New York: The Dial Press, 1999.

Budapest, Z. "How the Grinch Stole Winter Solstice." *The Lesbian Tide* 5.4 (January/February 1976): 29.

———. "The Movement Should Support Its Stars." *The Lesbian Tide.* 6.5 (March/April 1977): 14–15.

———. ". . . Responses on S&M." *The Lesbian Tide* 6.6 (May/June 1977): 26.

Buhle, Mari Jo, and Paul Buhle, *The Concise History of Woman Suffrage: Selections from History of Woman Suffrage, Edited by Elizabeth Cady Stanton, Susan B. Anthony, Matilda Joslyn Gage, and the National American Woman Suffrage Association.* Urbana: University of Illinois Press, 2005.

Bulkin, Elly. "Hard Ground: Jewish Identity, Racism, and Anti-Semitism." In Elly Bulkin, Minnie Bruce Pratt, and Barbara Smith, *Yours in Struggle: Three Feminist Perspectives on Anti-Semitism and Racism.* Ithaca, NY: Firebrand Books, 1984.

Bulkin, Elly, Minnie Bruce Pratt, and Barbara Smith. *Yours in Struggle: Three Feminist Perspectives on Anti-Semitism and Racism.* Ithaca, NY: Firebrand Books, 1984.

Bunch, Charlotte, and Nancy Myron, eds. *Class and Feminism: A Collection of Essays from The Furies.* Baltimore: Diana Press, Inc., 1974.

Bunch, Charlotte, and Sandra Pollack, eds. *Learning Our Way: Essays in Feminist Education.* Trumansburg, NY: Crossing Press, 1983.

Buss, Shirl. "Clinic Fires Doctor for Racist, Fatist Attitudes." *The Lesbian Tide.* 6.6 (May/June 1977): 20.

"Califia Land Project." *The Lesbian Tide* 6.3 (November/December 1976): 26.

"Califia Plans Urban Commune." *The Lesbian Tide* 6.4 (January/February 1977): 16.

Califia, Pat. *Public Sex: The Culture of Radical Sex.* Pittsburgh: Cleis Press, 1994.

Carmichael, Stokely, and Charles V. Hamilton. *Black Power: The Politics of Liberation in America.* New York: Vintage, 1967.

Carter, Lewis F. *Charisma and Control in Rajneeshpuram: The Role of Shared Values in the Creation of a Community*. New York: Cambridge University Press, 1990.

Carvajal, Doreen. "L.B. Women's Studies Instructor to Resume Teaching Duties in Fall." *Press Telegram*. August 21, 1982: 1.

———. "Turmoil Seen for CSULB Women's Studies." *Press Telegram* (July 2, 1982): B1, B5.

Cassell, Joan. *A Group Called Women: Sisterhood and Symbolism in the Feminist Movement*. New York: David McKay, 1977.

Cheney, Joyce, ed. *Lesbian Land*. Minneapolis: Word Weavers, 1985.

Chesler, Phyllis. *Women and Madness*. New York: Avon, 1972.

Cleaver, Eldridge. *Soul on Ice*. New York: Dell, 1968.

Coontz, Stephanie. *The Way We Never Were: American Families and the Nostalgia Trap*. New York: Basic Books, 2000.

Cordova, Jeanne. "Towards a Feminist Expression of Sado-Masochism." *The Lesbian Tide*. 6.3 (November/December 1976): 14–17.

Cordova, Jeanne, Karla Jay, Gudrun Fonfa, and Janie Elven. "Community Mows Under 'Flowers of Evil.'" *The Lesbian Tide* 4.5 (January 1975): 16–18.

Covina, Gina, and Laurel Galana, eds. *The Lesbian Reader: An Amazon Quarterly Anthology*. Oakland: Amazon Press, 1975.

Crain, Mary Beth. "Strange Bedfellows, Dangerous Precedents." *L.A. Weekly* (May 24–30, 1985): 39–40.

Crow, Barbara A., ed. *Radical Feminism: A Documentary Reader*. New York: New York University Press, 2000.

Cruz Rodriguez, Marilynn. "Pretty in Pink. Y Que?" *The Lesbian News*. 12.2 (September 1986): 35–36.

Currie, Elliott, Robert Dunn, and David Fogarty. "The Fading Dream: Economic Crisis and the New Inequality." In Karen V. Hansen and Ilene J. Philipson, eds. *Women, Class, and the Feminist Imagination*. Philadelphia: Temple University Press, 1990.

Dallek, Matthew. *The Right Moment: Ronald Reagan's First Victory and the Decisive Turning Point in American Politics*. New York: Free Press, 2000.

davenport, doris. "The Pathology of Racism: A Conversation with Third World Wimmin." In *This Bridge Called My Back: Writings by Radical Women of Color*, edited by Cherríe Moraga and Gloria Anzaldúa. Watertown, MA: Persephone, 1981.

Davis, Flora. *Moving the Mountain: The Women's Movement in America since 1960*. New York: Simon & Schuster, 1991.

Densmore, Dana. "Ja Shin Do." *Country Women* 16 (June 1975): 58–59.

"Dirty Street Fighting." *Human Behavior* (October 1973): 17.

Dixon, Marlene. "The Restless Eagles: Women's Liberation 1969." In *The New Woman: A Motive Anthology of Women's Liberation*, edited by J. Cooke, Charlotte Bunch-Weeks, and Robin Morgan. Indianapolis: Bobbs-Merrill, 1970.

Dobkin, Alix. *Alix Dobkin's Adventures in Women's Music*. New York: Tomato Publications, Ltd., 1979.

———. "View from Gay Head." *Lavender Jane Loves Women*. Women Wax Works, 1973.

Duggan, Lisa. *The Twilight of Equality?: Neoliberalism, Cultural Politics, and the Attack on Democracy*. Boston: Beacon Press, 2003.

Duggan, Lisa, and Nan D. Hunter. *Sex Wars: Sexual Dissent and Political Culture*. New York: Routledge, 1995.

Dunbar-Ortiz, Roxanne. *Outlaw Woman: A Memoir of the War Years, 1960–1975.* San Francisco: City Lights, 2001.

Dyani. "Self Defense." *Country Women* 12 (August 1974): 47.

Echols, Alice. *Daring To Be Bad: Radical Feminism in America 1967–1975.* Minneapolis: University of Minnesota Press, 1989.

Editorial and Political Collective, The. "Editorial: But Who Would Support the Movement?" *The Lesbian Tide* 6.5 (March/April 1977): 14–15.

Ehrenreich, Barbara. "What is Socialist Feminism?" In *Material Feminism: A Reader in Class, Difference, and Women's Lives,* edited by Rosemary Hennessy and Chrys Ingraham. New York: Routledge, 1997.

English, Deirdre, Barbara Epstein, Barbara Haber, and Judy MacLean. "The Impasse of Socialist Feminism: A Conversation." In *Women, Class, and the Feminist Imagination,* ed. Karen V. Hansen and Ilene J. Philipson. Philadelphia: Temple University Press, 1990 [1986].

Enke, Anne. *Finding the Movement: Sexuality, Contested Space, and Feminist Activism.* Durham: Duke University Press, 2007.

Epstein, Cynthia Fuchs. "Ten Years Later: Perspectives on the Women's Movement." *Dissent* (Spring 1975): 169–176.

Evans, Lee. "Dykes of Poverty: Coming Home." *Lesbian Ethics* 4.2 (Spring 1991): 7–18.

Evans, Sara. *Personal Politics: The Roots of Women's Liberation in the Civil Rights Movement and the New Left.* New York: Vintage, 1980 [1979].

———. *Tidal Wave: How Women Changed America at Century's End.* New York: Free Press, 2004 [2003].

Evans, Thomas W. *The Education of Ronald Reagan: The General Electric Years and the Untold Story of His Conversion to Conservatism.* New York: Columbia University Press, 2006.

Faderman, Lillian, and Stuart Timmons. *Gay L.A.: A History of Sexual Outlaws, Power Politics, and Lipstick Lesbians.* New York: Basic Books, 2006.

Fallingstar, Cerridwen. ". . . Responses on S&M." *The Lesbian Tide* 6.6 (May/June 1977): 26.

"Fat Underground Communique." *Sister* 5.4 (July 1974): 4.

Fields, Jonathan. *Uncertainty: Turning Fear and Doubt into Fuel for Brilliance.* New York: Portfolio/Penguin, 2011.

Firus, Randi. "Brooks—Profile in Unsubtle Persuasion." *Daily Forty-Niner* (October 17, 1979): 12.

Fisher, Joy. "The Califia Experiment." *The Lesbian Tide* 6.2 (September/October 1976): 4.

Fishman, Sara Golda Bracha. "Life in the Fat Underground." *Radiance: The Magazine for Large Women* (Winter 1998).

Freeman, Jo. *The Politics of Women's Liberation: A Case Study of an Emerging Social Movement and Its Relation to the Policy Process.* Authors Guild Backinprint.com, 2000 [1973].

Freespirit, Judy, and Aldebaran. "Fat Liberation Manifesto." *Sister.* 5.4 (July 1974): 4.

———. "Fat Liberation Manifesto." In *Shadow on a Tightrope: Writings by Women on Fat Oppression,* edited by Lisa Schoenfielder and Barb Wieser. San Francisco: Aunt Lute Books, 1983.

Freire, Paulo. *Pedagogy of the Oppressed. 30th Anniversary Edition.* Translated by Myra

Bergman Ramos. With an introduction by Donaldo Macedo. New York: Continuum, 2000 [1970].

Frye, Marilyn. "Some Reflections on Separatism and Power." In *Feminist Social Thought: A Reader*, edited by Diana T. Meyers. New York: Routledge, 1997.

Gagehabib, La Verne, and Barbara Summerhawk. *Circles of Power: Shifting Dynamics in a Lesbian-Centered Community*. Norwich, VT: New Victoria Publishers, 2000.

Gay Revolution Party Women's Caucus, "Realesbians and Politicalesbians." In Karla Jay and Allen Young, *Out of the Closets: Voices of Gay Liberation*. New York: Jove/HBJ, 1977 [1972]: 177–181.

Germain, Diane F. "Feminist Art and Education at Califia: My Personal Experience." In Charlotte Bunch and Sandra Pollack, eds., *Learning Our Way: Essays in Feminist Education*. Trumansburg, NY: Crossing Press, 1983.

Gladney, Margaret Rose. "A Chain Reaction of Dreams: Lillian Smith and Laurel Falls Camp." *Journal of American Culture* 5.3 (Fall 1982): 50–55.

Glen, John. *Highlander: No Ordinary School*. 2nd ed. Knoxville: University of Tennessee Press, 1996.

Gluck, Sherna Berger. "Reflections on Linking the Academy and the Community." *Frontiers: A Journal of Women's Studies* 8.3 (1986): 46–49.

Gluck, Sherna, with Maylei Blackwell, Sharon Cotrell, and Karen S. harper. "Whose Feminism, Whose History?: Reflections on Excavating the History of (the) U.S. Women's Movement(s)." In *Community Activism and Feminist Politics: Organizing Across Race, Class and Gender*, ed. Nancy A. Naples. New York: Routledge, 1998.

Gluck, Sherna Berger, and Daphne Patai, eds. *Women's Words: The Feminist Practice of Oral History*. New York: Routledge, 1991.

Gosse, Van. *The Movements of the New Left: 1950–1975: A Brief History with Documents*. Boston: Bedford/St. Martin's, 2005.

Gould, Cheryl. "New ♀ Institute Opens." *The Lesbian Tide* 4.5 (January 1975): 11, 29.

Griffith, Robert, and Paula Baker, eds. *Major Problems in American History Since 1945*. 3rd ed. Boston: Houghton Mifflin, 2007.

Hale, Sandra. "Our Attempt to Practice Feminism in the Women's Studies Program." *Frontiers: a Journal of Women's Studies* 8.3 (1986): 39–43.

Hancken, Helen. "Bearded Womon Honors Ancestors." *The Lesbian Tide*. 5.3 corrected to 4 (January/February 1976): 28.

Hansen, Karen V. "Women's Unions and the Search for a Political Identity." In *Women, Class, and the Feminist Imagination*, ed. Karen V. Hansen and Ilene J. Philipson. Philadelphia: Temple University Press, 1990 [1986].

Hansen, Karen V., and Ilene J. Philipson, eds. *Women, Class, and the Feminist Imagination*. Philadelphia: Temple University Press, 1990.

Hara, Yukihiko. *Green Tea: Health Benefits and Applications*. Food Science and Technology series, edited by Owen R. Fennema et al. New York: Marcel Dekker, 2001.

Harrington, Michael. *The Other America: Poverty in the United States*. New York: Macmillan, 1962.

Hendley, Vicky. "Crowther Cuts Women's Studies." *The Summer Union: The Student's Newspaper Cal State University Long Beach* 2.2 (July 6, 1982): 1, 8. In Betty Brooks file, LLC.

Hewitt, Nancy, ed. *No Permanent Waves: Recasting Histories of U.S. Feminism*. New Brunswick, NJ: Rutgers University Press, 2010.

Hole, Judith, and Ellen Levine. *Rebirth of Feminism.* New York: Quadrangle Books, 1971.

Hollibaugh, Amber L. *My Dangerous Desires: A Queer Girl Dreaming Her Way Home.* Durham: Duke University Press, 2000.

Horton, Myles. *The Myles Horton Reader: Education for Social Change.* Edited by Dale Jacobs. Knoxville: University of Tennessee Press, 2003.

Howe, Florence, ed. *The Politics of Women's Studies: Testimony from 30 Founding Mothers.* New York: The Feminist Press at the City University of New York, 2000.

Hull, Gloria T., Patricia Bell Scott, and Barbara Smith. *All the Women Are White, All the Blacks Are Men, but Some of Us Are Brave: Black Women's Studies.* New York: Feminist Press, 1982.

Hyde Park Chapter, Chicago Women's Liberation Union. "Socialist Feminism—A Strategy for the Women's Movement." *Sisters* 4.2 (February 1972): n.p.

Inman, Mary. *In Women's Defense.* Los Angeles: The Committee to Organize the Advancement of Women, 1940.

Jacinto, Louis. "Lydia Otero: GLLU's Eighth Year Begins." *Unidad.* (February/March 1989): 1–2.

Jakobsen, Janet R. "Different Differences: Theory and the Practice of Women's Studies." In Elizabeth Lapovsky Kennedy and Agatha Beins, eds., *Women's Studies for the Future: Foundations, Interrogations, Politics.* Piscataway, NJ: Rutgers University Press, 2005.

———. *Working Alliances and the Politics of Difference: Diversity and Feminist Ethics.* Bloomington: Indiana University Press, 1998.

James, Selma. "Introduction to *The Power of Women and the Subversion of the Community.*" In *Materialist Feminism: A Reader in Class, Difference, and Women's Lives,* edited by Rosemary Hennessy and Chrys Ingraham. New York: Routledge, 1997.

Jankowski, Katherine A. *Deaf Empowerment: Emergence, Struggle, and Rhetoric.* Washington, DC: Gallaudet University Press, 1997.

Jargowsky, Paul A. *Poverty and Place: Ghettos, Barrios, and the American City.* New York: Russell Sage Foundation, 1997.

Jenkins, Philip. *Decade of Nightmares: The End of the Sixties and the Making of Eighties America.* New York: Oxford University Press, 2006.

Katz, Judy H. *White Awareness: Handbook for Anti-Racism Training.* Norman: University of Oklahoma, 1978.

Katz, Sue. "Kick Ass for Women." *Country Women* 14 (February 1975): 50–55.

Keating, AnaLouise. *Teaching Transformation: Transcultural Classroom Dialogues.* New York: Palgrave MacMillan, 2007.

Kennedy, Elizabeth Lapovsky. "Socialist Feminism: What Difference Did It Make to the History of Women's Studies?" *Feminist Studies* 34.3 (Fall 2008): 497–525.

Kennedy, Elizabeth Lapovsky, and Agatha Beins, eds. *Women's Studies for the Future: Foundations, Interrogations, Politics.* Piscataway, NJ: Rutgers University Press, 2005.

Kenney, Moira Rachel. *Mapping Gay L.A.: The Intersection of Place and Politics.* Philadelphia: Temple University Press, 2001.

Kessler-Harris, Alice. *In Pursuit of Equity: Women, Men, and the Quest for Economic Citizenship in 20th-Century America.* New York: Oxford University Press, 2001.

Kleiner, Catherine B. "Doin' It for Themselves: Lesbian Land Communities in Southern Oregon, 1970–1995." PhD dissertation. University of New Mexico, 2003.

Krieger, Susan. *The Mirror Dance: Identity in a Women's Community.* Philadelphia: Temple University Press, 1983.

Lappé, Frances Moore. *Diet for a Small Planet.* New York: Ballantine Books, 1971.

Lassiter, Matthew D. *The Silent Majority: Suburban Politics in the Sunbelt South.* Princeton, NJ: Princeton University Press, 2006.

Lesh, Cheri. "Big Hipped, Beautiful, and Fierce." *The Lesbian Tide.* 7.3 (November/December 1977): 8–9.

———. "Wicca Is Rebellion, Not Mysticism." *The Lesbian Tide.* 6.5 (March/April 1977): 19.

Lewis, Jacqueline J. *The Power of Stories: A Guide for Leading Multi-racial and Multicultural Congregations.* Nashville: Abingdon Press, 2008.

Limmer, Melissa. "A World Apart: Lesbian Separatists Hold the Line for Women's Energy." *The Advocate* (October 10, 1988): 26–27.

Linden, Robin Ruth, et al., eds. *Against Sadomasochism: A Radical Feminist Analysis.* East Palo Alto, CA: Frog in the Well, 1982.

Lipsky, Laura van Dernoot, with Connie Burke. *Trauma Stewardship: An Everyday Guide to Caring for Self While Caring for Others.* San Francisco: Berrett-Koehler, 2009.

Lobel, Kerry. "Domestic Violence Hits Close to Home." *The Lesbian News* 8.3 (October 1982): 1–2.

Lobel, Kerry, ed. *Naming the Violence: Speaking Out about Lesbian Battering.* Seattle: Seal Press, 1986.

Lorde, Audre. *Sister Outsider.* Freedom, CA: The Crossing Press, 1984.

Madrone, Hawk. *Weeding at Dawn: A Lesbian Country Life.* Binghamton, NY: Harrington Park Press, 2000.

Martin, Del. *Battered Wives.* San Francisco: Glide Publications, 1976.

Matthews, Nancy A. *Confronting Rape: The Feminist Anti-Rape Movement and the State.* New York: Routledge, 1994.

———. "Feminist Clashes with the State: Tactical Choices by State-Funded Rape Crisis Centers." In *Feminist Organizations: Harvest of the New Women's Movement,* edited by Myra Marx Ferree and Patricia Yancey Martin. Philadelphia: Temple University Press, 1995.

———. "Surmounting a Legacy: The Expansion of Racial Diversity in a Local Anti-Rape Movement." In *Violence against Women: The Bloody Footprints,* edited by Pauline Bart and Eileen Geil Moran. Newbury Park, CA: Sage, 1993.

Maureen. "Self Defense." *Sister: Los Angeles Women's Center* 4.2 (February 1972): 9.

McCall, Cheryl. "Maya Angelou: The Writer-poet Continues to Find Art in Her Life as She Makes an Emotional Return to Her Native South." *People Weekly* 17.9 (March 8, 1982): 92, 95–96, 99.

McDonald, Sharon. "Z Budapest, Witch in Progress." *The Lesbian Tide.* 9.5 (March/April 1980): 6–7.

McGirr, Lisa. *Suburban Warriors: The Origins of the New American Right.* Princeton, NJ: Princeton University Press, 2001.

McLean, Barbara. "Diary of a Mad Organizer." *The Lesbian Tide* (May/June 1973): 35–41.

Mendenhall, George. "Classroom Spies Accuse Prof. of Teaching Porn." *Bay Area Reporter* (March 27, 1986): 10, 13.

Merchant, Carolyn, and Roger S. Gottlieb. *Ecology: Key Concepts in Critical Theory*. Atlantic Highlands, NJ: Humanities Press International, 1994.

Messer-Davidow, Ellen. "Acting Otherwise." In *Provoking Agents: Gender and Agency in Theory and Practice*, edited by Judith Kegan Gardiner. Urbana: University of Illinois Press, 1995.

Meyerowitz, Joanne J., ed. *Not June Cleaver: Women and Gender in Postwar America, 1945–1960*. Philadelphia: Temple University Press, 1994.

Mishler, Paul C. *Raising Reds: The Young Pioneers, Radical Summer Camps, and Communist Political Culture in the United States*. New York: Columbia University Press, 1999.

Mitchell, Greg. *Tricky Dick and the Pink Lady: Richard Nixon vs. Helen Gahagan Douglas: Sexual Politics and the Red Scare, 1950*. New York: Random House, 1998.

Moira, Fran. "Maya Angelou on the 'Child Stealing' Case." *Off Our Backs* 26.3 (March 31, 1986): 20.

Moraga, Cherríe. *Loving in the War Years: lo que nunca pasó por sus labios*. Boston: South End Press, 1983.

Moraga, Cherríe, and Gloria Anzaldúa, eds. *This Bridge Called My Back: Writings by Radical Women of Color*. Watertown, MA: Persephone, 1981.

Morgan, Robin. "Lesbianism and Feminism: Synonyms or Contradictions?: Keynote Address at Lesbian-Feminist Conference, Los Angeles, April 14, 1973." *The Lesbian Tide* (May/June 1973): 30–34.

———. *Going Too Far: The Personal Chronicle of a Feminist*. New York: Vintage Books, 1978.

Mosbacher, Dee, et al., prod. and dir. *Radical Harmonies*. San Francisco: Woman Vision, 2002.

Murphy, Marilyn. "Aging in April." *The Lesbian News* 12.8 (April 1987): 27.

———. "And Baby Makes Two—Part I." *The Lesbian News* 12.2 (September 1986): 34.

———. "And Baby Makes Two—Part II." *The Lesbian News* 12.2 [should be number 3] (October 1986): 30–31.

———. "And the Walls Came Tumbling Down." *The Lesbian News* 12.12 (July 1987): 28.

———. *Are You Girls Traveling Alone? Adventures in Lesbianic Logic*. Los Angeles: Clothespin Fever Press, 1991.

———. "At a Celebration for Hitler's Birthday." *The Lesbian News* 15.11 (June 1990): 25.

———. "Beachtree: My Kind of Place." *The Lesbian News* 11.4 (November 1985): 43–44.

———. "Califia Community." In Charlotte Bunch and Sandra Pollack, eds. *Learning Our Way: Essays in Feminist Education*. Trumansburg, NY: Crossing Press, 1983.

———. "Color Me Lavender." *The Lesbian News* 10.9 (April 1985 [August 1982]): 46.

———. "Do We 'Only Hurt the Ones We Love'?" *The Lesbian News* 8.12 (July 1983): 24.

———. "Feminist Yesterdays." *The Lesbian News* 9.10 (May 1984): 23–24.

———. "It Could Have Been Worse." *The Lesbian News* 11.10 (May 1986): 53–54.

———. "Letter from Florida." *The Lesbian News* 13.10 (May 1988): 34.

———. "Money, Homophobia & Death in the Closet." *The Lesbian News* 11.2 (September 1985): 44–45.

———. "More About Wills." *The Lesbian News* 11.3 (October 1985): 48–49.

———. "Mother of the Groom." *The Lesbian News* 10.6 (January 1985): 30–31.

———. "Old Is In: The West Coast Celebration by and for Old Lesbians." *The Lesbian News* 12.10 (June 1987): 30–31.

———. "One of the Murphy Girls." In *Out of the Class Closet: Lesbians Speak*, ed. Julia Penelope. Freedom, CA: The Crossing Press, 1994.

———. "'Our Proud Present.'" *The Lesbian News* 9.5 (December 1983): 22–23.

———. "Our Town." *The Lesbian News* 10.7 (February 1985): 34–35.

———. "Pretty in Pink." *The Lesbian News* 11.12 (July 1986): 46–47.

———. "RV Living: Lesbian Style." *The Lesbian News* 12.6 (February 1987): 26.

———. "She's Jewish, You Know!" *The Lesbian News* 13.5 (December 1987): 10.

———. "A Small Injustice." *The Lesbian News* 11.7 (February 1986): 52–53.

———. "Some Girls Never Learn." *The Lesbian News* 12.3 (November 1986): 29.

———. "The Summer of '73." *The Lesbian News* 10.12 (July 1985): 34–35.

———. "Thanksgiving Day." *The Lesbian News* 13.4 (November 1987): 29.

———. "Thinking about Bisexuality." *The Lesbian News* 9.7 (February 1984): 26–27.

"New Evidence in Witch Trial." *The Lesbian Tide* 7.1 (July/August 1977): 16.

Newton, Esther. "High School Crack-Up." In *Amazon Expedition: A Lesbianfeminist Anthology*, edited by Phyllis Birkby et al. Albion, CA: Times Change Press, 1973.

Olsson, Göran Hugo, Annika Rogell, Joslyn Barnes, Danny Glover, Axel Arnö, Angela Y. Davis, and Stokely Carmichael. *Black Power Mixtape 1967–1975: A Documentary in 9 Chapters*. New York: IFC Films, 2011.

Orton, William and Vicky Hendley. "A Voice from the 'Right.'" *The Summer Union: The Student's Newspaper Cal State University Long Beach* 2.2 (July 6, 1982): 1, 7, 8. In Betty Brooks file, LLC.

Pate, Marty, with Jill Wilson. "Tai Chi: A Learning Cycle." *Country Women* 28 (March 1978): 6–7.

Payne, Charles. *I've Got the Light of Freedom: The Organizing Tradition and the Mississippi Freedom Struggle*. Berkeley: University of California Press, 1997.

Pearce, Diana. "The Feminization of Poverty: Women, Work, and Welfare." *Urban and Social Change Review* 11.1–2 (February, 1978): 28–36.

Penelope, Julia, ed. *Out of the Class Closet: Lesbians Speak*. Freedom, CA: The Crossing Press, 1994.

Penelope, Julia, and Susan J. Wolfe, eds. *Lesbian Culture: An Anthology: The Lives, Work, Ideas, Art and Visions of Lesbians Past and Present*. Freedom, CA: The Crossing Press, 1993.

Pharr, Suzanne. *Homophobia: A Weapon Of Sexism*. Little Rock: Chardon Press, 1988.

Pomerleau, Clark A. "Empowering Members, Not Overpowering Them: The National Organization for Women, Calls for Lesbian Inclusion, and California Influence, 1960s–1980s." *Journal of Homosexuality* 57.7 (2010): 842–861.

"Purge of Feminists in ♀'s Phys Ed." *Sister: Los Angeles Women's Center* 5.5 (August 1974): 1.

Radicalesbians. "The Woman-Identified Woman." In *Out of the Closets: Voices of Gay Liberation*, edited by Karla Jay and Allen Young. New York: Jove/HBJ, 1977 [1972].

Ramakers, Mica. *Dirty Pictures: Tom of Finland, Masculinity, and Homosexuality*. New York: St. Martin's Press, 2000.

Raymond, Janice G. *The Transsexual Empire: the Making of the She-Male*. Athene Series. New York: Teachers College Press, 1994 [1979].

Reagon, Bernice Johnson. "Coalition Politics: Turning the Century." In *Home Girls: A Black Feminist Anthology*, ed. Barbara Smith. New York: Kitchen Table: Women of Color Press, 1983.

Reger, Jo. *Everywhere and Nowhere: Contemporary Feminism in the United States*. New York: Oxford University Press, 2012.

Reid, Frances, and Judy Dlugacz, prod. and dir. *The Changer: A Record of the Times*. Oakland: Olivia Records, 1991.

Retter, Yolanda G. "On the Side of Angels: Lesbian Activism in Los Angeles, 1970–1990." Dissertation, American Studies. University of New Mexico, 1999.

Rich, Adrienne. "Compulsory Heterosexuality and Lesbian Existence." *Signs: Journal of Women in Culture and Society* 5.4 (1980): 631–660.

Robins, Joan. "Betty Brooks: One Woman Wave Maker." *Sister: Los Angeles Women's Center* 5.6 (September 1974): 1.

Rodríguez, Amardo. *Diversity as Liberation (II): Introducing a New Understanding of Diversity*. Cresskill, NJ: Hampton Press, Inc., 2003.

Rosen, Ruth. *The World Split Open: How the Modern Women's Movement Changed America*. New York: Viking, 2000.

Rosenberg, Marshall B. *Nonviolent Communication: A Language of Compassion*. 5th print. Encinitas, CA: PuddleDancer, 2001.

Roth, Benita. *Separate Roads to Feminism: Black, Chicana, and White Feminist Movements in America's Second Wave*. Cambridge: Cambridge University Press, 2004.

Rubin, Gayle. "Thinking Sex: Notes for a Radical Theory of the Politics of Sexuality." In *Pleasure and Danger: Exploring Female Sexuality*, edited by Diana T. Meyers. Boston: Routledge & Kegan Paul, 1984.

Rubin, Henry. *Self-Made Men: Identity and Embodiment among Transsexual Men*. Nashville: Vanderbilt University, 2003.

Ruth, Barbara. "Cathexis (on the nature of S&M)." *The Lesbian Tide* 6.6 (May/June 1977): 10–11.

Salpiers, Roberta. "U.S. Government Surveillance and the Women's Liberation Movement: A Case Study." *Feminist Studies* 34.4 (Fall 2008): 431–455.

Sanday, Peggy Reeves. *A Woman Scorned: Acquaintance Rape on Trial*. New York: Doubleday, 1996.

Sandilands, Catriona. "Lesbian Separatist Communities and the Experience of Nature: Toward a Queer Ecology." *Organization & Environment* 15 (June 2002): 131–163.

Schlafly, Phyllis. "ACLU Leaps to the Defense of Lesbianism Course." *Oklahoma City Times* (October 15, 1982): 42.

Schlosser, Eric. *Fast Food Nation: The Dark Side of the All-American Meal*. New York: Perennial, 2002 [2001].

Schultz, Constance B., and Elizabeth Hayes Turner. *Clio's Southern Sisters: Interviews with Leaders of the Southern Association for Women Historians*. Columbia, MO: University of Missouri Press, 2004.

Seajay, Carol. "Violence between Women." *Country Women* 26 (September 1977): 16–18.

"Self-Defense for Women." *Sister: Los Angeles Women's Center* (February/March 1977): 9.

Shilts, Randy. *And the Band Played On: Politics, People, and the AIDS Epidemic.* New York: St. Martin's Griffin, 1987.

Sievers, Sharon L. "What Have We Won, What Have We Lost?" *Frontiers: A Journal of Women's Studies* 8.3 (1986): 43–46.

Smith, Barbara. "Between a Rock and a Hard Place." In Elly Bulkin, Minnie Bruce Pratt, and Barbara Smith, *Yours in Struggle: Three Feminist Perspectives on Anti-Semitism and Racism.* Ithaca, NY: Firebrand Books, 1984.

Smith, Barbara, ed. *Home Girls: A Black Feminist Anthology.* New York: Kitchen Table Women of Color Press, 1983.

Sprecher, Katharine Matthaei. "Lesbian Intentional Communities in Rural Southwestern Oregon: Discussion on Separatism, Environmentalism, and Community Conflict." MA thesis, California Institute of Integral Studies, 1997.

Springer, Kimberly. *Living for the Revolution: Black Feminist Organizations, 1968–1980.* Durham: Duke University Press, 2005.

St. Joan, Jackie. "The Ideas and the Realities: Sagaris, Session I." In Charlotte Bunch and Sandra Pollack, eds., *Learning Our Way: Essays in Feminist Education.* Trumansburg, NY: Crossing Press, 1983.

Stearns, Carol Zisowitz, and Peter N. Stearns. *Anger: The Struggle for Emotional Control in American History.* Chicago: University of Chicago Press, 1986.

Stein, Julia. "Women, Resistance and Revolution: A Marxist-Feminist View." *Sisters* 5.12 (April 1975): 10.

Sue, Nelly, Dian, Carol, and Billie. *Country Lesbians: The Story of the Womanshare Collective.* Grants Pass, OR: Womanshare Books, 1976.

Taylor, Verta, and Leila J. Rupp. "Women's Culture and Lesbian Feminist Activism: A Reconsideration of Cultural Feminism." *Signs: Journal of Women in Culture and Society* 19.1 (Autumn 1993): 32–61.

Terrell, Mary Church. *A Colored Woman in a White World.* Classics in Black Studies. Amherst, NY: Prometheus Books, 2005.

"There Is Good News and Bad News." *The Lesbian News* 8.3 (October 1982): 3.

Thompson, Mark, ed. *Leatherfolk: Radical Sex, People, Politics, and Practice.* Los Angeles: Alyson Books, 2001 [1991].

Tilchen, Maida. "Lesbians and Women's Music." In *Women-Identified Women*, edited by Trudy Darty and Sandee Potter. Palo Alto, CA: Mayfield, 1984.

Tillmon, Johnnie. "Welfare Is a Women's Issue." *Ms. Magazine* (Spring 1972): 111–116.

Valk, Anne. *Radical Sisters: Second-Wave Feminism and Black Liberation in Washington, D.C.* Urbana: University of Illinois, 2008.

Wann, Marilyn. *FAT!SO?: Because You Don't Have to Apologize for Your Size!* Berkeley: Ten Speed Press, 1998.

Weigand, Kate. *Red Feminism: American Communism and the Making of Women's Liberation.* Baltimore: Johns Hopkins University Press, 2001.

White, Edith. "Is Upward Mobility Wrong?" *Sisters* 5.12 (April 1975): 11.

Whittier, Nancy. *Feminist Generations: The Persistence of the Radical Women's Movement.* Philadelphia: Temple University Press, 1995.

Wieman, Henry Nelson. *Creative Freedom: Vocation of Liberal Religion.* Edited by Creighton Peden and Larry E. Axel. New York: The Pilgrim Press, 1982.

Wolf, Naomi. *Fire with Fire: The New Female Power and How to Use It.* New York: Random House, 1994.

Wolverton, Terry. *Insurgent Muse: Life and Art at the Woman's Building*. San Francisco: City Lights, 2002.
X, Malcolm. *By Any Means Necessary: Speeches, Interviews, and a Letter by Malcolm X*. Edited by George Breitman. New York: Pathfinder, 1970.
Yamamoto, Takehiko, et al., eds. *Chemistry and Applications of Green Tea*. Boca Raton: CRC Press, 1997.

WEBSITES

Bronski, Michael. "Why Reagan Ignored AIDS." *The Advocate: Online Exclusives*. Posted 9 June 2004, last accessed 27 August 2004. http://www.advocate.com/html /stories/917/917_reagan_bronski.asp.
Brooke. "Feminist Conference: Porn Again." *Off Our Backs* 9.10 (Washington: November 30, 1979), 24. Accessed 4 January 2011. http://www.webcitation.org/query?url =http://www.geocities.com/wikispace/oob.1979.html&date=2009-10-26 +00:12:27.
Denger, Mark J. "Spanish and Mexican California: Explorations and Conquest of California." California State Military Department, The California Military Museum: Preserving California's Military History website. http://militarymuseum.org/Ex ConXA.html.
"History Highlight: Women Veterans and the WWII GI Bill of Rights." History & Collections: Women in Military Service for America Memorial Foundation, Inc. website. http://www.womensmemorial.org/H&C/History/historyhl.html.
"National Women's Studies Association Constitution." Last accessed 12 December 2003. http://www.nwsa.org/constitution.htm.
"Poverty Status of People by Family Relationship, Race, and Hispanic Origin: 1959–2000." Table 2, last accessed 18 January 2010. http://www.census.gov/income /histpov/histpov02.txt.
Retter, Yolanda. "Los Angeles Lesbian Chronology, 1970–1980." Lesbian History Project. http://www-lib.usc.edu/~retter/main.html (1996).
"The Sexes: Really Socking It to Women," *Time* 109.6 (February 7, 1977). Accessed January 3, 2011. http://www.time.com/time/magazine/article/0,9171,914772,00. html.
"U.S. Department of Labor Bureau of Labor Statistics." http://stats.bls.gov/cps/prev _yrs.htm. Last accessed 29 July 2004.
Valvo, Pauline. "Nikolaj Frederik Severin Grundtvig: 1783–1872." National-Louis University Resources for Adult Education website (1 May 2005). http://nl.edu /academics/cas/ace/resources/nfsgrundtvig.cfm.
Women's Graphic Collective. "Many Waves, One Ocean." (Poster). Chicago Women's Liberation Union, 1972. http://cwluherstory.org/Online-Store.html, under "Large Poster Reprints."

Photographs in the plate section are designated with *pl.*

Little Red Book (Mao), 16
Lobel, Kerry, 95
LOC. *See* Lesbians of Color
Los Angeles, 4; and feminist institutions,
23–33
Los Angeles Commission on Assaults
Against Women, 28, 35, 78, 202n15
Los Angeles County Board of Super-
visors, 83
Los Angeles Gay and Lesbian Commu-
nity Service Center, 170
Los Angeles Gay Community Services
Center, 45
Los Angeles Women's Center, 23, 105
Los Angeles Women's Community Cho-
rus (LAWCC), 30, 31, 130
Los Angeles Women's Union, 35
Los Angeles Women's Yellow Pages, 33
Louderback, Llewellyn, 26; *Fat Power*,
25
Lundberg, Ferdinand: *Modern Woman*,
102
Lyon, Phyllis, 70

Mabel-Lois, Lynn, 26
MacKinnon, Catherine "Kitty," 83, 155
Magical Goddess Slide Show, 32
Malcolm X, 208n6
Malibu/Califia Land Management, 58
"Man-Hating as Taboo" (Jetter), 76–77
Manov, Ariana, 26–27, 51, 57, 60, 61,
106, 167; and class, 116; on sado-
masochism, 87–88
Maoist Chinese Revolution, 6
Martin, Del, 70
Martínez, Adel, 162–163
Martínez, Elizabeth Sutherland, 186n16
Marx, Karl, 101
Marxism, 6, 109, 120
Masters and Johnson, 24
McAfee, Lynn. *See* Mabel-Lois, Lynn
McCarthyism, 100, 103
McGrievy, Susan, 154
McLean, Barbara, 29
meat industry: critiques of, 64–65; and
environment, 65; and sexism, 65–66
Medvec, Emily, 38

Menaces, Lavender, 72
mental health, 24; and feminism, 59–61,
109–110, 198n127
Merriam, Eve, 199n1
Merry, Karen, 49, 60–61, 71, 73, 134;
and class, 110–111
Methodist Church, 192n1
methodology, x–xi
Mexican Americans, 23
Meyer, Mina. *See* Robinson, Mina
Meyerowitz, Joanne, 12
Michigan Womyn's Music Festival, 87
middle-class women, 107–109, 110–111;
vs. working-class women, 111–117
Millett, Kate, 70, 83
misogyny: and Califia, 46, 91–92; in soci-
ety, 90–92
Modern Woman: The Lost Sex (Farnham &
Lundberg), 102
Moosewood Cookbook, 145
Moraga, Cherríe, 128, 142
Moran, Barbara, 70
Morgan, Robin, 28–29, 71; on porn, 81–
82, 84
Morro Bay, 42, 194n31
Movimiento Estudiantil Chicano de
Aztlán (MEChA), 135
Ms., 39, 71, 118
multiculturalism, 181–182; and Communism, 20–21; and feminism, 5, 6, 7
Multi-Ethnic Gay and Lesbian Exchange
(MEGLE), 163
Murphy, Jeanne, 47, 61, 196n81
Murphy, Marilyn, 34, 36–37, 129, 150,
152, 165, 196n81, 214n4, *pl.*; and activism, 109–110, 195n52; and bisexuality, 73; and Califia, educational
focus of, 45–46; and Califia, founding
of, 37–38, 41–42, 45–46; and Califia, representative of, 165–166; and
class, 106, 111, 113–114; and consumer culture, 76; and custody case,
156–157; and feminine appearance,
75–76; and Feminist Primer, 70–71;
vs. heterosexuality, 172–173; "Lesbianic Logic," 171–174; and lesbianism,
69, 71–72; on motherhood, 173; and